Kadonowaki-cho and Minamihama-cho in Ishinomaki City wiped out by tsunami and ensuing fire. Photo taken about 8:40 a.m., March 13, 2011

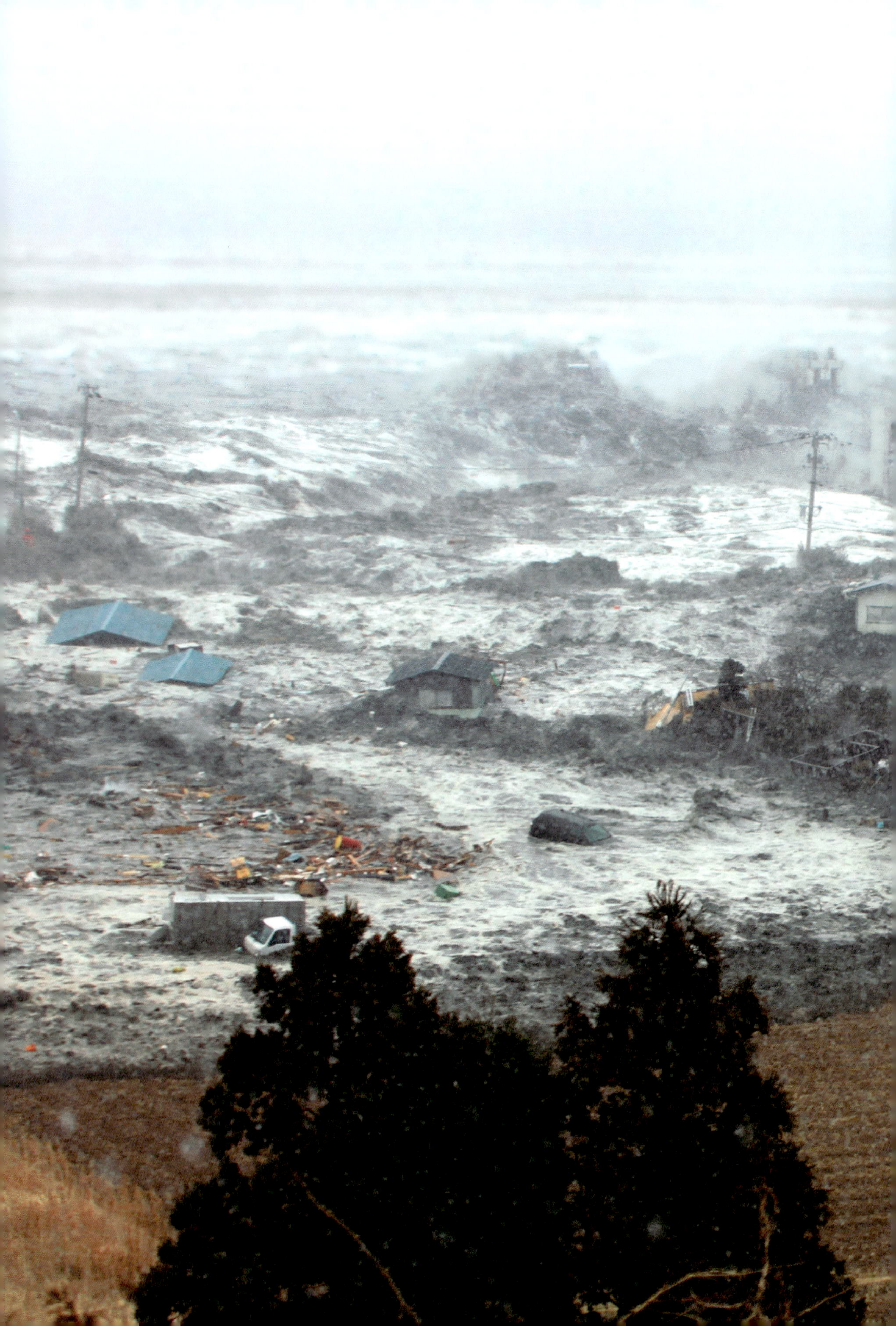

Raging tsunami closing in on houses in Jusanhama, Ishinomaki City. Photo taken at 3:31 p.m., March 11, 2011, courtesy of Tohoku Chiikizukuri Kyoukai

Tsunami increasing its force as it surged into residential streets in Sumiyoshi-cho 1-chome, Ishinomaki City. Photo taken about 3:50 p.m., March 11, 2011

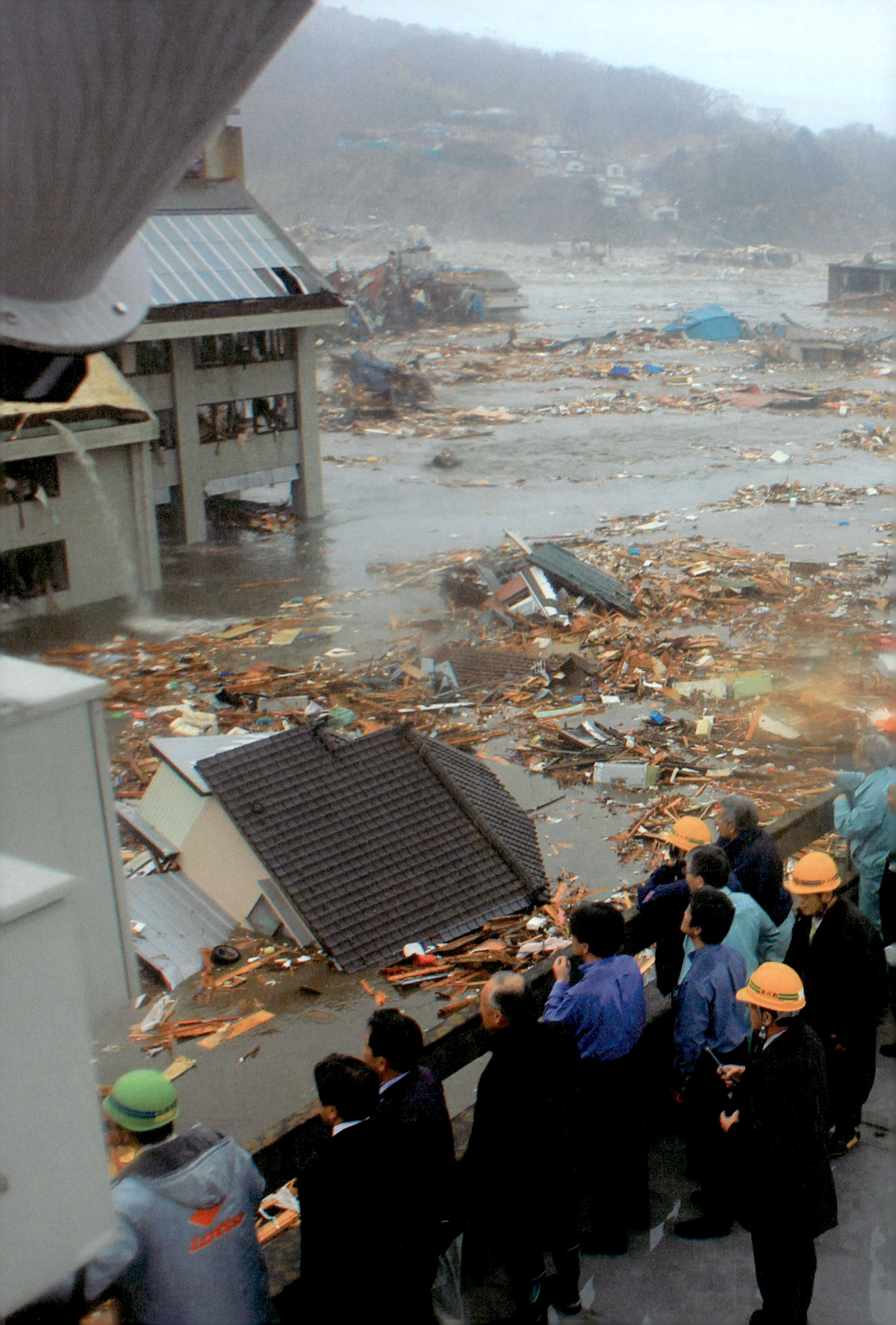

Stunned Onagawa residents staring down at tsunami as it tore homes to pieces. Photo taken at Onagawa Town Hall, 3:47 p.m., March 11, 2011

Many pupils and school staff fell victim to the tsunami at Okawa Elementary School in Ishinomaki City. Backpacks and other school things found in and around the school were gathered together. Photo taken in Kamaya around 3:15 p.m., March 29, 2011

[英語版] 津波からの生還　東日本大震災・石巻地方100人の証言

SURVIVING THE 2011 TSUNAMI

100 Testimonies of Ishinomaki Area Survivors of the Great East Japan Earthquake

Editorial Office of The Ishinomaki Kahoku
A Daily Newspaper of Sanriku Kahoku Shimpo

JUNPOSHA

Copyright © 2014 by Sanriku Kahoku Shimpo Co.
First printing, 2014

Published in 2014 by Junposha Co,. Ltd
2-14-13 Mejirodai, Bunkyo-ku, Tokyo 112-0015 Japan
www.junposha.com

Printed in Japan by Chuo Seihan Printing Co.

All rights reserved. No part of this book may be reprinted or reproduced or utilized in any form or by any electronic, mechanical or other means, now known or hereafter invented, including photocopying and recording, or in any information storage or retrieval system, without permission in writing from the publisher.

ISBN978-4-8451-1351-4

Foreword

This book contains the interview series that was run under the title "My March 11" in *The Ishinomaki Kahoku*, a daily newspaper published by Sanriku Kahoku Shimpo serving the Greater Ishinomaki Region—Ishinomaki City, Higashi-Matsushima City, and Onagawa Town. The entire serial, run in 100 installments for nine months starting three months after the disaster in June 2011, has been translated into English practically in its original form.

The tsunami inundated the first floor of the corporate headquarters building of Sanriku Kahoku Shimpo with the resultant failure of the editorial and production systems. However, we resumed the publication of our newspaper, two pages back to back, three days later. The staff members were all safe, but everybody had suffered from the disaster in varying ways including the loss of homes, and a few had lost their loved ones. Forty or so residents of the neighborhood were taking shelter in our building for a while after the disaster because of the fear of the tsunami.

While we continued to cover the towns that had turned into what seemed like battlefields because of the tsunami and the fire afterwards, we asked ourselves these questions: what should we do as a regional media that is based in the most severely damaged area and what is it that we can do as a company that is the most intimately connected to the distressed area. "My March 11" was the answer.

To carry the firsthand testimonies of the people who were attacked by the massive tsunami in as much detail as space would allow, focusing on the people who had narrowly survived the disaster at various places on that day, and aim to record the massive tsunami in its true forms; and to enable the people in our area to share the valuable experiences of those who had survived—this, we thought, would be a strong protection against future major tsunamis. Quite a few people had not recovered from the trauma of the disaster, and our requests for interview were often refused with the reply, "I don't want to remember it." What drove our reporters to keep on moving forward whenever they were declined an interview was their conviction that this project would surely be a response to the yearning that the people who had unfortunately fallen victim to the disaster must have had.

It was fortunate that Mr. Naomasa Tanabe, executive editor of the Tokyo publishing house Junposha, took notice of the interview series carried in a regional newspaper that was unknown outside of the Ishinomaki area. "To be able to go up close to the people and to lend your ear to them so you can single-mindedly hear what they have to tell—this style has something in common with the work of the noted American interviewer Studs Terkel"—Mr. Tanabe's appreciation of our project led us to see the series published in a book form, which was something that we had never thought of.

The publication of the English translation came about from a chance encounter as well. In the summer of 2012, Dr. Hitomi Nakanishi, assistant professor of the University of Canberra, who happened to visit our head office as part of an inspection tour of the disaster-stricken area, read this book and said, "This is something I would like people in the world to read." She suggested that the book could be translated by volunteers. I was incredulous about this unexpected proposal, but after returning to Australia, Prof. Nakanishi rallied support for the project on the Internet, to which 26 Japanese residing in various places in Japan and Australia responded, offering to translate the book as volunteers. Furthermore, 16 Australian friends of Prof. Nakanishi kindly participated in the checking of the manuscript as native speakers of English. Within a matter of six months, the English manuscript of all the 100 interviews was delivered to me from Australia. Mr. Tanabe of Junposha readily agreed to publish what would be the publisher's first book in English. The manuscript was given another careful checking by a few translators who are familiar with the region, and the English version of the book finally came to completion as we are about to reach the third-year anniversary of the disaster.

The importance of the *bond* of the family and of the people of the community was reaffirmed following the great disaster of 2011. The word has even become a motto for the restoration support effort. I believe that the publication of this English edition is in fact a product that was woven by the bond of the people who were united, beyond the borders of a region and of nations, in their earnest desire to help spread the lessons of the disaster around the world.

I would like to convey my gratitude to the many people who supported the translation project. It is my hope that this book will be of help to the foreign readers as they deepen their understanding of the Great East Japan Earthquake, a once-in-a-millennium event, and prepare for potential major earthquakes and tsunamis.

—**Yoshihisa Nishikawa**
President
Sanriku Kahoku Shimpo Co.

*The occupation and age of the people in the text are as of the time of interview unless specified otherwise. Longer place names that appear in the text may have a hyphen inserted within each name for the sake of readability. When searching for such place names, the hyphen may be deleted.

CONTENS

Foreword — 003

Photographic record of the Great East Japan Earthquake and Tsunami
—from Greater Ishinomaki — 013

I Ishinomaki City

[Ishinomaki Region]
Overview of damage with maps of inundated areas and aerial views — 053

Colossal wave engulfs the Okada Theater—Horrible sounds made me think *This is the end*
—Kiyoto Sugawara — 061

Clinging onto deck post for life—Surviving frightening night on second floor
—Eiko Matsuno — 062

Escaping car and hanging onto roof gutter—Stranded boat blocking tsunami current saved life
—Masaaki Takasuka — 064

Muddy water invades car—Surviving one night on rooftop while exposed to cold
—Yuka Hamaya — 066

Daring to drive the wrong way to escape—Breaking away from crowd to rescue child
—Masato Kusajima — 067

Tsunami: the lesser of two evils—Fear of fire pushed me to jump into water
—Masayoshi Kotono — 070

Slipping into unconsciousness in water—Floating rooftop was my lifesaver
—Katsuju Ogata — 071

Churned as if in a washing machine—Evacuating into factory after being washed away 200 meters
—Masahide Yoshida — 073

24,000-ton freighter with 31 on board washed away
—Massive force of tsunami cut off thick mooring rope, sending ship adrift
—Tomofumi Abe — 075

Isolated after being washed away, house and all—Jumping into water saved my life
—Toshiji Fukuda — 076

Pain pierces body while getting out of flooded car—Climbing to store roof to stay above water
—Nobuaki Miura — 078

Baby in arms, mother runs for life
　　—Handing baby to husband on rooftop
　　—Miho Asano —————————————————————————————— 079

"I had this sheer desire to save my grandchild"—I waded out into a sea of rubble to seek rescue
　　—Yoshiji Mogi ————————————————————————————— 081

Flooding besieged City Hall
　　—Responding to overwhelming needs as City Hall chief despite losing family members
　　—Hideyuki Sugawara ————————————————————————— 082

Sudden onslaught sends chill up my spine
　　—Houses jamming into Utsumi-bashi Bridge
　　—Seitaro Omori —————————————————————————————— 084

Strong quake during an operation—Hospital staff helped all 150 inpatients escape with SDF support
　　—Kimie Ito ———————————————————————————————— 086

Hotel turned into shelter for 300—Devoted staff helped manage shelter over two months
　　—Munenori Goto —————————————————————————————— 087

Frantic run from the surging tsunami—Crossing makeshift bridge from school building to back hill
　　—Yukiteru Moriyama ———————————————————————————— 089

Over 1,000 employees safely evacuated—With bodies buried in rubble, debris was removed with caution
　　—Yoshikatsu Murakami ——————————————————————————— 090

Restored 17th century sailing ship survives tsunami
　　—Sant Juan Bautista Museum's Dock Hall submerged in waters
　　—Hiroshi Sudo ———————————————————————————————— 092

Kindergarten principal takes children to roof—The tsunami came surging in two layers
　　—Hiroaki Tsuda ———————————————————————————————— 094

Tsunami closes in on police car—Cry for help drew rescue response for mother and child
　　—Takeyuki Kanno ——————————————————————————————— 096

Rescue operation in a sea of debris—Fighting a fire approaching hillside
　　—Rikio Konno ————————————————————————————————— 097

Examining patients at evacuation centers—Doctor brothers reassured evacuees
　　—Fumihiko Sato ———————————————————————————————— 099

Setting up aid station at school—Cooperating with fellow health professionals
　　—Satoko Tsuda ————————————————————————————————— 100

Receiving the support of 800 volunteer pharmacists
　　—Coordinating prescriptions and hygiene guidance
　　—Yoshiro Tanno ———————————————————————————————— 102

Attacked by tsunami in the dark—Candlelight saved my life
　　—Sadao Owada ————————————————————————————————— 104

Golden wall of water closes in—Aitopia Street turns into sea of sludge
　　—Kiyoko Abe —————————————————————————————————106

Water almost reaches ceiling—Helping elderly parents dive under doorway
　　—Yoshihide Okumura ————————————————————————————108

Ships knock down electric power poles—The gushing water was like a horizontal waterfall
　　—Nanae Onodera ——————————————————————————————109

First floor of school: Sea of sludge—Staff immediately respond to needs of students and evacuees
　　—Toshiyuki Fukuhara ————————————————————————————111

Wall of white wave behind us—Desperate getaway with family in car
　　—Chika Unakami ——————————————————————————————112

Murky water shooting out between houses—Running for dear life to Hiyoriyama hills
　　—Hiroyuki Suda ——————————————————————————————114

Bookshelf becomes lifeboat—Evacuee gives birth to baby at school
　　—Nobutaka Shoji ——————————————————————————————115

Restaurant owner and staff brace up to rescue people
　　—Seventy people took shelter at Chinese restaurant
　　—Yuko Yamamoto ——————————————————————————————116

Battle for life on top of car—Each time I fell I thought *This is the end*
　　—Shota Ito ————————————————————————————————118

Tsunami rushes in at breakneck speed—House struck second floor of office building
　　—Maki Shiratori ——————————————————————————————119

Tsunami engulfs tide barrier pine trees—Large cargo ship under construction slides into ocean
　　—Mamoru Onuma ——————————————————————————————121

Heading for shelter with invalid family—Escaping disaster with help of many
　　—Hideki Saito ——————————————————————————————124

First floor submerged in sea—The river turned into a black writhing horizon
　　—Katsuhiro Suzuki —————————————————————————————125

My soon-to-be-born baby must wait for help!—Enduring the pain
　　—Yukako Sasaki ——————————————————————————————127

Escaping to a slope, just in the nick of time—The tsunami swallowed up a line of cars
　　—Yoshietsu Sasaki —————————————————————————————130

Water gushing out at front approach to Makiyama
　　—"A tsunami is approaching!" I yelled to a line of cars
　　—Hitomi Chiba ——————————————————————————————131

Traffic jam hampers evacuation—Water comes to chest on 2nd floor
　　—Kenichi Abe ——————————————————————————————132

Getting washed away in car—With no time to escape, my car floated in the water and started drifting
  —Ryuji Hayashi ————————————————————— 134

Helping 20 escape to station rooftop—Rescuing people trapped in flooded cars
  —Kaichi Nishino —————————————————————— 136

Big black waves wash away neighbor's house—Three children rescued from rooftop
  —Yasuhiro Kikuchi —————————————————————— 137

Massive wave fended off by skillful boat maneuvering—Split-second decision saves life
  —Shuichi Utsumi ——————————————————————— 139

[Oshika, Kahoku, Kitakami, and Ogatsu Regions]
Overview of damage with maps of inundated areas and aerial views —— 141

Boat out of control—Fellow fishermen support via wireless
  —Satoru Watanabe ——————————————————————— 149

Boat suspended from six-meter wave—Battered by sprays of flotsam
  —Tsutomu Hiratsuka —————————————————————— 150

A devastated seaside community—Working for our "Large Catch"
  —Hidenori Abe ————————————————————————— 152

Steering frantically in turbulent waves—A village that disappeared without a trace
  —Fumio Kimura ————————————————————————— 153

Houses washed away into ocean—First wave engulfs cars
  —Fumiko Toda —————————————————————————— 155

Barber shop washed away by second tsunami—Restarting as barber at shelter
  —Tadao Takeda ————————————————————————— 156

Drawback of tsunami reveals sea bottom
  —It reminded me of a scene from the movie *The Ten Commandments*
  —Toru Sasaki —————————————————————————— 158

Tsunami walls close in on fishermen—Devastation leaves seaside village in despair
  —Katsuyuki Atsumi —————————————————————— 160

Muddy tsunami hit rooftop—Diving into torrent to swim for life
  —Noriko Watanabe ——————————————————————— 161

Family carried away offshore, house and all—Spending night on drifting boat
  —Kyuetsu Abe ——————————————————————————— 163

Mother disappears in whirlpool—Water roars as it recedes
  —Kiyonori Naganuma ————————————————————— 167

Hamlet becomes remote island—Five who won't be returning home
  —Senichiro Suenaga ————————————————————— 168

Muddy waters reach high ground—Men rescue elderly woman
—**Shoji Sanouchi** ———————————————————————————— 170

Man swims across waters with floating log—The tsunami was like Niagara Falls
—**Michio Komatsu** ———————————————————————————— 172

Tsunami attacks school from two sides—Teachers save stranded woman with rope
—**Shigeru Tamura** ———————————————————————————— 173

Saving two girls stranded in school—Making path with boards for barefoot girls
—**Hiroshi Sasaki** ———————————————————————————— 175

Tsunami attacks from two different directions—Stranded residents rescued by fishing boat
—**Shigeo Ogawa** ———————————————————————————— 177

Tsunami swallows homes in Nagatsura district
—Collapsing in tears while holding body in arms
—**Hisaji Nishimura** ———————————————————————————— 178

Aquaculture farmer hangs from tree branch—Too busy struggling to feel any fear
—**Takashi Oyama** ———————————————————————————— 180

House after house swept away in whirling waters—Warning neighbors to evacuate
—**Kiyoshi Oyama** ———————————————————————————— 181

Screaming to pupils, "Run up the hill!"—Graduation ceremonies on the street in six different venues
—**Seinosuke Katakura** ———————————————————————————— 183

Bridge girders swept away by wave's impact—Rice paddies and villages becoming just like sea
—**Yasuo Sasaki** ———————————————————————————— 184

II Onagawa Town

Overview of damage with maps of inundated areas and aerial views ———— 189

Chased up antenna tower by tsunami—Capsized fishing vessel came bearing down
—**Kazuyoshi Noda** ———————————————————————————— 193

Waiting out tsunami perched on ladder—Dozens of cars falling as if in waterfall
—**Kenichi Hino** ———————————————————————————— 195

Massive waves go over supermarket roof—Drifting alone in sea for over 14 hours
—**Akihito Kimura** ———————————————————————————— 196

Escaping to maintenance tower—20-ton ship closing in on Town Hall
—**Koya Kimura** ———————————————————————————— 198

Tsunami reaches hospital on hill 16 meters above sea
—Hospital staff respond to patients and evacuees
—Kaoru Cho ——————————————————————————————199

Husband and wife carried away into bay—Her last words: "I want to see my grandkids"
—Hayato Aso ——————————————————————————————201

Floating away in my attic refuge—Running to shrine when waters recede
—Tadashi Yamada ————————————————————————————203

Astonished to be swept away in my home—Waiting on roof to be rescued
—Miki Mochida ——————————————————————————————204

Tossed around in my ship out at sea—Saving life by jumping onto rocky tract
—Hideki Ueki ——————————————————————————————206

Friend's ship washed away—Salmon farming facilities destroyed completely
—Yoshiaki Kimura ————————————————————————————207

III Higashi-Matsushima City

Overview of damage with maps of inundated areas and aerial views —————————211

Tumbling into water as house collapses—Unable to move in muddy torrent
—Atsuko Ogata ——————————————————————————————219

Whirling current like a plunge pool—Clinging to floating beam
—Nobuaki Atsumi ————————————————————————————220

Tsunami sweeps man into river—Hanging on to floating object for three kilometers upstream
—Masaru Ogata ——————————————————————————————222

Tree stops car from being swept into bay—Evacuating into canal's control center
—Harue Kanno ——————————————————————————————223

Narrow escape: train stopped on high ground—Caring gestures keep hearts warm overnight
—Yasuko Konno ——————————————————————————————225

Swallowed by tsunami, prepared to die—Mom was saved because of a cranny
—Kenichi Saito ——————————————————————————————226

Losing elderly residents in tsunami—Engulfed during transport to evacuation center
—Teruo Oizumi ——————————————————————————————228

Tsunami goes over first floor of school—Classroom packed with 400 evacuees
—Satoko Ishimori ————————————————————————————229

Plowing through water to nursery school—Late night rescue of sleeeping children
—Akihiro Onodera ————————————————————————————231

Evacuation with elderly on back—Muddy dental records used to identify tsunami victims
  —Hiroshi Kawashima ——————————————————————— 232

Big wave hits car in traffic jam—Washed away in car, prepared to face death
  —Keiko Sato ——————————————————————————— 234

Family rushes to truck to avoid tsunami—Huddling together in attic to survive cold night
  —Kana Takeda —————————————————————————— 235

Tsunami smashes through walls and windows
  —Withstanding onslaught by holding on to staircase handrail
  —Masayuki Okuda ————————————————————————— 237

Jet black wave assaults car—Car eventually lands on slope of mountain
  —Koki Yamauchi ————————————————————————— 238

Saved by running up hill—Dumbfounded at wretched sight
  —Keiko Kikuchi —————————————————————————— 240

Entire car engulfed in muddy stream—Prepared to die as car started sinking
  —Sonosuke Endo —————————————————————————— 241

The appearance of silent black water—Rescuing three people from veranda
  —Yoshiaki Ninomiya ————————————————————————— 242

Narrow escape from tsunami—Taking 25 elderly people to shelter on bus
  —Kazuo Suzuki —————————————————————————— 244

Chased up the hill by tsunami—Climbing over huge rock to reach even higher ground
  —Kenichi Inatomi —————————————————————————— 245

Helicopters washed away from SDF Base—Frustrated rescue staff use dinghies instead
  —Momoei Koseki —————————————————————————— 247

Translators / Messages from translators ——————————————————————— 250

Map Labels

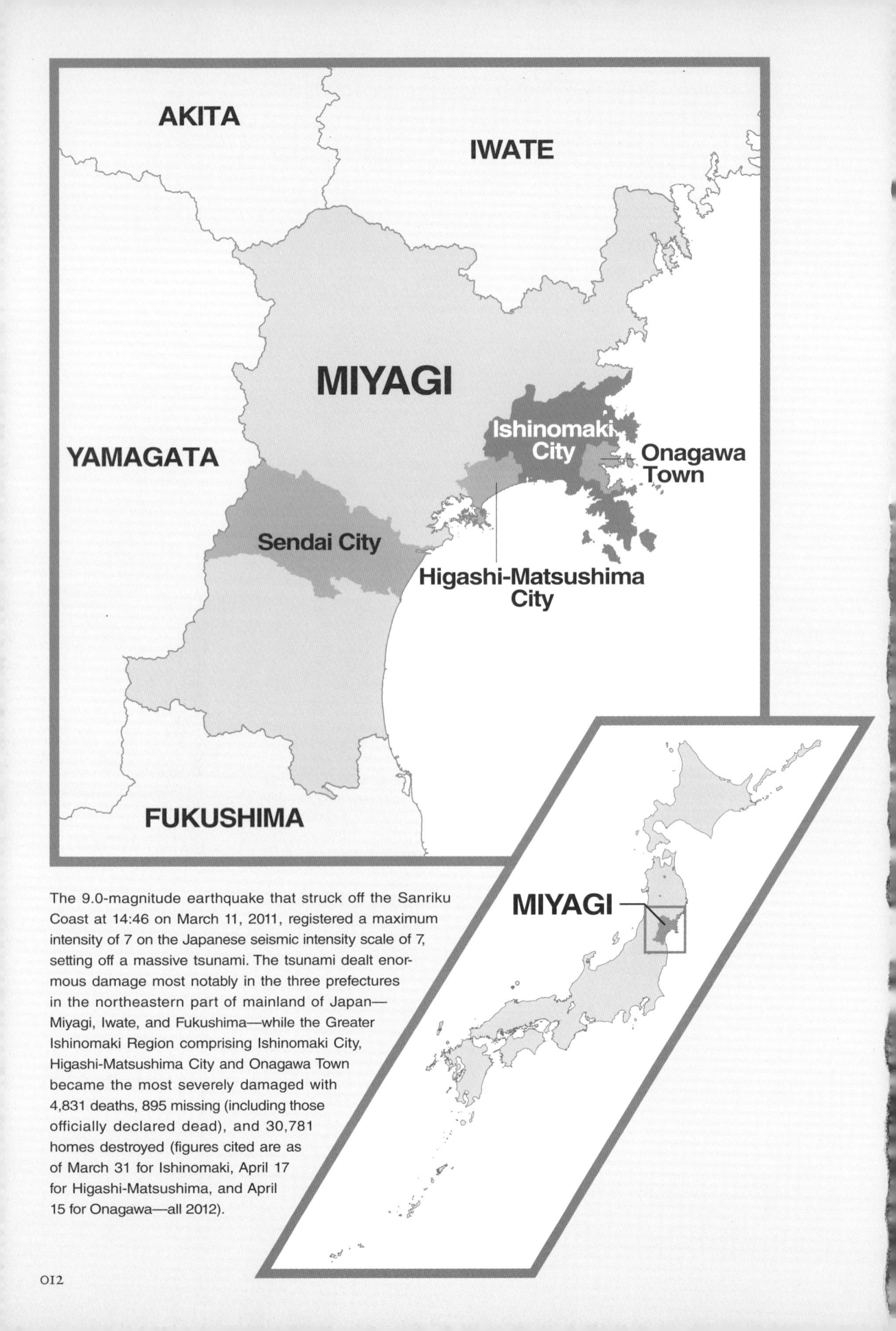

AKITA

IWATE

MIYAGI

YAMAGATA

Ishinomaki City

Onagawa Town

Sendai City

Higashi-Matsushima City

FUKUSHIMA

MIYAGI

The 9.0-magnitude earthquake that struck off the Sanriku Coast at 14:46 on March 11, 2011, registered a maximum intensity of 7 on the Japanese seismic intensity scale of 7, setting off a massive tsunami. The tsunami dealt enormous damage most notably in the three prefectures in the northeastern part of mainland of Japan—Miyagi, Iwate, and Fukushima—while the Greater Ishinomaki Region comprising Ishinomaki City, Higashi-Matsushima City and Onagawa Town became the most severely damaged with 4,831 deaths, 895 missing (including those officially declared dead), and 30,781 homes destroyed (figures cited are as of March 31 for Ishinomaki, April 17 for Higashi-Matsushima, and April 15 for Onagawa—all 2012).

Shopping street in Chuo 3-chome in Ishinomaki turned into scrapyard. Photo taken around 7:00 a.m., March 12, 2011

Two pleasure boats washed away from Kyu-Kitakami-gawa River blocking intersection of shopping streets in Ishinomaki's Chuo 2-chome. Photo taken around 7:00 a.m., March 12, 2011

Kadonowaki Elementary School in Kadonowaki-cho 4-chome, Ishinomaki City, burned out by fire that broke out after tsunami attack. Photo taken around 2:30 p.m., March 15, 2011

After the Quake

Shopping street Aitopia in Chuo 2-chome in Ishinomaki filled with sludge and rubble, blocked further by stranded car. Photo taken around noon, March 12, 2011

Before the Quake

Aitopia shopping street before quake, trees along street adding nice touch. This photo taken in December 2008 shows same street as above, but from opposite direction.

Disaster victims heading for shelter on flooded National Route 398 in Okaido-Minami, Ishinomaki City. Photo taken around 11:10 a.m., March 12, 2011

Rolls of paper readied for shipping lying scattered in yard of Nippon Paper Industries Ishinomaki Mill in Nanko-cho, Ishinomaki City. Photo taken around noon, March 21, 2011

Collapsed transit shed at Ishinomaki Fish Market in Sakanamachi 2-chome, Ishinomaki City, left no clue as to what it used to be like. Photo taken about 12:35 p.m., March 21, 2011

Miyagi Prefecture's fishing training vessel washed up onto seawall in front of Ishinomaki Fish Market in Sakanamachi. Photo taken in morning, April 2, 2011

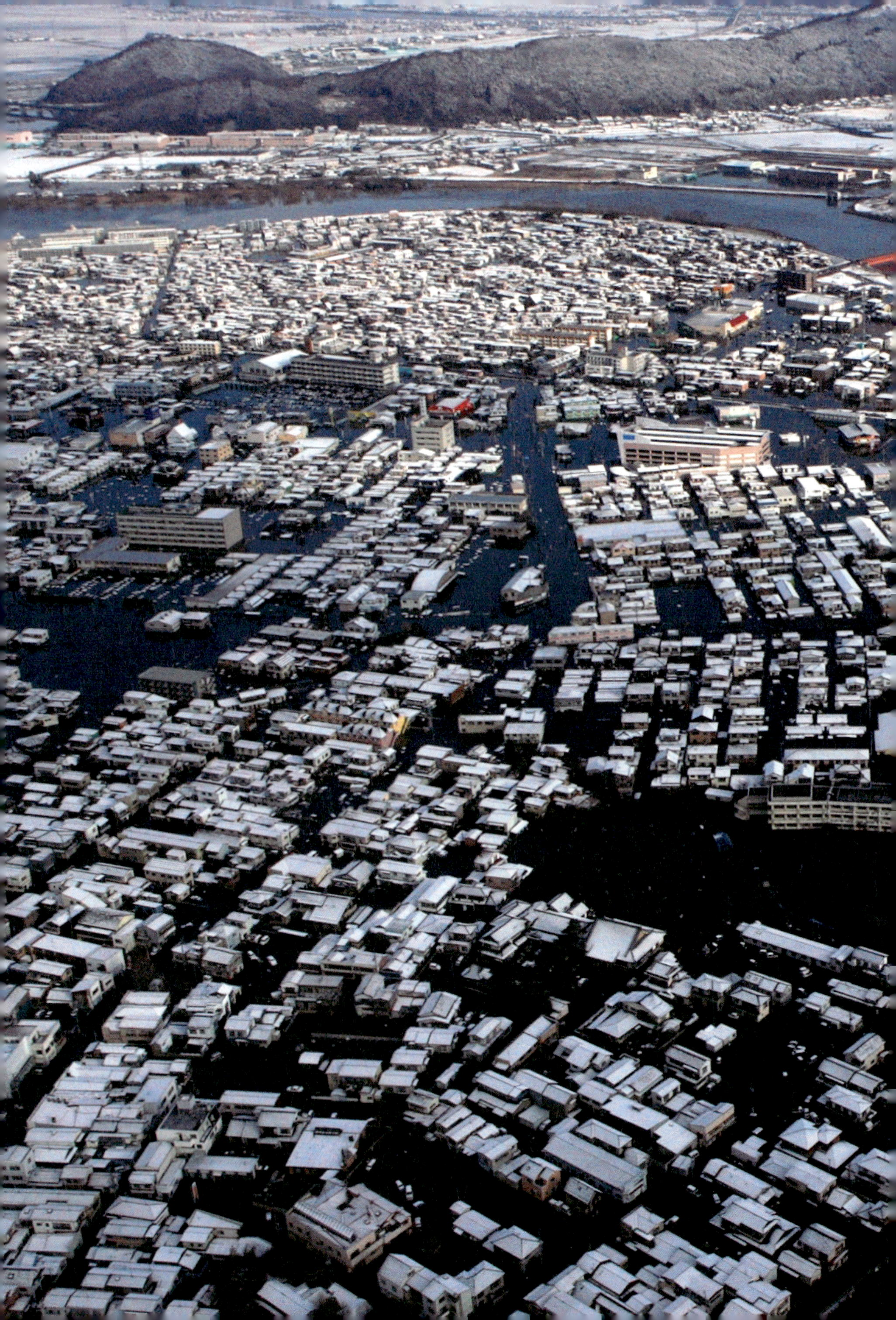

Flooded area of Central Ishinomaki. Building with large round roof in center of photo is Sumiyoshi Elementary School. Bridge on right is Ishinomaki-ohashi Bridge. Photo taken at 7:40 a.m., March 12, 2011

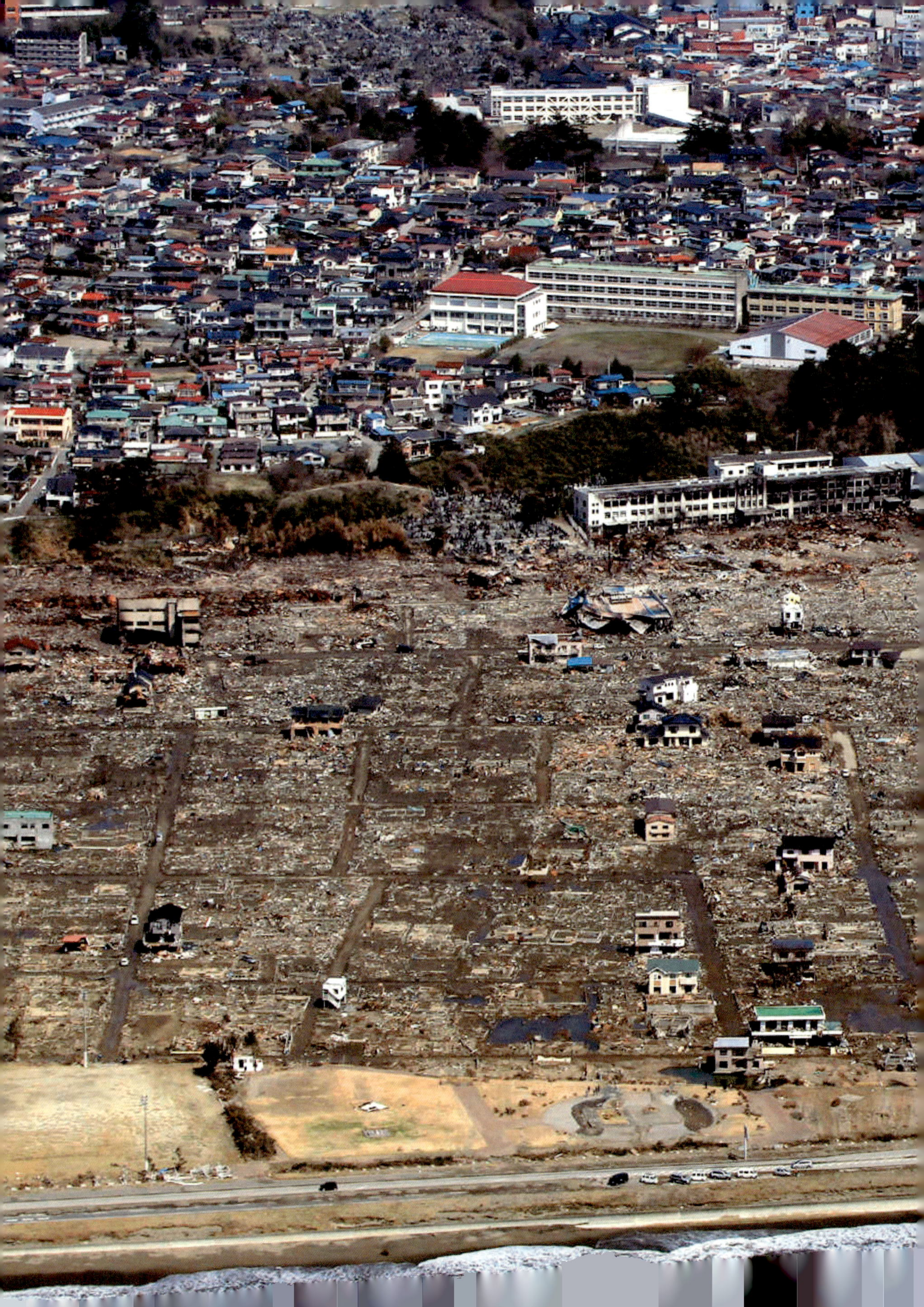

Devastated Minamihama-cho and Kadonowaki-cho in Ishinomaki City. Debris scattered from coast to bottom of Hiyoriyama hills in back. Photo taken in morning, April 10, 2011

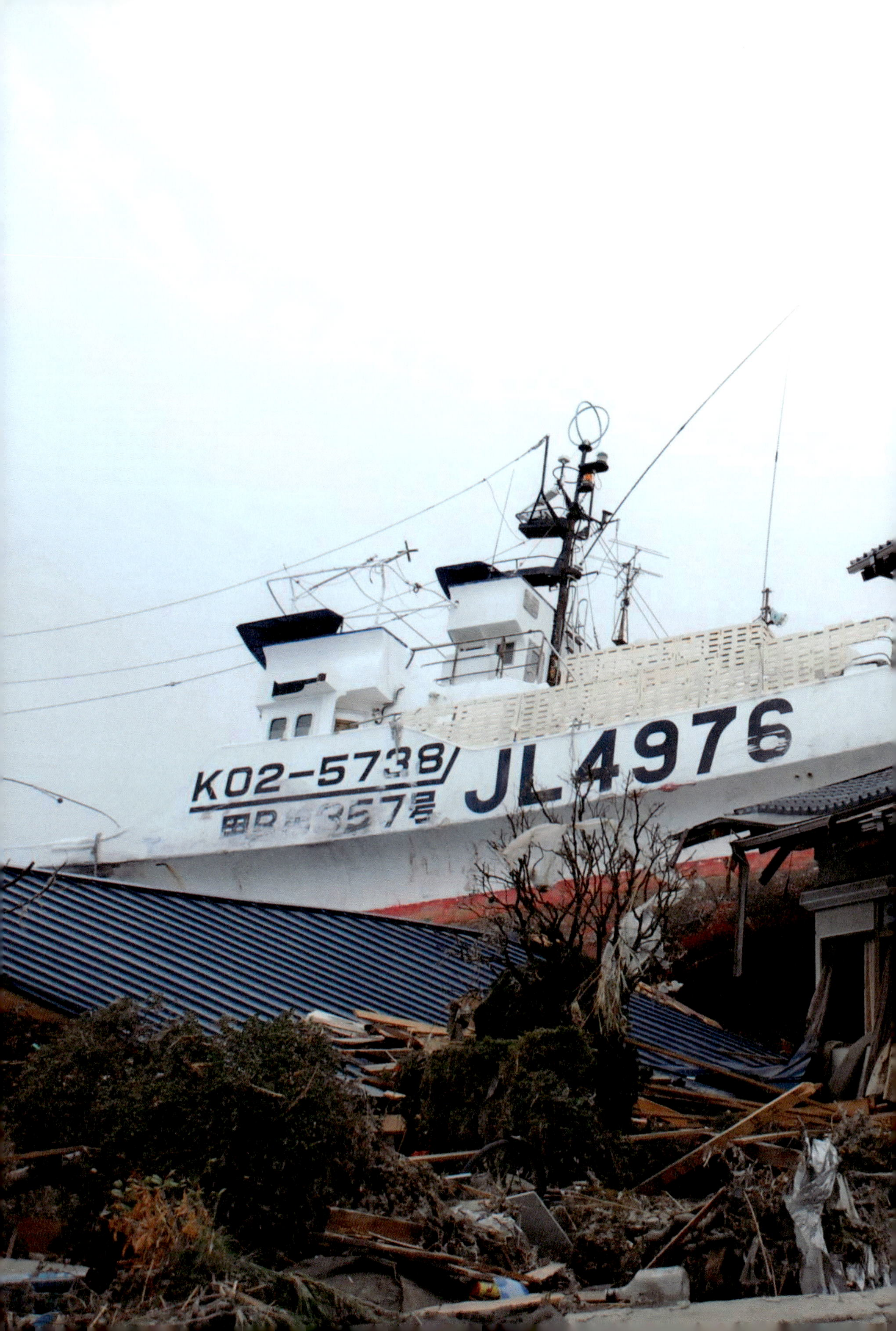
K02-5738
JL4976

Fishing vessel landed in backyard of house in Kawaguchi-cho, Ishinomaki City. Tsunami brought unbelievable horror to numerous places. Photo taken about 4:10 p.m., March 24, 2011

Yoriiso Fishing Port in Ishinomaki being attacked by tsunami

① Cars being swept, piling up in spaces among houses. Photo taken about 3:15 p.m., March 11, 2011

② Raging tsunami smashing against seawall. Photo taken at 3:40 p.m.

③ Heaving black tsunami barreling along, destroying fishing village. Photo taken at 3:40 p.m.

Seabed of strait between Kinkasan Island and Oshika Peninsula exposed after powerful drawback of tsunami

Waves from both north and south clash against each other, making sea surface swell high. Both photos taken by Mr. Ryo Higashino from Kinkasan Island at 3:36 p.m., March 11, 2011

Tsunami surging in from Nobiru Beach in back right. Houses inundated up to ceiling of first floor of two-story homes. Photo taken by Ms. Eri Watanabe at Tona, Higashi-Matsushima City around 4:00 p.m., March 11, 2011

Man escaping from car being washed away. After forcing door open, he fled into Ishinomaki Kahoku building just in front of him. Photo taken at Sengoku-cho, Ishinomaki, at 3:52 p.m., March 11, 2011

Coastal village in Nagatsura, Ishinomaki City, inundated after tsunami attack remaining isolated. Body of water at top is Kitakami-gawa River. Photo taken in morning, April 10, 2011

Town of Ayukawa at end of Oshika Peninsula devastated as well. Up front is Oshika Whale Land. Photo taken in morning, April 8, 2011

After the Quake

Oshika Whale Land scattered with debris. In back, catcher boat *No. 16 Toshimaru* escaped getting washed away. Photo taken about 2:30 p.m., March 20, 2011, Ayukawahama, Ishinomaki City

Before the Quake

Oshika Whale Land before disaster—reminiscent of prosperous whaling days of Ayukawa Port as whaling base. Photo taken December 2007

Collapsed homes in Oginohama, Ishinomaki City. Tiled roofs on ground—painful reminders of tsunami's power. Photo taken about 10:50 a.m., April 24, 2011

Oshika's monument for welcoming tourists submerged after tsunami attack. Photo taken at Ayukawa Port, Ishinomaki City, about 2:30 p.m., March 20, 2011

Tatami factory in Monou-cho, Ishinomaki City, totaled by earthquake. Inland areas were not affected by tsunami but earthquake damage occurred at numerous places. Photo taken April 18, 2011

Many sought shelter at public facilities in inland areas. Photo taken at Ishinomaki City's sports center in Kanan, about 11:15 a.m., April 20, 2011

Only foundations remain of homes in fishing village next to Ogatsu Port; washed-up wreckage of homes gives no clue where they came from. Photo taken at Ogatsucho Mizuhama, Ishinomaki City, about 1:40 p.m., April 6, 2011

Dumbfounded victims at site of what was their home in Ogatsucho Karakuwa, Ishinomaki City. Photo taken at 10:40 a.m., March 14, 2011

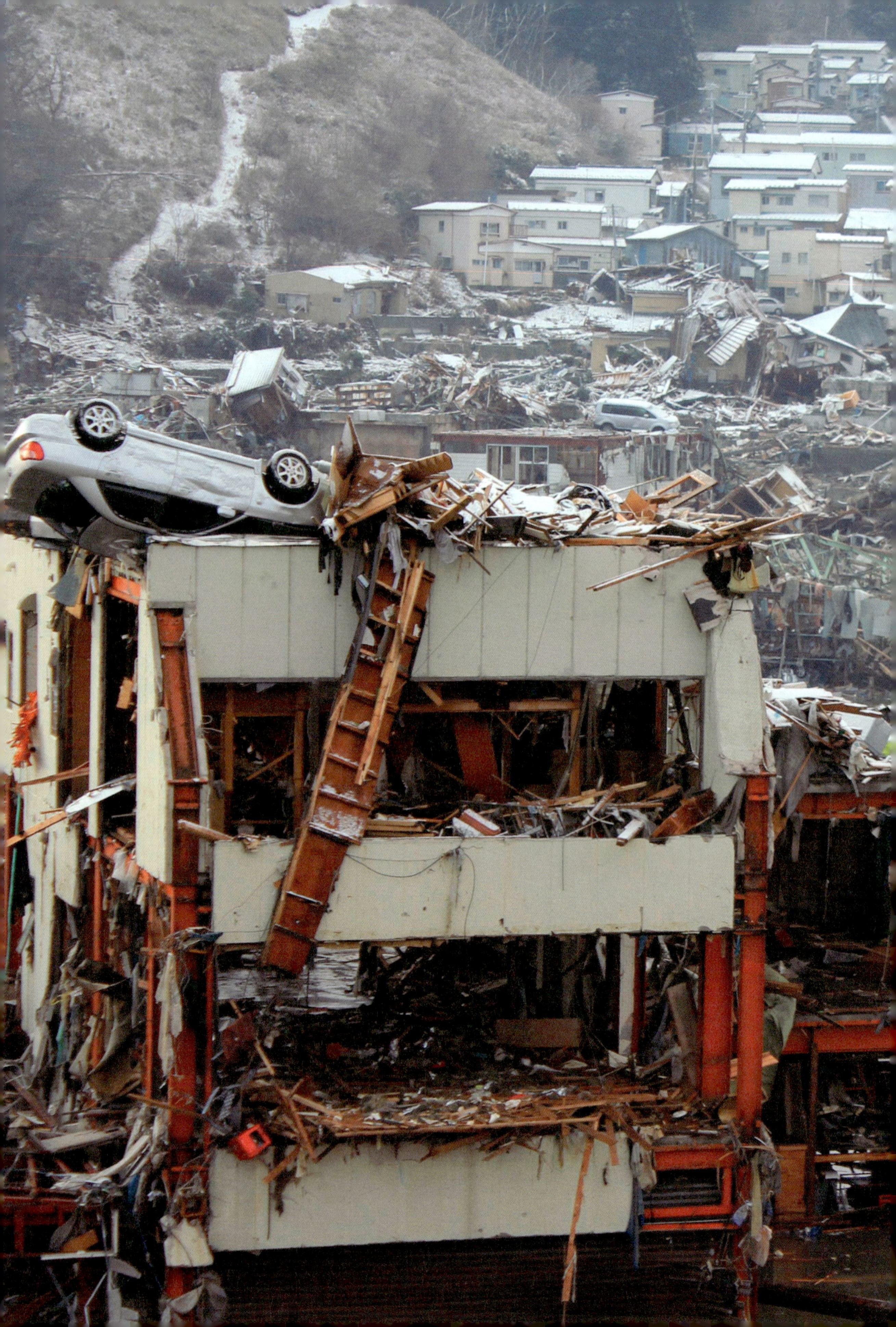

Cars washed up on top of three-story buildings in central Onagawa. Photo taken at Koganehama, about 7:10 a.m., March 12, 2011

Train car of Japan Railway's Ishinomaki Line washed up on cemetery ground scattered with tombstones. Photo taken in Onagawahama, Onagawa Town, afternoon, March 25, 2011

Firefighters put all-out effort searching for missing amid washed-up boat, wreckage of buildings and debris in Onagawahama, Onagawa Town. Photo taken in afternoon, March 18, 2011

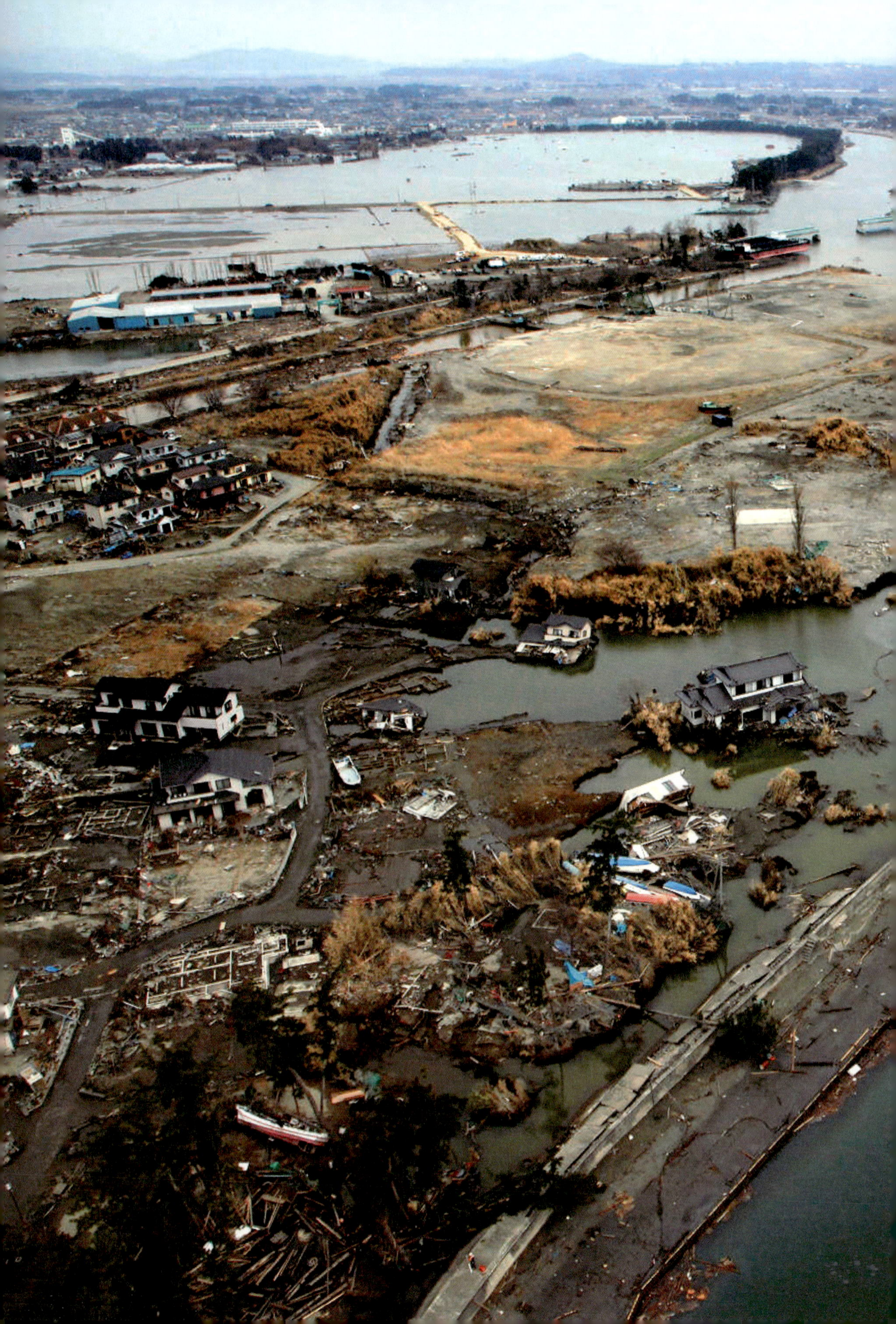

Large cargo ship stranded in devastated town after getting washed up by tsunami. Photo taken in Omagari, Higashi-Matsushima City, in afternoon, April 8, 2011

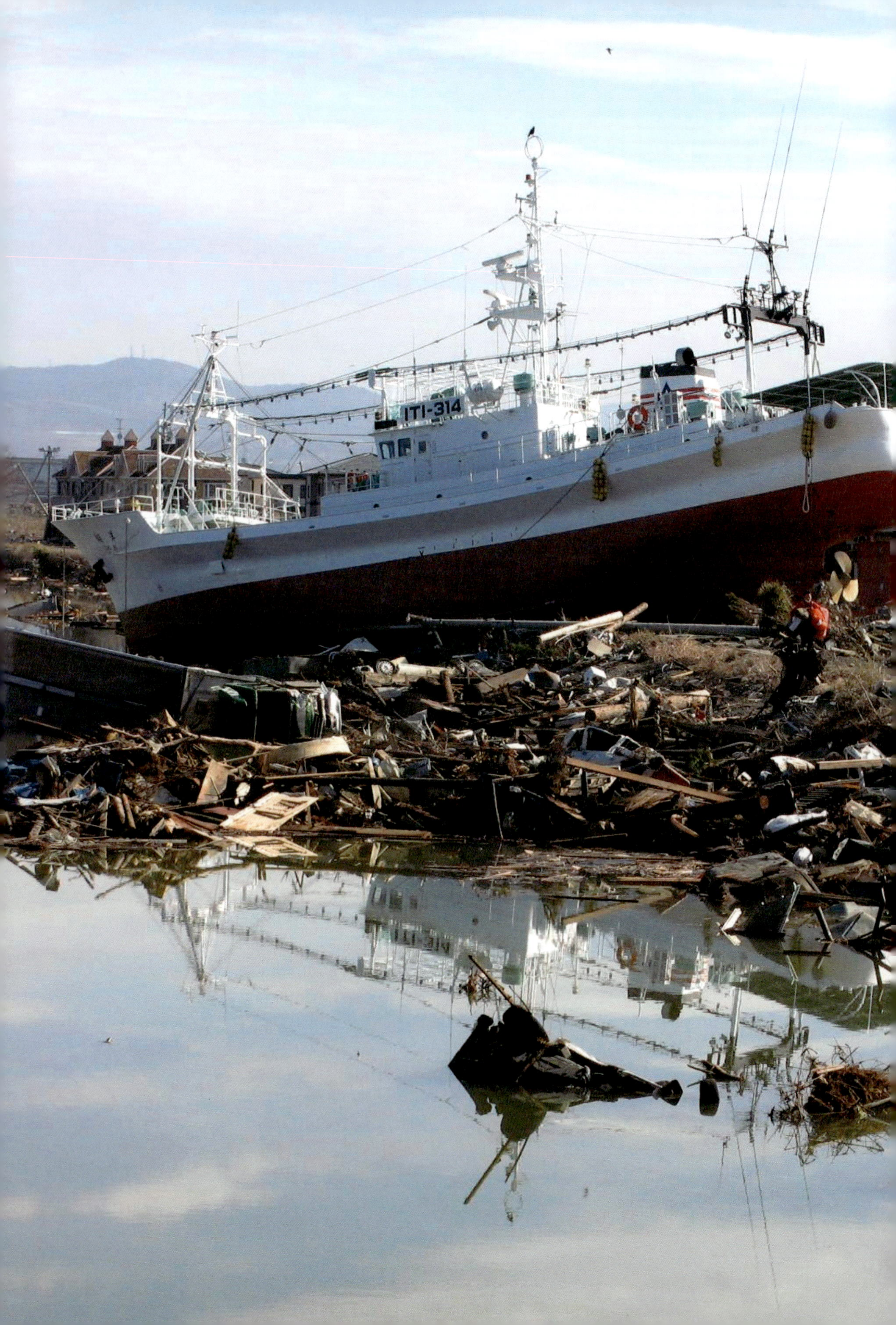
ITI-314

Fishing vessel washed up onto residential area in Omagari, Higashi-Matsushima City. Photo taken about 8:35 a.m., March 19, 2011

Commuting street for Yamoto Nichu Junior High School students remaining flooded, scattered with logs. Photo taken in Akai, Higashi-Matsushima City, March 18, 2011

Whole village vanished in devastated Omagarihama. Photo taken in Omagari, Higashi-Matsushima City about 8:00 a.m., March 19, 2011

Two-story house floating in Tona Canal in Nobiru, Higashi-Matsushima City. Photo taken about 4:10 p.m., March 15, 2011

Railroad tie sticking high up in air and twisted rails—testimony to destructive power of earthquake and tsunami. Photo taken at Japan Railway's Tona Station on Senseki Line, about 12:40 p.m., April 4, 2011

Bent-up train swept off of rails on Japan Railway's Senseki Line. Photo taken in Nobiru, Higashi-Matsushima City, about 11:20 a.m., March 18, 2011

Overturned piano and podium on 5-centimeter-deep layer of mud inside Nobiru Elementary School gym, Higashi-Matsushima City. Photo taken April 11, 2011

Great number of volunteers removing massive amounts of garbage and rubble. Photo taken in Tachimachi, Ishinomaki City, about 11:00 a.m., April 10, 2011

Pupils volunteering to clean up their mud-filled school. Photo taken at Omagari Elementary School, Higashi-Matsushima City, 10:30 a.m., March 27, 2011

"We've come to know how grateful we are to have food." Victims eat curry rice and pork soup provided at shelter. Photo taken at Osu Elementary School, Ishinomaki City, about noon, April 2, 2011

Super long line in front of supermarket due to shortage of food and essential daily commodities. Difficulty of getting gasoline forced most people to walk to store. Photo taken in Okaido-Higashi, Ishinomaki City, about 11:25 a.m., March 13, 2011

U.S. servicemen visiting with victims at evacuation shelter, April 14, 2011. Photo, taken by Mr. Yosuke Kimura at Ishinomaki High School, won the Shiraken Kamaboko Inc. Award in the 1st Ishinomaki Kahoku Restoration Photography Exhibition.

Children practicing baseball without giving in to harsh environment. Photo, taken by Mr. Shigenao Takahashi at Kadonowaki Elementary School on October 22, 2012, won Ishinomaki Kahoku Award and Onagawa Town Mayor Award in the 2nd Ishinomaki Kahoku Restoration Photography Exhibition.

Onagawa Town Hall staff cleaning photos retrieved from debris, hoping they will be claimed by owners. Photo taken at Onagawa Municipal Gym, 10:45 a.m., March 24, 2011

City of Ishinomaki starting to be recovered with smoke rising from Nippon Paper Industries Ishinomaki Mill after having been plunged into darkness. While fishing industry is mainstay of Ishinomaki, paper mill is another symbol of the town. Photo, taken in Ishinomaki by Mr. Tomezo Suganomata in 2011, won Nippon Paper Industry Award in the 1st Ishinomaki Kahoku Restoration Photography Exhibition.

People preparing lanterns to console the souls of disaster victims. Photo, taken by Mr. Masaharu Nakagawa on March 11, 2012, won the Ishinomaki Kahoku Award in the 2nd Ishinomaki Kahoku Restoration Photography Exhibition.

I

Ishinomaki City

Damage Report of Ishinomaki City (as of end of December, 2013)

Casualties	
Dead	3,415 (including 249 related deaths)
Missing	434 (including 424 officially declared dead)
Peak number of evacuees	50,758 (March 17, 2011)
Date all shelters closed	October 11, 2011

Extent of inundation by tsunami	
Inundated land area	73 km²
Municipal land area	556 km²
Population of inundated area	112,276

Number of damaged homes	Number of homes
Total collapse	19,973
Partial collapse	13,099
Partial damage	23,615
Total damaged homes	56,687
Total homes before earthquake	74,000

Temporary housing	
Number of temporary housing	6,523 (7,102) units
Occupants	14,824 (16,788)
Houses/apartments as temporary housing	4,604 (5,808) units
Occupants	12,012 (15,482)

*Figures in parentheses indicate peak count.

Inundated areas in central Ishinomaki

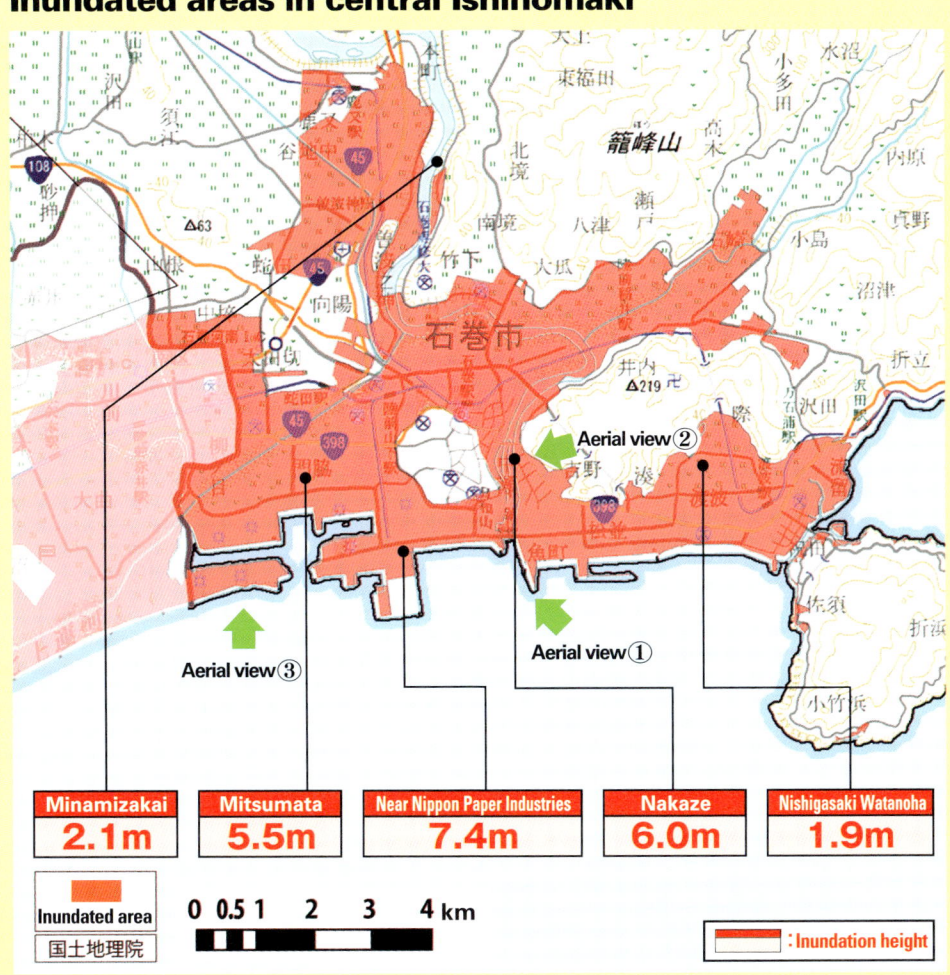

Minamizakai	Mitsumata	Near Nippon Paper Industries	Nakaze	Nishigasaki Watanoha
2.1m	5.5m	7.4m	6.0m	1.9m

Aerial view ①
Kadonowakicho and Minamihamacho

View of Kyu-Kitakami-gawa River from above Ishinomaki Fishing Port. In center of pre-disaster photo is Ishinomaki City Hospital, large white building by harbor with small boats. Long white building in front of green hill at top right is Kadonowaki Elementary School. (Photos Top: November 1999 Bottom: April 17, 2011)

Aerial view ②
Area around Nakaze islet

Egg-shaped building on Nakaze islet, sandbar in Kyu-Kitakami-gawa River, is Ishinomori Mangattan Museum. (Photos Top: September 2001 Bottom: April 17, 2011)

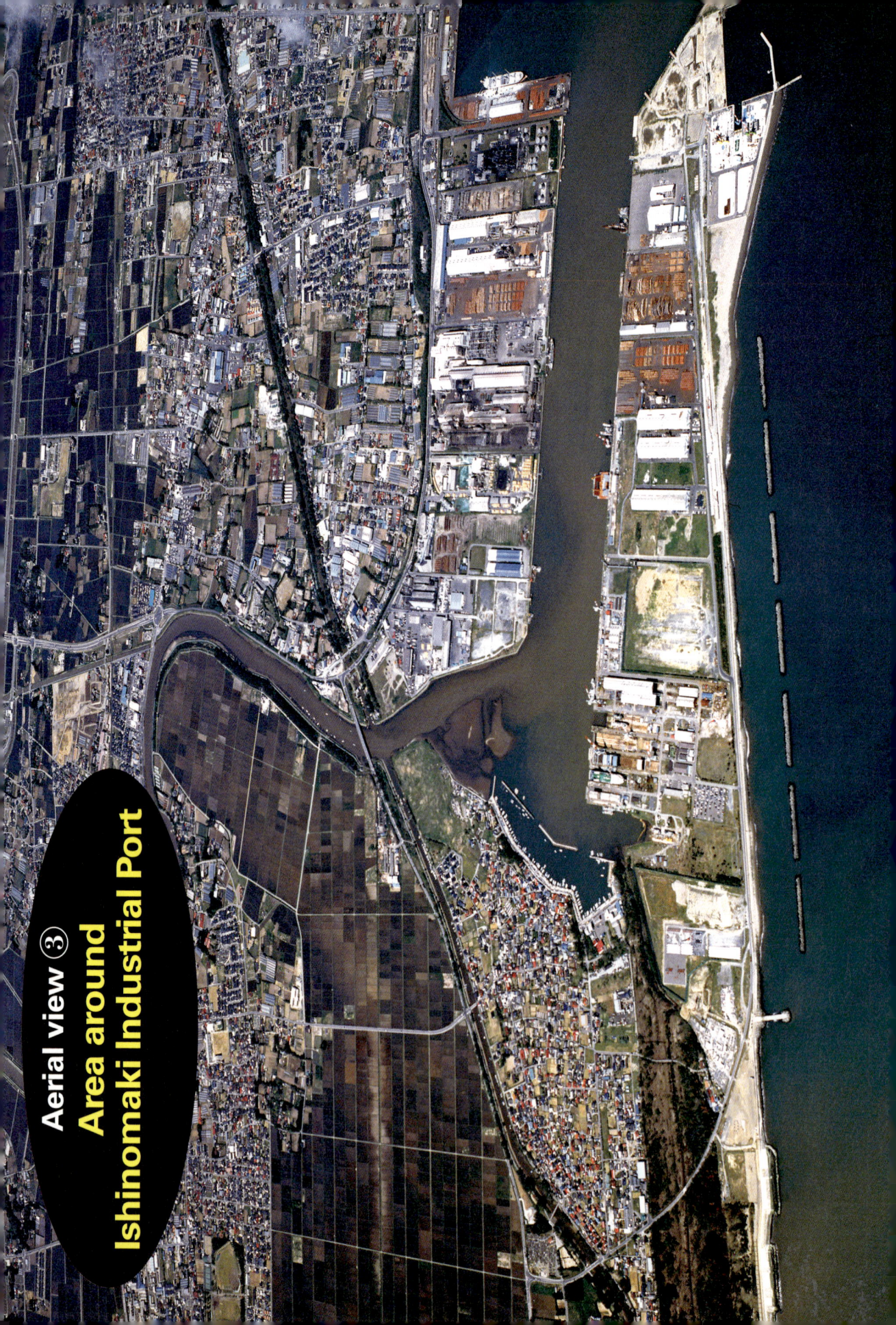

Aerial view ③
Area around Ishinomaki Industrial Port

Jo-gawa River meandering from top left through center. Left of river is Omagari, Higashi-Matsushima City. 24,000-ton ship under construction at Yamanishi Corporation was swept away and stranded at Omagari Fishing Port. Dark green line running from top right toward bottom left is Kitakami Canal. (Photos Top: May 2001 Bottom: April 17, 2011)

Central Ishinomaki
Japan Red Cross Ishinomaki Hospital
Sanriku Expressway
Ishinomaki Senshu University
JR Ishinomaki Line
Hebita
Hebita Station
JR Senseki Line
Rikuzen-Yamashita Station
Kadonowaki
Kitamura Camera
Kama Elementary School
Okaido
Miyagi Nissan Dealer
Mitsumata
Pekin-Daihanten
Nakaura Shintate
Okaido Elementary School
York Benimaru Okaido Store
Port Authorities' Office
Shigeyoshicho
Ishinomaki Koiki Clean Center (waste incineration plant)
Jo-gawa River
Yamanishi
Ishinomaki Industrial Port
Kaihoku Elementary School
Sumiyoshi Junior High School
Suimei-kita
Rikuzen-Inai Station
Ishinomaki Station
Ishinomaki-ohashi Bridge
Ishinomaki-Ogatsu Road
Fudocho
Civic Auditorium
City Hall
Ishinomaki Police Station
Route 7
Chuo
Nakaze
Izumicho
Ishinomaki-Onagawa Road
Hiyorigaoka
Nippon Paper Ishinomaki Mill
Ishinomaki Municipal Hospital
Kadonowakicho
Minamihamacho
Nankocho
Hibarino Park
Hiyori-ohashi Bridge
Hibarinocho
Kyu-Kitakamigawa River
Ishinomaki Bay
Hachimancho
Minato
Tateyama Park
Makiyama Civic Forest
Minato Elementary School
Tafukuin Temple
Yoshinocho
Minatocho
Kawaguchicho
Daimoncho
Myojincho
Matsunami
Route 398
Sakanamachi
Ishinomaki Fish Market
Ishinomaki Fishing Port
Kazuma
Kazuma Elementary School
Watanoha
Watanoha Elementary School
Watanoha Station
Watanoha Community Center
Mangokubashi Bridge
Mangokuura Station
Mangokuura
Sant Juan Bautista Museum
Dogen-in Temple
Sasuhama Fishing Port
Ishinomaki Station
Civic Auditorium
Ishinomaki Grand Hotel
Ishinomaki Police Station
Utsumi-bashi Bridge
Aitopia Street
Shunchoro
Okada Theater
Ishinomaki Mangattan Museum
Kodama Hospital
Ishinomaki Elementary School
Kadonowaki Junior High School
Ishinomaki Junior High School
Ishinomaki High School
Hiyoriyama
Kashimamiko Shrine
Saikoji Temple
Ishinomaki Municipal Girls' High School
Sato Internal Medicine Clinic
Kyu-Kitakamigawa River
Nippon Paper Ishinomaki Mill
Kadonowaki Elementary School
Shohoji Temple
Ishinomaki Municipal Hospital

Colossal wave engulfs the Okada Theater

Horrible sounds made me think *This is the end*

Kiyoto Sugawara
male, 41, president of the Okada Theater

I had taken some time off and was visiting a friend in the Hebita district, Ishinomaki City. The intensity of the quake was beyond any that I had ever felt, making me think This one's serious.

THE VERY FIRST THING THAT WORRIED ME was the Okada Theater. My father, 74, the owner, and my wife, 35, were working there along with four employees, so I tried to rush back there in my car. The traffic lights in town had gone out. I was stuck in traffic when I got as far as Chuo Koban police box. I abandoned my car there and ran toward Nakaze, a small islet near the mouth of the Kyu-Kitakami-gawa River.

I could hear a policeman trying to stop me shouting, "Don't go in that direction! The tsunami's coming!" Cars were stuck in a jam on the Utsumi-bashi Bridge. I was relieved when the Okada Theater came into view. Since the building was quite old, I was awfully worried that it might have collapsed entirely.

I went inside and called out but nobody was there. Most likely they had fled to the hill called Tateyama in the Minato district, which gave me a momentary sense of relief.

I was aware that a major tsunami warning had been given. I paid attention to the change in the water level of the Kyu-Kitakami-gawa River. I had heard that a tsunami wave comes only after the river water has receded, which made me think I was still safe.

My relatives, an elderly couple, lived along the river on the Minato side of the Utsumi-bashi Bridge. I lived next door, so I had them take refuge on the second floor of my house. Then one of the employees, 55, got back from Tateyama. I checked the river again, and saw that there was no change. *Is a tsunami really coming? Even if one came, it would be no more than 50 centimeters or one meter at the most*—I was wrong to have kept my guard low.

I was halfway up the stairs to the second floor when I heard some glass breaking downstairs. *What—a tsunami?* The Okada Theater stood right across the river from where we lived, and I could now see the theater being engulfed by the tsunami. Boats were crashing against the Utsumi-bashi Bridge. *This can't be true*—I couldn't believe my eyes. As I looked toward the sea, I could see a much bigger tsunami pushing up the river past the Hiyori-ohashi Bridge, carrying a ship on it.

THERE HAD BEEN NO SIGN. The tsunami came all too suddenly. This humongous wave engulfed the Okada Theater and went on past the Utsumi-bashi Bridge. Hearing all these horrible sounds—crashing,

Nothing remains of the long-established Okada Theater in Nakaze.

creaking, splitting—of houses being destroyed by the tsunami, I braced myself thinking that my house would be next, thinking *This is the end*. And now the water came rushing in, sweeping the employee away first, and then me.

My body sank in the muddy current all at once. I was now tossed about by the pitch-black mass of water amidst these squishing sounds. It was as if I was thrown into a washing machine and being churned.

In the next instant, my head came up out of the water. I clung to a thick wooden post, but it was flowing so fast that it seemed like it would go smashing right into a house being swept away by the tsunami. I let go of the post thinking it was too dangerous, and I was churned again. When I resurfaced, a heap of junk was surging my way, and I held onto it.

I'm not sure that I would be here now if I had been swept away toward the middle of the river. I must have been lucky that I was swept toward Civic Auditorium (Shimin Kaikan). The tsunami went over the riverbank, invading the residential areas. I was carried to a Toyota Corolla dealership's parking lot along the prefectural highway connecting Ishinomaki and Ogatsu (Prefectural Route 192). I must have been carried about 700 meters.

The entire area was covered with blackish water. It was starting to get dark. I was barefoot and it was starting to snow. I was shivering uncontrollably on the mass of junk. I was afraid of a strong receding tide, but the water went down gradually.

Some 20 minutes must have passed. I could sense the presence of people at the Saito's kerosene store across the street, so I waded in the chest-deep water and sought help. I was given a change of clothes and spent the night there.

THE NEXT MORNING, I walked a mountain path to head for Tateyama. I got to see my father and wife there. My wife was ever so surprised to see me the way I was. She had thought all along that I was safe because I was in Hebita visiting a friend.

A few days later, we found that the employee who had been swept away was safe. My only regret is that I was not able to save my relatives. The Okada Theater disappeared completely. Three hundred seats were all swept away. The power of the tsunami was way beyond what I had ever imagined.

But I didn't want to give in. I set up a prefab office behind Kodama Hospital in the Yamashita-cho district and started to offer traveling shows at different locations within the same month. A few days ago I gave a popular music show at a spa town in Fukushima where evacuees were staying. Seeing the smiles of the audience convinced me that it was good to have resumed show business.

Clinging onto deck post for life
Surviving frightening night on second floor

Eiko Matsuno
female, 46, homemaker

I came back from work at 2 p.m. After preparing an oden *pot for dinner, I was taking a break and watching a press conference on TV showing the governor of Tokyo Shintaro Ishihara announcing his decision to run in the gubernatorial election for a fourth term. Suddenly the quake started with a lateral jolt and the TV was cut off.*

THE BOOKSHELF FELL OVER and was blocking the passage to the stairway. I was worried about my mother, 73, who was upstairs, and so in the middle of the shaking I climbed over the bookshelf and managed to make my way up to her room. I could see that all the roof tiles had fallen off of our next-door neighbor's house. My mother said to me, "Go see the next-door neighbors." I hurried outside to find the 83-year-old husband bracing himself against the house which seemed about to collapse, and his 78-year-old wife crying.

My mother went to check the neighborhood. When she came back, I heard her mumbling, "Just a while ago I noticed the water level of the river was going down, but now the tip of Nakaze (an islet in the Kyu-Kitakami-gawa River) is hidden under water."

It wasn't until then that I thought a tsunami might be coming. I decided to get my mother and the couple next door in my car and evacuate to the Hiyoriyama hills. I put in a bag some warm clothes, sweet buns and rice crackers that were on the living room table, and said to my mother, "Go find the next-door neighbors and get them in our car." The street by our house which runs along the Kyu-Kitakami-gawa River was packed with cars heading toward the Minato district, giving rise to a vague sense of unease within me.

While I was locking up my house and turning the lock on the front door, I heard from behind me this dreadful roaring sound. I turned around to see that the water had risen some 50 centimeters over the river bank in front of our house, and a huge muddy torrential wave that looked high enough to engulf the Utsumi-bashi Bridge was coming toward us.

The black torrent ran over the embankment in no time, running into our neighbor's parking space and reaching my feet. For a second, I wondered whether I should go back inside the house, but the water was rising fast, reaching my knees and then rising up as high as my chest. I climbed onto the handrail of the wooden deck by the front entrance of my house.

I WAS THINKING I HAD TO SAVE MY MOTHER, and inched my way down the 20-centimeter-wide handrail all tense, grabbing the deck post by the front gate. My mother was sitting petrified on the landing of the outside stairs, clinging onto the handrail. She was so scared of the tsunami that she was about to black out.

The black waves had reached my hands, making me slip many times, but I held onto the post. I had my family and I was determined to live no matter what. The wave subsided about ten minutes later. I came down from the handrail, waded across the chest-deep water and went inside the house through a broken window of the first floor.

The first floor of the house was a sea of muddy water. Broken pieces of boats and a ship's buoy had stabbed through the house wall and were embedded in the living room. I went upstairs, unlocked the door to the outside stairs and went down to rescue my mother. "The tsunami had come before I went to the next-door neighbor's," she said in a daze.

As I waited for the chance to evacuate, I checked for the second and ensuing waves. It was snowing now. I decided to keep my mother inside the front entrance, and prayed and prayed that the roaring and threatening waves would not reach the second floor.

By the time the water subsided somewhat, it was already dark. I took the candles out of the family Buddhist altar, lit them and placed them at the top of the stairs to the second floor. We fought the cold by bundling ourselves in one blanket, back to back with disposable body warmers in between. We had one sweet bun to share.

Only the outside staircase remains of Eiko Matsuno's house in Chuo 3-chome.

I WAS EXTREMELY WORRIED about the movements of the tsunami. I went down the stairs again and again to see if there was any chance of evacuating, but the street was a sea about three meters deep. At around 10 p.m., I heard a helicopter approaching. I signaled for help with a flashlight but to no avail. I tried the same thing every time a helicopter flew by, but was never successful. I was overcome with sadness and despair.

The water in the river would be making these big sounds as it receded, and then it would come back up again with surging sounds even past midnight. We waited for daybreak in the darkness, daunted by these frightening sounds of the waves.

Early next morning, the water level by the outside stairs receded to waist level. After it went down to knee level, my mother and I rolled up our pant legs and took to the street in slippers.

We made our way to a shelter, and after a few days there, we were informed that our house had burned down in a fire that had broken out in the neighborhood.

Escaping car and hanging onto roof gutter
Stranded boat blocking tsunami current saved life

Masaaki Takasuka
male, 66, owner of home fuel business

I was washed away in my car when the tsunami wave came flowing back up the Kyu-Kitakami-gawa River, but made a narrow escape. I believe the reason I managed to find refuge in a building was that a fishing boat that was stranded on land had formed a wall, shielding me from the torrent of the tsunami.

I HAD DONE SOME REPAIR WORK at a house in the Minamihama-cho district and was tidying up my things in the driver's seat of my small car. The quake started out with an intense rocking that made my car bounce. I turned on the radio and held onto the steering wheel tightly. The shaking would start to subside, but then it would become strong again. When the third jolt started to subside, I heard the radio giving a tsunami warning—that it was expected to reach three meters in height.

I had a female employee, 27, in my Hachiman-cho office. Although she had been instructed to evacuate in case of a disaster, I was worried and decided to drive over. While driving north down Prefectural Route 7 which runs parallel to the Kyu-Kitakami-gawa River, I was checking to see if my clients' homes had not collapsed.

The lane for turning right toward the Utsumi-bashi Bridge was in a jam from around the former Chuo-1 post office. I got stuck in the jam in front of Shoei Car Park Building. I tried to call my employee but the telephone line was dead and time only slipped away.

I think it was nearly 3:30 p.m. Just after I heard a major tsunami warning over the community wireless system, I saw in the rearview mirror a tsunami with its foaming crest approaching from the direction of the sea. At that very moment, a big wave from Kyu-Kitakami-gawa River to my right came overflowing my way, lifting my car like a float. It brought my car up to the height of the roof of a one-story building, carrying it to the parking lot of a restaurant called Shunchoro which was located some 60 meters to the north.

The car turned around twice before it hit a fir tree and stopped, after which it started to sink and only the roof remained above the water. The water was coming inside the car rapidly now. I thought I might die, but I grabbed my money bag which I had placed under the passenger seat, held it under my left arm, and pressed the power window button. Fortunately the window opened and I could slip out of my car.

I got a hold of a fir tree branch and tried to float up above water, but my foot got stuck on something and I couldn't stay afloat. I swallowed water twice, but managed to break the surface of the water.

The fishing boat that blocked the tsunami, Chuo 2-chome. The bakery was on the right side of the boat.

THE FIRST FLOORS OF ALL THE BUILDINGS in the surrounding area were submerged. I was now being swept away, but I was able to grab hold of the roof gutter of a one-story bread bakery which was next door to Shunchoro to the south. The water was flowing at an amazing speed to the west through the gap between the bakery and Shunchoro restaurant. It was like a jacuzzi and I was just barely managing to keep a hold of the roof gutter. Then I noticed the house standing next to the bakery on the west side had a recess in the wall, about 10 centimeters deep, where the current was not directly hitting. I squeezed myself into that space to try to avoid the current.

After a short while, the torrent of the water suddenly weakened. In a photo I saw later, I noticed that a fishing boat that was always moored on the south side of the Utsumi-bashi Bridge was blocking the street. That boat, most likely, blocked the flow of the water. I was now able to move, grabbed a joint in the roof gutter with my hands, numb with cold, and crawled up onto the roof of the bakery.

Before long, however, the bakery started to groan. No sooner had I hastily jumped over to the eaves of the next house on the west side than the roof of the bakery collapsed. It was snowing now and the wind was strong. As I stood trembling in the freezing cold on the 30-centimeter-wide eaves, I heard a woman's voice saying, "Come on up here!" It was the proprietress of Shunchoro restaurant, 47, shouting from the third-floor window.

I had lost my glasses in the torrent and couldn't see well, but dove into the water and was able to enter Shunchoro based on what sense of direction I had. My jacket was heavy after being in the water. I dragged myself up the stairs with my legs all numb.

When I got to the third floor, I found the proprietress taking shelter all alone. She took down a banquet hall curtain, which, after removing my wet clothes, I wrapped around my whole body, head and all, and sat down on a chair.

I COULDN'T KEEP FROM SHAKING all night long because of the cold. Falling asleep would have meant falling into a state of hypothermia. Without leaning against the chair back, I kept on talking until morning. Once in a while, we heard the surging sounds of the approaching tsunami—I noted at three times these big and distinctive sounds. I kept trying to send a text message to my employee but it never went through, so I prayed for her safety.

At 7 o'clock the next morning, I left for my house in Hachiman-cho 2-chome in my underwear and the curtain wrapped around me. I went by way of the Ishinomaki-ohashi Bridge since the Utsumi-bashi Bridge was blocked. I tried to walk where the water was lower, making my way over all the rubble.

When I got home after walking for eight hours for a mere 2.5 kilometers in distance, I was relieved to see my wife and mother safe on the second floor. Some days later, however, I was informed that my employee had died of hypothermia in a shelter. I regret that I couldn't save her.

Muddy water invades car
Surviving one night on rooftop while exposed to cold

Yuka Hamaya
female, 35, helping family business

My family lived in a two-story wooden house where my father, 68, had a portion of the house set aside for a traditional Japanese confectionary shop. It was near the front approach to a Shinto shrine called Kashima Miko Jinja on the Hiyoriyama hills with a Buddhist temple called Shohoji standing on the south side from us.

AT THE TIME OF THE EARTHQUAKE, my father was making steamed buns in the shop on the first floor while I was making preparations for the packaging. I was totally stunned by the sudden and intense shaking, and shortly the electrical appliances including the TV went out with the power outage.

My father was the leader of the local unit of the volunteer fire company. He turned off the gas for the steamer, and left for the fire-fighting post saying to me, "Are you all right? You be sure to evacuate!" I decided to wait for my brother, 32, at home since it was about time he returned from shopping and I didn't want him to be at a loss. The story of the 1933 Sanriku earthquake and tsunami that I had heard from my grandmother and the fact that our house stood on a somewhat higher lot made me think that the tsunami would not get there.

Seeing that my brother came back in the small car, I grabbed some drinks, a boxed lunch that hadn't been opened, my purse, then put on some extra clothes for warmth and got into the passenger seat of the car. We could hear our father announcing from the fire truck, "A major tsunami warning has been issued!"

Since it was cold, my brother and I stayed in the car and were observing the situation, when suddenly we noticed a tsunami coming from the direction of Kadonowaki Elementary School. Black muddy water came surging to my side of the car. I thought that if I had the door shut I wouldn't be able to open it, so I opened it at once. But then the muddy water came inside, so I shut it. The car was floating now, and was tilting to the driver's side. My brother's head was starting to be submerged in the muddy water.

I WAS SO DESPERATE that I don't remember well, but I somehow got to open the passenger side of the window and got outside of the car, and then pulled my brother out. My legs couldn't touch the ground. We were like swimming and then put our hands on the roof of a house that came flowing toward us. This house happened to bump into the roof of our own house, which had remained in place without being swept away.

We got up on the roof together. We were kind of in between the two roofs and couldn't see around us well, but we did notice there were currents on both the north and the south, and thought, if we got swept away, that would be the end.

We wrung out our clothes—they were soaking wet. It was snowing and cold. I looked down at the water by our feet and found the rooftop of the car we had been riding in. The back door of the car was open. Fortunately there were a lot of boxes of tissue that my brother had just bought. I asked my brother to get them out of the car. The plastic wrapping had kept the tissue dry, so I took some out and stuffed it around the sleeves and inside the hoods of our jackets to fight the cold.

At long last just before dark, a helicopter came flying our way. We frantically shouted for help, but it went flying away. Then a man on a pile of debris came streaming by. Someone who was on the roof of a nearby factory guided him with a flashlight to a window of another building and rescued him.

We could hear a series of explosions from the direction of the sea. To our northwest, something must have been burning and it was turning the sky red. We were scared that the fire might come spreading our way. We could also hear gas tanks flowing past us making hissing sounds. We felt awful.

It was so cold that I thought we might not be

able to make it—we were so distressed and I was unable to talk to my brother—my mouth had stiffened from shaking. Then I noticed what might have been some flashlights on the steps of the front approach to the Hiyoriyama hills, moving up and down, one here and another there. That's when I decided *We're going to survive this no matter what*.

As it started to get a little lighter, I sensed the presence of people nearby. I called out for help, and a voice came saying, "We'll come to help you after it gets a little brighter, so you wait there!" In a little while, three men appeared and they helped us get down from the roof—it was slippery because of the snow. They told us to go up to Hiyoriyama from behind Saikoji Temple, and left us saying, "We've got to rescue more people."

WHERE WE CAME OUT was in front of the high fence wall of Saikoji Temple near the steps to Hiyoriyama. There I was astounded to find on top of the wall my father with his fire-fighting crew members. "So that was you," said my father with such a happy tone. He said that while he was worried about the two of us he was doing his best rescuing and guiding people to safety. Then he and the crew members pulled us up onto the wall. "Mother should have found shelter at either Ishinomaki Junior High School or Kadonowaki Junior High School," said my father.

We went up the steps of the front approach to Hiyoriyama, and then walked through the residential section, the two of us all muddy. Somebody told us on the way that our mother should be in the Ishinomaki Junior High School gym, and when we got there, we found her in the very back. "It's so great that we've survived." The three of us—our mother, my brother, and I—hugged one another in the warm embrace of our mother. Everybody around us clapped for us, and some of them were even crying with us.

Daring to drive the wrong way to escape
Breaking away from crowd to rescue child

Masato Kusajima
male, 51, home tutor

The sea shouldn't have been there in front of my eyes, but there it was, swollen up high. It simply couldn't be true. There was no time to feel any fear at this unbelievable sight so I put my small car into reverse. The drama of my getaway from the tsunami had begun.

I WAS DRIVING NORTH near Ishinomaki Senshu University when the earthquake happened. My car shook violently. I was worried about my second daughter, 20, and my son, 18, who were supposed to be at home in the Hibarino district so I turned around and set off back home.

On the way, I tried to stop at Ishinomaki Chuo Post Office, where my oldest daughter, 22, worked. However, I had to give up the idea because there was a traffic jam on the Ishinomaki Bypass. Luckily, the road that ran alongside the Kyu-Kitakami-gawa River was not closed to traffic despite the fact that there were cracks and bumps in the road.

I did hear the radio saying, "A tsunami a meter high has reached Onagawa Town." However, I didn't think it was such a big deal. I could see people standing on the embankments of the Kyu-Kitakami-gawa River and Hibarino Beach to check the water level.

The door of my house in Hibarino-cho 1-chome was open, and inside the house was a mess, with books, plates everywhere. There was no one home, not even the cat. I went to my in-law's home nearby, but their car was gone. I headed to Kadonowaki Elementary School, the designated evacuation center, but I couldn't find my family there.

Quite a few people were going back home after evacuating once, so I thought I might have missed my family on the way to the school. So, once again, I drove back home.

Just as I turned left on to an incline from a narrow street in Minamihama-cho 2-chome, I saw water flowing on the gentle slope, which sometimes gets covered with seawater during storms and spring tides. *I just hope it won't flood above the floor level of our home*—that was the extent of my grasp of the situation.

As I was pulling back, I saw the sea to my right. Normally I wouldn't see it from that spot. The surface of the sea was an unruffled gentle slope, but had swollen up high. The color of the sea was the color it was normally, but at the tip of the slope, I could see that the crest was raging.

I DROVE THE CAR BACK in reverse gear. A house was being washed away gently now, with no resistance, and it crashed into the house next door, and that house slowly crashed into another house. Then I heard a huge explosion and saw thick dust swirl up into the air. A cloud of dirt and rubble came together as a wall looming toward me. The speed of the tsunami seemed to have slowed, so I pulled into a driveway and turned around. In retrospect, I suppose the tsunami must have been over six meters high.

If I drove up to the Hiyoriyama hills, I should be safe—I made myself believe. I used narrow streets as much as possible because I thought the tsunami might rush up more quickly on wider roads. I headed west after I came to Prefectural Route 240 connecting Ishinomaki and Onagawa.

I soon got stuck in a traffic jam so I drove down the opposite lane going against traffic, trying to enter the side street leading up to the Hiyoriyama hills. However, there was a car left diagonally on the street, blocking traffic. I got out of my car and started to run, tapping the windows of cars on the road, yelling, "A tsunami is coming! Get out of your car and run!" However, only one person paid attention to me. On the way to Route 240, I had done the same thing, too, calling out to people to warn them of the tsunami. But few people became aware of the oncoming tsunami.

I ran up the hill as fast as I could, and almost reached the Ishinomaki High School grounds. Some people were coming down the hill, so I started back, too. What I saw before me was an ocean full of floating rubble. People who lived on higher ground were trying to rescue people who were still trapped in the tsunami by throwing down sheets and ropes from the retaining wall. I heard that a child was trapped under a house that had been washed up.

LESS THAN A HUNDRED METERS AWAY, fires blazed up in two spots. It was snowing. I could also see a man on a pile of rubble yelling for help. Taking off my suit jacket, I jumped down on the rubble in my leather dress shoes, and crawled under a wrecked roof. I found the boy everyone was talking about. His lower body was buried in the rubble. I tried to pull him out by digging with my bare hands, but his foot was stuck and it wouldn't come out.

I went back on the retaining wall to get some help. Only three of about a hundred people helped me. It may not be a nice thing to say, but to me, the others seemed to be simply a crowd of curious onlookers. We dug out the rubble with a shovel someone who lived in the area had lent us. After about half an hour, the four of us rescued the boy. He said he was a sixth grader, and had been trying to escape with his mother. However, his mother was nowhere to be seen. I still wonder what had happened to her.

I was dead tired by the time we boosted the boy up onto the retaining wall. I was so exhausted I couldn't climb up on my own. I then realized that the man on the pile of rubble who had been yelling for help had disappeared—without me even noticing.

Victims heading for their destinations on road to Makiyama hills scattered with debris and damaged cars. Photo taken in Yoshino-cho 2-chome, Ishinomaki City, around 10:30 a.m., March 14, 2011

Waters remain in section of residential area where street had caved in. Photo taken near Watanoha Port around 11:55 a.m., April 24, 2011

Tsunami: the lesser of two evils

Fear of fire pushed me to jump into water

Masayoshi Kotono
male, 49, corporate employee

Houses and cars being washed away by the tsunami, raging with fire, were now coming toward me. I would rather drown than be burned to death—I said to myself and jumped into the water. It was perhaps this desperate decision that determined my fate.

WHEN THE EARTHQUAKE STRUCK, I was at my workplace, a fish processing plant in the Sakanamachi district. From outside of the plant, loud sounds of electricity poles toppling down could be heard, getting some 40 people who were inside to burst out in clamor.

When the shaking settled down, I knew instinctively that a tsunami would come. My boss instructed us to leave the plant. My workplace and home were both right next to Ishinomaki Bay. I was worried about my parents, who lived with us, so I immediately drove home to the Kadonowaki-cho district.

From the car radio, a major tsunami warning was being aired along with information that the tsunami had already reached Ayukawa in Oshika Peninsula. There was a big traffic jam on the road to the Hiyoriohashi Bridge and I think that it took me nearly 30 minutes to get home, a journey which usually only takes five minutes. I became frustrated and irritated. There was a traffic jam in front of my house, too, so it was obvious there was no way of escaping by car. I yelled to my parents who were trying to clean up our house, "A tsunami is coming! Run to the Hiyoriyama hills quick!" telling them to evacuate on foot.

After seeing my parents get out of the house, my thoughts turned to helping the elderly man living next door to us and evacuating with him. Though he was physically fit, he was in his eighties and moved quite slowly. When I went to his house, he seemed to be on the phone talking to his wife who was in a nursing home. I waited impatiently for him for five to ten minutes in front of the entrance to his house. Thinking back now, I should have made him hang up the phone and gotten him out of the house right then and there. Because his steps were uncertain, I practically picked him up and took him outside.

AFTER RUNNING DOWN A PATH ALONG THE HOUSE for some 30 meters, the water came to lap at our feet. As I turned around and looked into the far distance, white waves forming something like a wall came heading our way. Some cars were being washed away as if they were surfing. In a few seconds or less, a huge wave that was higher than a two-story building came closing in on us, accompanied with these roaring sounds. I thought we would die if we got caught in the maelstrom of surging water.

There was also the fear of getting smashed by the cars being swept away. My neighbor and I went into someone's yard and tried to find shelter behind its wall. Just then, I was hit by a wave coming over the top of my head. I held on to a tree there as tightly as I could with both arms so I wouldn't get swept away by the torrent. But it was at that moment that I lost sight of my elderly neighbor.

I swallowed water many times. Not being able to understand what was happening, I flailed my arms and feet around. Finally my foot hit some rubble, and I was able to stand on it. Just in front of me, the second floor of someone's house could be seen emerging from the water. I was relieved to find a human figure moving inside it. The man in the house was offering a helping hand to me, so I struggled through the water and managed to enter it through a window.

The man who helped me out of the water was in his sixties or seventies. About 15 minutes after I had thanked him, what must have been the second tsunami came through. The house leaned a little and it was then that I realized that it had been separated from the ground and was floating in the water. Several other houses were being washed away just like the one I was in and they were making creaking sounds as they all piled up against a hillside.

Inside the house, the water had reached my knees. I heard sounds like something was exploding nearby, and from the window, I saw some red lights. I soon realized that the houses and cars were on fire.

I GOT OUT OF THE HOUSE from the second-floor window where I had been rescued, and shimmied down to the roof of the first floor to leave the house. The fire burning toward the hillside was growing, so I scampered from rooftop to rooftop of the floating houses trying to escape the fire. Suddenly, a few dozens of meters ahead of me, I saw a building with human figures inside on the second floor. *If only I could get there. . . .* Fear of the nearby fires gathering strength pushed me to take the chance of jumping into the water. To be honest, I was prepared for death.

No matter how hard I tried to swim, I was swept back to the hillside again and again by the force of the waves. I couldn't reach the building. Just when I felt the muscles in my arms and legs had reached their limits, I grabbed on to some rubble that just happened to come floating toward me. I was washed away several hundred meters and then managed to crawl onto a house I had landed on by chance.

After I sat down on the roof I looked toward the Hiyoriyama hills. I saw the lights of a fire company team. I yelled with every fiber of my body and soul. "Help me!" It was the loudest I had ever screamed in my whole life. The fire company team yelled back, "Are you okay, there?" They set up three long ladders to rescue me. By that time, I had no strength left in me.

Slipping into unconsciousness in water
Floating rooftop was my lifesaver

Katsuju Ogata
male, 66, restaurant owner

When I rushed out of my restaurant, surprised by the magnitude of the earthquake and how long it lasted, there were about 30 people on the street who had come out of their homes. They were waiting to see what would happen and no one was trying to get away.

THERE WERE NO SIRENS, no announcements over the emergency wireless—in fact there was no information available at all. After a while, somebody who was listening to the radio said, "A 3-meter tsunami at Ayukawa in Oshika Peninsula." *If that's the case, there's no way it will come here,* I thought. We were 800 meters away from the coastline.

Shortly before the earthquake struck, my ramen noodle restaurant was in the middle of the lull after the lunchtime rush, so I left the shop in the hands of my wife, 59, while I went to the barber for a haircut. The big quake hit just as I got back.

On the second floor of our place, my wife's younger sister, 54, had been visiting and was starting to clear up what had fallen down including the TV and furniture. My wife was gathering our valuables and other things we needed to take with us for evacuating. During this time, I started to see quite a number of cars driving the wrong way on the one-way street in front of the restaurant. *What an outrage!*—that's what I thought at the time, but now I realize that they were desperately running away from the tsunami.

Going back into the shop, I heard my wife, who had left her bag on the counter in the restaurant, calling her sister who was on the second floor. That's when it suddenly happened—the crash and the explosive wham! It felt as if the entire building was falling down on my head. Water came flooding around my feet. The backyard door swung open, its hook lock unhinged, and I could see an electronics store being washed away. An elderly lady in the neighborhood was running away screaming, "The tsunami's here!" I could hear my wife's voice calling, "Dear, watch out! It's a tsunami!' even though I could not see where she was. I think that those were her last words.

THE WATER NOW WENT OVER MY HEIGHT and I was being churned and was gradually losing consciousness. *Ah, I'm going to die,* I thought. I don't know how long I had been in the water—it could have been minutes or seconds—when I sensed light, which allowed me to know which way was up, and I was able to struggle to the surface of the water.

After catching hold of some wooden post which was flowing by me, I got to crawl up onto a tin roof which also came flowing alongside me. When I looked around me, what I saw was flames: the houses around me were on fire. The roof I was on bumped into one of the houses in the neighborhood and came to a stop. The elderly couple living in that home had escaped to the second floor. "The fire's going to spread, so come on over this way!" I yelled to them, helping them to move out to the tin roof I was on.

Then I realized we had come closer to land and were only two meters away from the concrete retaining wall at the base of the Hiyorigaoka heights. The elevation of the heights was about ten meters. *If we climb up there, we will be safe,* I thought. So we picked up some debris which came floating by and piled them up on the roof to make a path that extended toward the wall. It was about 1.2 meters to the top of the retaining wall. We got some pieces of rubble to lean against the wall to use like a stepladder and eventually made it up onto the concrete wall.

When we climbed up the hillside, we were on the property of somebody's home in Hiyorigaoka 4-chome. I walked 300 meters to the home of my relatives where I borrowed some dry clothes and changed into them. Then I started my way back home to search for my wife, but the area was a sea of fire and there was no way I could get near my house. You couldn't tell the sea from the land for that matter—all I could see was black water.

When it started to get dark, I was back at my relative's house and was keeping warm by the heater. Then an emergency response vehicle came around making this announcement: "Fire is spreading toward the hillside. Please evacuate to Ishinomaki Junior High School!"

Every corner of the school was filled with the evacuees. Everybody was covered up in blankets and looking down. I don't know when it started, but I was experiencing a racking pain on the left side of my chest and I couldn't raise my left arm. It was hard to even walk up the stairs. I found out later that three of my ribs were broken.

After spending the night at the junior high school, I went out looking for my wife. I walked to all the evacuation sites of that area and searched—

Only the steel skeleton remains of Katsuju Ogata's home and restaurant. Kadonowaki-cho 3-chome.

Ishinomaki Municipal Girls' Senior High School, Ishinomaki Junior High School and Ishinomaki High School. Nobody from my neighborhood had seen my wife, either.

ABOUT TEN DAYS AFTER THE EARTHQUAKE, I stopped by my restaurant and was looking around when I found two spatulas covered in mud. They were the very spatulas that my wife had used when making Ishinomaki *yakisoba* (fried noodles). Holding them in my hand, I was reminded of the promise my wife and I had made to enter the "B-1 Grand Prix," a soul food competition that was to be held down south in Himeji in November. I entered the competition with the mementos, setting up a booth named "Ishinomaki Brown Yakisoba Academy." I won 6th prize.

My plan now is to obtain a food truck to travel and offer Ishinomaki *yakisoba*. To all the people around the country, too, who have helped us in the reconstruction of Ishinomaki, I wish to pay a visit with Ishinomaki *yakisoba* to offer as a way to show my gratitude.

Even though my wife's body has never been found, I held her funeral on December 11. I believe my wife's funeral was the point at which I started to rebuild my life.

Churned as if in a washing machine

Evacuating into factory after being washed away 200 meters

Masahide Yoshida
male, 24, caregiver

I had finished my work outside the office and had just returned to the two-story office building of the nursing care company in Minamihama-cho 4-chome when the earthquake struck. This one's a bit bigger than the one two days ago—that was what I thought at first and I did not take it very seriously.

THE LATERAL SHAKING MOTION gradually increased in intensity and I had to hold onto the handrail to go up to the second floor. There were five or six staff workers, both male and female, in the upstairs office. The sight of so many objects such as files falling from the shelves and the copy machine shaking wildly about made me think that something extraordinary was occurring.

The quake settled down after a long while, and we went down to the first floor. That day, we had more than 40 elderly people at our care facility, located on the same premises, for short-stay and daycare services. We helped them into over a dozen vehicles, those in wheel chairs into minivans and others in the cars of staff workers, and headed for higher ground nearby.

Because the care center was near the Ishinomaki Industrial Port, we conducted evacuation drills twice a year in preparation for emergency events including fires, earthquakes and tsunamis. "Whatever happens, just run." As I look back now, I think that that experience was put to good use. With all the staff workers moving swiftly into action, we could evacuate to higher ground without getting caught up in the traffic jam.

I truly think that all had gone well until then. We were able to move everybody to safety with no casualties. But honestly, I didn't think that a huge tsunami would ever come—not at that point. I was also too absorbed in what actions we took till then to think to obtain any information from the emergency wireless system or the radio.

SNOW WAS FALLING NOW and it was absolutely freezing on the high ground. Thinking the elderly people needed something like blankets to survive the cold, I decided to go back to the office. My boss said to me, "You stay here, you hear me! Don't you dare move!" but I started to walk toward the office. I remember it was just after 3:30 p.m.

As I approached the office, this sight came into view where a woman, screaming at the top of her

Masahide Yoshida stands on the second floor of a tsunami-ravaged office near Nippon Paper Industries Ishinomaki Mill in Minamihama-cho 4-chome.

voice, was backing up in her car. A tsunami of about half a meter was encroaching. I still thought I was all right, and I even allowed myself time to change into slippers to go upstairs as I usually do.

Looking down from a second-floor window, the tsunami was still only 20 to 30 centimeters high, with some debris and pieces of wood being carried by it initially. I was still looking at this rather calmly, but then, with the water level rising, cars and houses now came crashing. When a second house came heading my way, I thought it was all over and I lost all hope. Along with these cracking sounds of outer walls and window panes being smashed, I was sent flying in a flash and got swallowed in the water.

The water had such a momentum that I could hardly move at all. It was as though I was being churned in a washing machine. It was fortunate that I used to take swimming lessons when I was in elementary school, which enabled me to deal with this, but I still can't forget the pressure of the water I felt then.

When the force of the tide ceased and I was able to get my head out of water, I found that I had been carried as much as 200 meters away to the west. I saw in front of me what appeared to be a building of Nippon Paper Industries Ishinomaki Mill, and I grabbed its fence to evacuate into it, which was about the height of a two-story building. Looking toward the Minamihama-cho district, practically all I could see were the roofs of two-story houses, and the rest was under the sea. That was the moment that I realized for the first time how serious the entire situation was. It was so stunning I could not help but ask myself: *Could it be that I'm the only one alive?*

WITH THE LAPSE OF TIME, I must have been overcome with exhaustion. I had fallen asleep inside that building without my knowing it. When I woke up, I could now see in the darkness the bright red flames consuming all the debris and buildings. The fire was spreading from one spot to the next, and was now encroaching on me. I was caught up in this illusion that maybe I was just watching TV or a movie.

As dawn came, I could hear from inside the factory somebody who I thought was an employee there calling out, "Is anybody there?"

I borrowed rubber boots, and I went outside the factory from a spot where the water had receded. I then headed out to Kadonowaki Junior High School, where I found all the company staff and the elderly people. We all rejoiced in being together again.

By any measure all this was a huge disaster. All the familiar sights and scenery became transformed before we knew it. Honestly speaking, I did not think that I would survive this. All I can say is that I was simply lucky. I still wish that it had been just a dream. What I personally learned from this disaster was to never go back, never go near the place where you have evacuated from—once you have left it. This is the one lesson that I have taken to heart.

24,000-ton freighter with 31 on board washed away

Massive force of tsunami cut off thick mooring rope, sending ship adrift

Tomofumi Abe
male, 39, manager, Yamanishi Corporation

Just before 3 p.m. on March 11, I was in the pilothouse of the 24,000-ton freighter the Sider Joy, *which was docked in the Nishihama district at the shipyard of Yamanishi Corporation where I was employed.*

THE *SIDER JOY* HAD JUST BEEN BUILT and was scheduled to be delivered in five days. There were 31 people on the ship including the Italian captain and we had to spend an anxious night after being washed away by the tsunami.

When the earthquake occurred, we did not feel the effect as much on the ship as we would have on land. We thought it would be over soon as was the one two days before. The shaking, however, kept on increasing in intensity. The Italian captain and those who were with him were extremely terrified by the long-lasting quake, but I convinced them to stay on the ship since it was more dangerous on land.

The pilothouse was at a height of the seventh or the eighth floor of a building, and this allowed us a good command of the view of the surrounding area. The crane nearby was shaking wildly with these rattling sounds, and I was afraid that it might topple down. But then a scene more shocking still came into view. The *Tulipan*, a cargo ship that was being built, was shaken off of its platform and was sliding down into the harbor. She was the same model as the *Sider Joy*; her launching ceremony was scheduled to be held seven days later on March 18.

After the shaking settled down, a few people came hurrying onto the *Sider Joy* to evacuate. The shipbuilding dock is located between the open sea and the Ishinomaki Industrial Port with no tall buildings in the surrounding area, so this made the ship an optimal evacuation site.

Although I do not remember how much time had passed, I saw through the hazy snow a tsunami surging toward us from the open sea. It was at least six meters high when it was about to reach land. When it got to the shipyard, it went smashing through the wooden structures, and easily washed away even the steel parts of a ship's body.

ALL WE COULD DO was to helplessly watch this devastation from on board the ship. I also felt how powerless humans could be in the face of an unbelievable menace of nature.

As for the *Sider Joy*, the ship we were on, the massive force of the tsunami had cut off her thick mooring rope, and she went adrift in the Ishinomaki Industrial Port. She was not free from danger there. Her bow went colliding against the side of the *Tulipan*, the ship that had earlier slid off of the platform into the sea. The *Sider Joy* was pushed around by the tsunami a number of times before she finally came to rest.

Because of the snowstorm I do not remember the view around us very well, but when the sun came out briefly just before sunset, I could tell that we had been carried to the north of Omagari Fishing Port in neighboring Higashi-Matsushima City. From the ship, we could see the rice fields in the Omagari district had been inundated by the tsunami.

What was the extent of the damage caused by the earthquake and tsunami? How bad was it? There was no way I could imagine the entire picture since all I could tell was limited to what view I had from the ship. My cell phone would not be connected, and it wasn't until I finally got a text message that I learned that those who had remained inside the shipbuilding dock had climbed up onto the rooftop of the two-story reinforced concrete building, where they had evacuated safely.

THE *TULIPAN*, in the meantime, had gone aground in the shallow waters near the bridge by the mouth of the Jo-gawa River, and was taking in water due to the damage from the collision, facing the risk of sinking. Fishing and other boats that had been moored at the dock for repair had all been washed away as well; most of them had either foundered or gone aground while a few had crashed into some of the homes in the Omagari district.

Being a freight ship, the *Sider Joy* had a flat bottom, and this prevented her from being capsized; she did not go drifting any further, either, for that matter. In the engine room, however, muddy water giving off an oily smell seeped through the opening in the damaged section, and it had flooded the engine, the heart of a ship.

There were a number of big aftershocks before daybreak. Although the ship was equipped with an emergency generator, heating was not available. The 31 people on the ship gathered together in the pilothouse, where we spent the night covered up in things such as plastic bags and curtains to keep ourselves from the cold.

The *Tulipan*, on the other hand, had no windows or insulation—it was merely a box made of iron and the best it could do was just to keep out the snow. So when a helicopter came for us at night, we tried to urge the crew to rescue the people on the *Tulipan* first by means of gestures and pointing toward the mouth of the Jo-gawa-River, but they did not get the message. It wasn't until the following morning that I learned that the receding tide had washed the *Tulipan* away to the opposite side of the Ishinomaki Industrial Port during the night. Afterwards, the Coast Guard and other rescue workers came to our rescue and all 31 of us on the *Sider Joy* were able to disembark the vessel safely.

The *Sider Joy* underwent a large-scale repair work since then and was eventually delivered to the client on October 24. She was one lucky ship—not only did she protect 31 people from the tsunami, but she was fully restored as well. My wish now is for her service to be blessed by good fortune as well and for many of the local businesses to achieve a prompt recovery from the disaster.

Isolated after being washed away, house and all
Jumping into water saved my life

Toshiji Fukuda
male, 77, retired

I was practicing Japanese poetry recitation during our regular meeting at Minato-so, one of Ishinomaki's public welfare centers, which was in my neighborhood. The quake was such that I could hardly keep standing, and I had to endure the long-lasting shaking by clinging to one of the table legs.

THE PRACTICE WAS IMMEDIATELY CALLED OFF and everybody started for home. I dropped in at Minato Nursery School where I served as a member of the board before hurrying home. After meeting my wife, 73, at home in the Hachiman-cho district, we set off for Minato Elementary School together. When we walked about 200 meters, however, I alone turned around and went back home. I wanted to move our valuables to the second floor. Just as I had finished doing that and come downstairs, I heard someone screaming from outside, "The tsunami's here!"

When I came out of the front door, the water was almost at my feet. I thought there was no way I could run, so I went back inside and was looking outside through the staircase window. The tearing sounds of my neighbors' homes breaking apart reverberated in my ears. The front door of my own house was broken now and water was rushing in, leaving me no choice but to be driven upstairs, where there was nothing I could do.

The spectacle outside was visible throughout. My next-door neighbor's house collapsed; then it was washed away, and came colliding right into our house. Then another house that was being washed away from a different direction collided into ours also, forcing it to tilt steeply with a big *wump*, and now our house, too, started to be washed away.

Only the foundation remains of Toshiji Fukuda's home. In the background is the Hachiman-cho pedestrian bridge where he landed after swimming across the flooded area.

OUR HOUSE WAS CARRIED AWAY about half a hundred meters to the north, where it ended up on top of three other houses that had also been washed away. Then still another house came, which piled up over ours and stopped. This last house then was carried away with the backrush. I suppose that if it had not been for that house, ours could have been the one to be carried out to the sea.

I broke a window and got outside once, but it was water all around. I mustered up my courage and jumped in, but my feet couldn't touch the bottom and I got back inside the house. I didn't care if I seemed frantic—I cried out in a loud voice, "Help! Help me!" But nobody was there any more to hear me.

A tatami mat* came floating by, which I pulled into the house through a window, and I placed my own self on it. What was impending now was the cold, exhaustion, and hunger. I was overcome with extreme loneliness and despair, and thought that it was all over. It was then that the second tsunami wave came and I noticed a pile of debris that was flowing back up Kyu-Kitakami-gawa River, right in the middle of the river. In the middle of that pile was a whole roof of a house—with a man on top of it. Just when I thought *Oh no, that guy's not going to make it,* the pile hit Utsumi-bashi Bridge and was bounced toward the bank, enabling the man to make his way over the debris to the land and escape.

There's no reason why I couldn't be saved—that was the kind of courage I felt rising within me then. When the force of the second tsunami wave ceased, I decided to go ahead and jump in the water. I tried to swim toward the Utsumi-bashi Bridge street, but my clothes were hindering me, and I was getting cold and tired, finding it harder and harder to keep on swimming. But just then, my feet just barely hit the ground.

The Hachiman-cho pedestrian bridge was now in front of me, so I plowed my way toward it through the water which was at waist level, but I was caught in deep water again. I managed to struggle out of it, and eventually made it to the bridge, completely exhausted and with no energy left to climb up. Half of my body was in the water, and I was not able to move any more. A young man came down the steps just then, and he pulled me out of the water. I looked for him later at the evacuation center, but could never find him.

From the pedestrian bridge, I could see the window on the second floor of Sakuma Eye Clinic, where Dr. Sakuma appeared and kindly said, "Come over to our place!" The five people who were on the bridge including me went over to his place, where we found five people including Dr. Sakuma and the nurses.

I was dripping wet, my legs were numb with cold and exhaustion, and my frozen hands would not move at my will. At the clinic, there happened to be an acquaintance of mine who had come down to see the situation from the Minato-Tateyama district up the hill. He went to the trouble of fetching a pair of pants and a shirt for me from his home. By chance he was the same man who had given me shelter in the 1960 Chilean earthquake and tsunami disaster. I was really grateful to have a change of clothes, but it did not stop me from feeling cold. I used newspapers and plastic bags to cover my feet, took down some curtains and wrapped myself in them to endure the cold.

AFTER STAYING TWO NIGHTS at Sakuma Eye Clinic, I moved to Minato Elementary School, the designated evacuation center, on the third day. The second floor was set aside for accommodating the injured and the disabled, and that was where I found my wife. Her hand was injured and was swollen up like a baseball glove. She told me she had been caught up by the tsunami just before reaching the elementary school and was swept to the path along the school building. Some of the people who had climbed up on the roof of the school kitchen pulled her up, where she apparently lost consciousness.

I feel that it was fortunate that our lives at least were safe thanks to luck and to the many people who helped us.

*Tatami mats—180 centimeters long by 90 centimeters wide, 5 centimeters high, 30 kilograms—are flooring materials commonly used in traditional Japanese-style rooms. Tightly woven rush grass covers the mat core made of packed rice straw. Fitted tightly to form the floor surface, tatami mats can float in water if homes are flooded.

Pain pierces body while getting out of flooded car
Climbing to store roof to stay above water

Nobuaki Miura
male, 55, marketing manager, Ishinomaki Fish Market

I was on the fish market pier supervising the landing of Japanese sand lance, a spring season fish, when the earthquake struck. It was a big jolt with a powerful uplift. The roof of the steel-frame building started to creak, so I ran toward the quay but the quay itself was undulating.

THE BOAT STOPPED ITS LANDING TASK at once and moved away from the port at maximum speed. Waves were overlapping one another irregularly, making the sea look ominous. The quake continued for quite a long time. Parts of the quay had collapsed, and cracking and caving had occurred at many spots.

All the employees of the fish market evacuated immediately after the major tsunami warning was issued, but I stayed there to tidy things up and soon found myself alone. Looking back now, I realize that I had an inadequate sense of the impending crisis. It was after 3:20 p.m. when I got into my car.

As I headed north from the fish market, I saw that the biggest street was jammed with cars. The road leading to the city center from the Hiyoriohashi Bridge and the one to Watanoha were both overflowing with cars.

I somehow managed to cut across this traffic and headed toward National Route 398. There were few cars on the back street that I used for commuting and was familiar with. Feeling relieved, I drove to the point where Daimoncho 3-chome became Minatocho 4-chome and got on to Route 398, but the traffic there was heavily jammed. I couldn't believe how many minutes it took just to go one hundred meters.

Just then I looked ahead and saw that the street was flooded. *Could that be a tsunami?* I was not convinced. But then I saw the water level rising higher and higher. *It would be dangerous to stay in the car.* I saw a convenience store ahead on the other side of the street and turned into its parking lot in a hurry. The water level had already risen to the bottom of the car door. No sooner had I kicked the door open with all my strength than the water came rushing inside. Something hit my leg just then. The impact was awful and an acute pain pierced my whole body. I was backed into a corner now. Dragging my pain-stricken leg, I managed to clamber out of the car.

BY THEN THE WATER was rising to my waist, and then up to my chest. There was a shed behind the convenience store. I climbed up the fence and managed to get on top of the roof of the shed. About a dozen people were already up there. The street had turned into a river now, and all we could do was to helplessly watch cars with people inside being carried away. The tsunami level was getting higher and higher now. *It might reach the roof of the shed.* I was overcome with inexplicable horror.

Can't we do anything?—everybody was at a loss, but right then these wooden forklift pallets came floating by. They must have been used at the fish market or some marine product processing plant. We tried to use one as a ladder to reach the roof of the convenience store which was higher than the shed, but it wasn't long enough. Putting our heads together, we placed a pallet on the roof of the shed so that half of it stuck out from the roof, and several men held the other end to secure it. This served as a foothold from which everybody, one by one, could climb up to the roof of the store. The last person was pulled up by the arms.

The water level was way over 2.5 meters in height now and the shed had become warped. If our group of over ten people had stayed on that roof, it might have caved in. Even after we got on top of the convenience store roof, our fear remained strong.

A car with a man still left in it had been thrust into the convenience store. We managed to pull him out, but his clothes were soaking wet, and the added weight made it extremely hard for us to lift him up to the roof.

Across the street from us, people on the second floor of the bank were trying to get the people being swept away out of the water with a makeshift rope made out of towels. We also saw a man swim over to a person who was trapped in some debris and rescue him.

WHEN THE NIGHT FELL, we were seized by the cold. Fearing it could be fatal for some, we decided to move over to the next building on the west side. One young man bravely jumped down onto the shed and then came back with a ladder. The water was still at waist level, but we all moved to the next building and took refuge on the fourth floor.

There were about twenty of us. The hot oolong tea we drank warmed us up. The people there let us borrow some spare clothes and we dried our wet pants by a space heater. We were able to procure food from the convenience store, and in the end I stayed there for two whole days.

On the third day, I was able to get back home, avoiding the flooded areas. I tried to take my rubber boots off, but my legs were so swollen I couldn't get them off on my own—I had to get someone to help me take them off. When I went to a hospital much later, I was diagnosed with a partial tear of the Achilles tendon in my right leg; in my left leg, part of the calf muscle tissue was found to have collapsed. I am lucky to be alive. I need to continue with my rehabilitation and try to get back to a normal life.

Baby in arms, mother runs for life
Handing baby to husband on rooftop

Miho Asano
female, 23, homemaker

With the tsunami rushing behind us, I held my then 7-month-old daughter Rio and ran for our lives. Wanting to protect my child, I climbed onto the roof of a house, and we survived by a hair's breadth. I can only say that it was a miracle that saved us both.

ON THAT DAY, Rio and I were at home on the second floor of our apartment at Minato-cho 3-chome. The earthquake happened right as we were getting ourselves ready to go out. The quake that sent me rocking made the baby walker I had sat Rio in start to lurch back and forth.

As I leaned over her quickly to protect her, the light shade fell off from the ceiling and hit my face. The apartment started to make big creaking sounds

Miho Asano with Rio stands on the lot where the house they entered for shelter used to be in Yoshino-cho 1-chome.

and I was afraid that it might collapse. While being rocked, I was all the while thinking about how I could protect Rio, should the building collapse.

When the rocking settled down, I held Rio in my arms and reassured her, "It's all right, it's going to be all right," though I couldn't convince my trembling self as the aftershocks continued. Although my eyelid was bleeding, I was not in the state of mind to be bothered by it. Surrounded by fallen furniture, I was at a loss as to what to do. My cell phone wasn't working, but I managed to text a message to my husband, 25, at work. I didn't hear anything from the community emergency wireless system, and I never imagined that a tsunami would be coming.

Around 15 minutes later, I received a reply from my husband saying "Go outside." The fallen fridge and cupboard obstructed the front entrance, but we squeezed through a slight gap. There were a few neighbors asking one another, "What should we do?" A woman among them who I knew said, "Let's go to the Makiyama hills." My husband had just returned from work and, following her suggestion, we set off for the hills in our car.

On our way to Makiyama, our car got caught in a traffic jam that was hardly moving. There was nothing we could do, so we turned left on National Route 398 and headed northwest, only to get stuck again near Ishinomaki Red Cross Nursing School.

MOMENTS LATER, the cars in front of ours started making U-turns one after another. As we were wondering what was going on, we saw a black wave rushing toward us, swallowing people, cars, and everything. "Help me!"—We heard cries like this from all around us. My husband steered hurriedly to the left but the wave was coming not only from behind but from the left as well. Quickly picking Rio up in my arms and opening the door, I dashed toward the mountainside with my husband alongside.

The place where we ran to was a dead-end, surrounded by concrete block walls enclosing residences. We clambered up a wall, but even then the muddy water was coming close by our feet. After handing Rio to my husband, who had climbed farther and reached the roof of a shed, I too climbed up. As my husband went up on the roof of a house which was higher still, the muddy water kept rising higher and higher. "Hurry up! Hurry up!" Thinking I may not make it, I hurriedly passed Rio to my husband, and at that moment the water which had almost reached the roof of the shed stopped rising. Hurriedly, I made it up to the roof of the house just as the shed was swept away.

There were roaring sounds of the water as well as splitting and tearing noises from houses coming apart around us. My feet slipped on the roof as the snow started falling heavily. I knocked on a window and found that it was unlocked and no one was home. Though we were a bit hesitant about trespassing, we couldn't bear the cold, so we entered through the window and pulled a nearby blanket to cover ourselves. The tsunami water had barreled through the first floor and the smell of what seemed like kerosene that filled the house gave me a headache.

I wrapped Rio's head in the blanket so the smell wouldn't affect her.

I noted Rio's diaper had become cold and her skin red. I tore up a bed sheet that was there, folded it and stuffed it inside the diaper. I used the remaining pieces as makeshift diapers for several days at Minato Elementary School where we later evacuated to. It was fortunate that I was breastfeeding her.

THROUGHOUT THE NIGHT, the tsunami rose up toward us time and time again with zooming and rumbling sounds similar to those accompanying an earthquake. Each time it came, I thought that the place we were at might no longer be safe.

The next morning, the water had receded to waist level, so we decided to go to Minato Elementary School. Using a baby sling, I carried Rio on my upper back and started to walk with my husband. It was only 300 meters away but the water was cold and it felt much farther to me. On the way to the school, we came across a construction site at the foot of the mountain, where some workers were making a fire and they let us dry our clothes out. I had been all tense until then thinking I had to protect Rio at all costs, but now I found myself relaxing for the first time after coming in contact with other people.

When the Great East Japan Earthquake happened, we didn't really have any provisions for such a disaster. I am now putting together the experiences my friends and I had to create an emergency handbook for mothers with small children. This is for all families who are raising children across Japan. Familiarizing yourself with escape routes, preparing emergency bags to carry on your back, packing a bed sheet or a bath towel that can be adapted for various uses—these are some of the lessons that I want to pass on as someone who survived this disaster.

"I had this sheer desire to save my grandchild"
I waded out into a sea of rubble to seek rescue

Yoshiji Mogi
male, 61, iron works factory owner

I had been taking care of my first grandchild Yuna during the day since the first of March. My daughter, 31, had given birth in December and her maternity leave had ended. On that day I fed Yuna around 2 p.m. and was cradling her like any other day when suddenly the severe quake struck.

WHEN I LOOKED OUTSIDE, the electric power pole across the street was shaking so much that it looked as though it would topple down at any moment. When the shaking stopped, the factory manager who was listening to the radio said, "A tsunami of more than six meters is coming!" I said to him, "I'm going to run, so you run too, you hear me!" The designated evacuation site for all residents in this area was the Makiyama hills. I wrapped the baby in a bath towel, jumped into the car, and headed for Makiyama. When we got onto National Route 398, we had hardly gone 30 meters before we got stuck in a jam. *We're going be swept away completely, car and all, if we are stuck here.* It didn't take long before I decided to make a U-turn.

When we returned to the factory, I ran into my second son, 35, who was employed at a nearby company and had come to see if the family was all right. The two of us carried to the office space above the factory such things as a space heater, flashlights, a sofa to use as a bed, and some kerosene. Just as I told my daughter that the four of us were safe, the cell phone call was disconnected.

Ten minutes or so after we got back, we heard these roaring sounds. At first, I thought it was rain. But then all of a sudden, this black, murky seawater came surging into our place. I think it took barely ten seconds for it to rise to more than two meters in height. After the water ceased to rise, we entered our house that was adjacent to the factory and groped in the mud for what we needed the most—things such as milk, diapers, and baby bottles. We were lucky to also find three 2-liter bottles of water and paper diapers which were still covered in plastic. Even so, baby Yuna had to be fed 140-160 milliliters of milk every three hours. I didn't drink a single drop of water.

ON THE SECOND DAY, we saw helicopters fly by in the sky many times. Though we sent SOS signals by waving towels again and again, there was no sign that they would come back for us. The baby, perhaps missing her mother, screamed all through the night. She cried so much that she started to intermittently stop breathing. This happened repeatedly during the night. *If this continues, her life will be at risk. I should go and make a request for rescue.* I made up my mind to go.

As soon as the sun started rising on the third day, I left the factory. As I got to the road along Kyu-Kitakami-gawa River, I saw that the road ahead was buried in rubble. The water level was around stomach to chest height. Because I had no idea of what was submerged in the water, I waded one slow step at a time, avoiding the rubble, using a wooden stick I found as a cane. Though I knew the place well, I had to repeatedly go back and forth along the way.

Shortly after I started to wade out into the sea of debris, I was faced with a heap of rubble which wouldn't budge either by pulling or pushing. There was no alternative route. I crawled onto the rubble that floated on the water and continued on. Right then, I put my hand on another mound of rubble, but it didn't have enough buoyancy and I fell into the water headfirst. It helped that the next pile of rubble I put my hand on was stable enough, but I almost got pinned under it. If that had happened, there would have been no saving me. I came across a situation like this two times.

HOW CAN I POSSIBLY MAKE IT?—I was seized by this anxious thought many times. Despite that, the reason I could keep on moving forward was because I had this sheer desire to save my grandchild. It was a two-and-a-half hour march to the Ishinomaki Area Fire Headquarters.

When I finally got there, the place was packed full with evacuees. People lined both sides of the corridors and the stairs sitting with their knees up, such that only one person could pass through at a time. I managed to make arrangements to have a helicopter dispatched, and I waded through the sea of rubble back to my factory.

The helicopter arrived in a short while. The view of the city from the helicopter was tragic. Everything—houses and all—was gone. It looked as though bombs had been dropped as in a war.

On the message board in the back of the Ishinomaki Red Cross Hospital where we were taken to, I wrote down the names of the four of us and left a message saying that we were safe. Then I went into the waiting room, where I could hear a voice calling "Yuna! Yuna!" I wondered, *Who could be calling the same name as that of my sweet grandchild's?*

As I looked in the direction of the voice, who should I see but my daughter and her husband looking for their own baby? There's never ever been a coincidence like that. It was a miracle. My daughter naturally cried out loud when she got to embrace Yuna, and even I cried out loud. I had never cried like that, ever. No matter how much I cried, tears just continued to come pouring out.

Flooding besieged City Hall

Responding to overwhelming needs as City Hall chief despite losing family members

Hideyuki Sugawara
male, 60, former City Hall chief

I was at Ishinomaki City Hall which was besieged by the flooding water that reached almost two meters at one point. My memories of the time spent there may be

muddled. For days, I was there around the clock.

WHEN THE EARTHQUAKE HAPPENED, I was in a meeting with some City Hall officials in a conference room on the fourth floor of City Hall. I held on tightly to the long desk during the intense quake, my body all tense. From the corridor, I could hear the loud sounds of framed paintings falling down. I even thought that the ceiling could come tumbling down. Immediately after the shaking subsided, we held a disaster response meeting. On that day, Mayor Hiroshi Kameyama was in Sendai City on business. I issued an order for a report on the condition of the designated evacuation spots and the damage each area had sustained. Cell phones had become useless, so I made contact over the city's wireless emergency system.

Since the City Hall building had an in-house power generator, we were assured of electricity for a few days. Watching scenes of the tsunami crawling over land on TV, I couldn't believe my eyes. My house, located in the Kamaya district, was about 100 meters away from Okawa Elementary School. *Looking back at history, as far back as 300 or 400 years even, no tsunami had ever reached the area. My home should be all right*—that was what I thought at that time.

After sunset, there were anywhere from 200 to 300 evacuees at City Hall. The first floor had been completely flooded before we knew it. It was impossible to go outside, and we were pressed to secure food. I directed some staff members to procure food from the supermarket that was on the first floor of the City Hall building, but only small quantities were delivered. They told me that the store was checking out the merchandise one by one. I went to the person in charge and said, "We'll pay you whatever it comes to later. Allow us to buy whatever you have here that can be eaten, all of it right now. We have a great number of evacuees here."

WE HANDED OUT those snacks and candies that escaped getting soaked by flood water to the evacuees. It was far from enough. The rice that was procured from the store was cooked and was handed out to the evacuees in the form of small rice balls with no filling. Out of concern for the evacuees, not one City Hall staff member ate any of them.

I noticed that the direction of Hiyoriyama hills was orange in color. It was a fire. Information reached us that it might reach Ishinomaki Municipal Girls' Senior High School, a designated evacuation site. I gave instructions to have the people at the school evacuate temporarily to higher ground on the Hiyoriyama hills.

The next morning, we tried to get out of City Hall by lining up long tables as a bridge. However, given the depth of the water, the table legs were not long enough to reach ground and they floated, no matter what we tried. Frustrated, I had the two staffers who had previously participated in a rowing match at a national athletic meet to head for a fishing tackle shop in the Hebita district. "I want you two to go buy a boat from there. If the shop is locked, go ahead and break the door, and come back with one," I said to them. Though this meant I was instructing my staffers to steal, I had no hesitation in asking this of them—we were driven into a corner.

I believe it was the third day. The two staffers had bought a boat and came back. Fortunately, the shopkeeper had been there. As the floodwater gradually receded, the long tables that were lined up started to function as a bridge, and some of our staffers went about gathering information.

I hadn't slept. I couldn't tell day from night. It was around this time that I noticed the words "Nagatsura, Okawa districts devastated" on the disaster response department bulletin board that was there to give updates on the damage.

I thought of my family. My wife was formerly a staff member of a government office. She was the kind of person who could make a level-headed decision under any situation. *She's all right*—that was what I believed.

It was probably the fifth day after the disaster struck. A letter was delivered to me during a meeting. It was from my granddaughter who lived with us, sent from an evacuation shelter. "To Grandpa: Grandma has been found. I'm all right."

THE MESSAGE was brief, but I understood what it meant. It meant that my daughter, my wife and my mother were not all right. I couldn't keep standing. *I'm not the only one who's in pain*—I kept telling myself, until I snuck behind the reception counter of a department that was empty of staff members, and collapsed into quiet sobs, trying not to allow my voice to escape. I had made this resolve: *I will never show any tears to my staff.*

The staff members were physical and mental wrecks, too. Many of them had lost their homes and families. Even when emergency supplies started to reach evacuation shelters, their nutrition level was poor. Even so, I had to urge them to carry on.

"Your response is slow"—we were berated over and over. That the number of staff members was overwhelmingly insufficient to handle a disaster of that magnitude—that was what I found so hard.

One female staff member who had lost her husband was turning the document in her hands to pulp with her tears. "You are not the only one who is having a hard time. You have to learn to live with the fact that your husband is gone." I knew too well it didn't help to say that, but I had no choice. Those kinds of days dragged on.

On June 30, I retired—after having my retirement extended for three months. I have more time now than I did back then, and I'm in a situation where I can look at the photos of my departed family members when I like. But,to be honest, because of this, perhaps it may well be that the present is an even harder time for me.

Sudden onslaught sends chill up my spine
Houses jamming into Utsumi-bashi Bridge

Seitaro Omori
male, 34, manager of the Mangattan Museum

I was driving my car to Ishinomaki City Hall for a meeting. As I came to the intersection with taverns in front of the station, a great rumbling of the earth and a strong quake shook me and I almost lost control over my steering.

AS THOUGH DANCING, the car bounced around but I brought it to a sudden stop. The buildings before my eyes rocked in billowing motions, and I heard the cracking sounds of things falling from somewhere around the top of the City Hall building. Sensing danger, I moved my car to a safe place and soon after, the quake settled down.

Is Ishinomaki Mangattan Museum all right?—as one of the managers of the museum dedicated to the manga works of Ishinomori Shotaro, this uneasy thought crossed my mind. Right away, I headed back to the museum. On the way back I could see that the walls of stores and display windows were damaged and traffic lights weren't working due to the power outage. There were lots of cars stopped in the streets, but I was able to get back to the museum within five minutes of the quake.

At the time of the quake, around 30 visitors were at the museum. Since the staff members were well prepared for emergencies, the visitors had already been taken to a safe place by the time I arrived. I locked up the museum, and took steps for an emergency closure.

A major tsunami warning had been announced over the city's wireless emergency system at an early stage. I instructed the staff to get away from Nakaze, a tiny islet in the Kyu-Kitakami-gawa River where the museum is located, and to go home. I stayed in the museum alone. It was around 3:10 p.m. then.

I was aware of the major tsunami warning. However, with no working TV and no radio, I didn't know the predicted height of the tsunami or its estimated time of arrival. Even if one came, I assumed it would only be about one meter high—about double the height of the tsunami that reached here after the 2010 Chile Earthquake. As a safety precaution, I moved my car to a parking lot on the opposite side of the river. After returning to the museum, I started taking pictures for a report on the damage due to the earthquake.

IT STARTED TO SNOW. Looking across the river at the opposite shore, I could tell that the water level was plummeting. I vaguely thought that a tsunami was about to come. I had heard that people had seen the bottom of the Kyu-Kitakami-gawa River before the tsunami that arrived as a result of the Great Chilean Earthquake in 1960.

The water level had not fallen to the point where the riverbed was visible so I thought it would still be a while. In the meeting area located on the first floor of the museum, I sat down in a chair to take a little breather, when suddenly the river water flowed backwards before my eyes, accompanied with what sounded like heavy rain. Confused by the gap between what I had heard before about a tsunami attack and the reality of it, I rushed up the ramp inside the museum.

As I looked back down on the first floor, I saw the lockers and information boards—set right outside the museum's front entrance—breaking through the glass and flowing into the building. In an instant, the sea water rushed in and all sorts of things were being washed away. The tsunami now came rushing up the ramp. *I am the only one in the museum. No one will come to my rescue.* Sensing danger, a chill ran up my spine and I made a dash for the third floor.

Looking out east toward the Minato district from the window in the library section, I could see the tsunami increasing its force and attacking the town. The water was gradually turning to a dark black, and, accompanied with what smelled like heavy oil, it was increasing its speed.

Over the Kyu-Kitakami-gawa River, cars had been left stranded on Utsumi-bashi Bridge because of the traffic jam. Those that were stuck on the east side of the bridge were mercilessly washed away. Houses and apartments near the museum were producing cracking sounds as they got torn apart, starting with those by the mouth of the river and spreading upstream.

CARS AND RUBBLE which I supposed came from the Minamihama-cho and Kadonowaki-cho districts washed up from the mouth of the river in increasing amounts. They had probably been destroyed in the first wave, and then washed back up the river by the second wave. There were lots of people desperately clinging onto the roofs of houses and the rubble. Most of the houses and rubble that were washed away jammed into the eastern portion of the Utsumi-bashi Bridge, where they got stuck.

Seitaro Omori points to the Utsumi-bashi Bridge from the ramp inside the museum.

The people who were being carried along by the water seemed to be struggling desperately to cope with the ever-changing circumstances they were in. Carried away and slamming into the bridge at speeds of around 50 kilometers an hour, the rubble kept piling up. There were people being buried under the humongous piles of rubble and disappearing, and others perishing when their foothold slid from slamming into the bridge, never to be seen again.

Being where I was on top of the museum, I couldn't call out to the people, let alone help them—I just stood there watching, stunned. It was starting to snow more heavily. Reverberating relentlessly around me were the ruthless blaring of car horns that had been washed away and short-circuited, and the sirens of the major tsunami warning.

Strong quake during an operation
Hospital staff helped all 150 inpatients escape with SDF support

Kimie Ito
female, 41, nurse manager

When the earthquake happened, I was in the middle of assisting an operation on the second floor of Ishinomaki Municipal Hospital.

WHILE THE STRONG AND LONG-LASTING SHAKING CONTINUED, all of our staff remained calm. This was, I believe, due to our routine training and preparation for disasters. Although I'm not sure exactly how many staff members were in the hospital at the time, each of us ran to check the condition of approximately 150 inpatients on the third and fourth floors.

The operation was to remove half of the stomach of a man in his 70s who had stomach cancer. Even if the shaking had stopped, the operation of the patient in front of us had not come to an end. While aftershocks intermittently followed, the surgeon calmly continued working on removing the affected area and closed the stomach temporarily. Because of a blackout, we lit up the operating table with several flashlights brought over by the staff.

As we were checking the equipment in the operation room, we heard a male staff member shouting somewhere. "The first floor is more than half way flooded by water! Run to the upper floors!" I recall that it was around 3:40 p.m.

Leaving the room in order to confirm the situation, I looked outside through a window in the hall and there I saw an unbelievable scene. Houses on fire were being washed away. It didn't strike me as reality at all. We put the male patient whose operation had just been completed onto an air-stretcher and carried him to the intensive care unit on the fourth floor. There was also a woman in her late 80s who was hooked up to an oxygen respirator in the same room, so we carried her to a room on the third floor.

As the time passed, some of the young nurses became concerned about the safety of their families and were starting to come out in tears. There was, however, no one who panicked. This was, I believe, because we all had the strong sense of duty to protect our patients. Since cell phones had become useless, we couldn't contact our families. My seven-year-old daughter and six-year-old son would have reached home about that time. If the timing was bad, they could have gotten caught in the tsunami, so I was extremely anxious.

AS IF A WAR HAD DEVASTATED THE LAND, all I could see was piles of rubble that were on fire. Anxiety permeated the conversations of the nurses. Since I knew that heavy oil tanks were near the hospital, I could well imagine the situation we would be in if they were to explode and the fire was to spread to the hospital.

I don't know who started to do this, but all the staff members suddenly started to help one another write personal identification information—name, address, date of birth—on our arms with a permanent ink marker. "This is just in case," we said. The information would enable us to be identified in the worst case scenario. None of us mentioned the word "death."

Because the emergency stockpile of food and water was all on the first floor, we couldn't go and get anything. It was strange I didn't feel hungry, but that was probably because I was keyed up. However, I drank some tea and juice and ate some snacks that we had on hand. We had divided ourselves into pairs and took turns checking on the patients. We continued doing this, but it seemed that most nurses hadn't slept. Encouraging each other, we kept trying to keep worry out of our minds.

During the night, we received word that a helicopter would come at 5:30 a.m. on the 12th for transporting those patients who were in the middle of operations at the time of the earthquake. Early in the morning, we gathered the documents that the patients would need to take with them, and then waited for the helicopter, looking out from the deck on the third floor. However, the helicopter failed to show up. A feeling of futility circulated among us.

I spent that day giving directions to the staff, and holding meetings to corroborate our plan of action. On the morning of the 13th, after it was confirmed that the water level had gone down, the chief surgeon and the deputy administrative officer left the hospital, wading through the knee-deep water. They did that in order to explain our condition to City Hall. Around noon, we received word from the Ishinomaki Red Cross Hospital—they had come to know about our situation—that help was on the way, and a disaster medical assistance team (DMAT) arrived at our hospital. It was as if gods had come to us. After the triage assessments were made on our patients, we carried all of the patients out of the hospital, with the assistance of the Japan Self Defense Forces who arrived later, working day and night until the night of the 14th.

I WAS ABLE TO LEAVE THE HOSPITAL on the morning of the 15th, four days after the earthquake. Since I had spent days worrying about the condition of the staff and patients, the time spent at the hospital seemed, and still seems, surreal for me. Returning home on foot on the morning of the 15th, my daughter and son jumped into my arms crying. Squeezing my daughter in my arms, I, too, could not hold back the tears that came streaming down.

Hotel turned into shelter for 300
Devoted staff helped manage shelter over two months

Munenori Goto
male, 52, president of Ishinomaki Grand Hotel

Just after the earthquake, I had my staff check the extent of injuries and property damage at our hotel as well as at Sun Plaza Hotel, an affiliated hotel across the street.

THERE WASN'T ANYONE INJURED OR TRAPPED IN THE ELEVATORS, but at Ishinomaki Grand Hotel, the marble had fallen off of the wall of the first floor, and water was flowing down from the ceiling of the second floor to the first floor.

I became worried about possible fires in the surrounding area so I went out to check. My home, which was a clothing rental shop in the nearby Tachimachi district, had collapsed completely. I came to realize later that I should not have left the hotel without telling the staff.

I returned to the hotel, and as I began to clean up with the staff, I was thinking about how to get in contact with those guests who were to attend banquets at our hotel or how to go about the repairs on the buildings. A major tsunami warning had been issued, so I was paying close attention to the direction of the Kyu-Kitakami-gawa River while I continued to clean up. Then a number of neighborhood residents came to our hotel seeking shelter, and we let them in, sending all of them up to the sixth floor. Shortly afterwards, a tsunami came surging in,

Tuna on rice was prepared for the people of the neighborhood as part of a relief effort organized jointly by the Ishinomaki Grand Hotel and a Tokyo publishing house. Front entrance area of the hotel, May 21

flooding up to about 40 centimeters above floor level on the first floor.

We asked the evacuees to write down their names on a list, and decided to have them stay in the banquet halls on the second and third floors. This was to make it easier for us to lead them to safety in any contingency since none of the disaster prevention equipment was functioning. There probably was a certain degree of dissatisfaction that we didn't allow them to use the guest rooms, but we put top priority on safety.

As for food, there was what had been prepared for banquets and other provisions. The water tank was full enough for the time being, plus we had some stock of beverages. Banquet candles were there for light. There were blankets and tabletop cooking stoves as well.

I called together the 80 or so evacuees to explain the situation we were in, including disaster updates so as to prevent any panic from developing. This done, I went on to make this announcement: "I don't want you to think that you can go home in just a day or two. We can provide meals twice a day including one hot meal. Three meals will be provided for those who require it for health reasons. During the daytime, you may go home to clean up. . . ."

IT'S IMPORTANT TO MAKE RULES when a lot of people live together in a shelter. I was able to apply what I had learned from volunteering as a member of the Ishinomaki Junior Chamber following the Great Hanshin earthquake in 1995. It takes one to two weeks before things settle down after a major disaster. Until then, water, food, protection against the cold, human waste, and medical care must be managed appropriately. There were about 80 evacuees plus 46 staff workers. We were all set for water, food and the cold.

The problem was bodily wastes. We decided on the following: males urinate outside; females urinate in the toilet without flushing; both males and females defecate in the toilet but with old newspapers stuffed in it, and no flushing; staff workers clear and clean the toilets once a day.

I had everybody gather together after the evening meal on the first night, where I explained these rules. There were a few people who couldn't follow them because of health conditions. From the fifth day on, the younger evacuees helped to clean the toilets voluntarily. As for medical care, I was able to have Dr. Takahashi from the gastroenterological clinic next door come for house calls a few times during the night. A volunteer medical team set up by a medical organization in Sapporo, Hokkaido, came to assist periodically for four weeks, for which I was very thankful.

From the second day on, the number of evacuees continued to increase, exceeding 300 on the fourth day. Every day before the evening meal, I explained what disaster updates I had obtained to the evacuees. With the damage so great and the aftershocks that continued, an increasing number of people were beset with anxiety over the situation where they could not return home anytime soon. Some of them came to share their feelings with me quite often.

I HAD ALSO TO THINK ABOUT the management of our hotel, a private enterprise. The fatigue on the part of the staff was also a concern. Around March 20, I had to go to Sendai to consult a financial institution about a loan.

March 25 was the hardest. I had to call the staff together and make this plea: "I can no longer keep you employed. I want to ask you to take a leave of absence. For some of you, I have to terminate employment. If I can reopen the hotel, I will rehire you. We still have evacuees here, however, and if possible, I would like to ask you to help out as volunteers now." Many of them did offer to help—one employee even took an hour and a half to walk all the way from Higashi-Matsushima. I was really glad.

It was early May when the last evacuee left the hotel. We could run the shelter because we had the conditions that enabled us to do so. I am thankful for the effort of the staff. They are my treasure.

Sun Plaza Hotel reopened for business in June, and Grand Hotel in August. On the evening of July 31, a memorial event was held for the souls of the victims as part of the Ishinomaki Kawabiraki Festival, the city's annual summer festival. I took this occasion to make a vow to look forward and carry on.

Frantic run from the surging tsunami

Crossing makeshift bridge from school building to back hill

Yukiteru Moriyama
male, 63, member of Ishinomaki City Assembly

I was visiting the General Affairs Department on the fourth floor of Ishinomaki City Hall taking care of some assembly matter. This horrendous jolt, the kind that I had never encountered before, hit right then.

"GET DOWN UNDER THE TABLE!"—I shouted to the people there, many of them female staff workers who had turned pale and were on the verge of panic. Although the quake subsided shortly, the sense of fear remained. The whole place was in an uproar. I headed out for the sixth floor of the parking lot where I had parked my car. Many of the staff workers were standing there in a daze.

A major tsunami warning was being aired over the community's emergency wireless system. *I should be able to get home (in the Inai district) in no more than an hour,* I thought. I agreed to give a ride to two City Hospital employees I had met at City Hall and decided to go back via the hospital. I had no qualms then about heading toward the sea coast.

After leaving City Hall, we headed for the hospital by going down Tachimachi street, past Aitopia street, and going over the hill. The road going over the hill was jammed with cars and I felt impatient, but we managed to go down the hill. From a ditch that was 300 to 400 meters inland from the Hibarino Beach, I could hear these heavy thumps.

As I looked beyond the direction of the sound, I could see a wave that was five to six meters high. *What in the world could this be!* I made a U-turn right away, and drove the wrong way down the one-way street. All three of us had the same idea: the only high ground nearby was Kadonowaki Elementary School, which was also a designated evacuation site. "Kado-sho, Kado-sho"—the name the school was commonly called was uttered among us, and we hurried to that destination.

THE SURGING TSUNAMI seemed as if it were chasing after my car, and the two hospital workers in the backseat were shaking with fear. The school yard came into sight now. A man was calmly directing cars. The school yard was already crowded with about a hundred cars. Once we got to the entrance of the building, we abandoned the car and ran desperately up the stairs that were near the entrance.

The tsunami was pushing houses and cars as it came surging closer to the school building. People were shouting, "Tsunami! It's the tsunami!" The sounds of objects scraping against each other resounded as we rushed up to the rooftop. The tsunami was rising up to nearly catch up with us.

I looked around to see the whole surrounding area was now under water and had been transformed into a sea of muddy water, where the only other things visible were the sign for Ishinomaki City Hospital and the triangular roof of Ishinomaki Culture Center. It was sleeting now and the cold was becoming more severe. There were anywhere from 70 to 80 people including elderly people who were trembling and mothers holding their infants.

The waves were flowing from west to east, and a number of houses were being carried away ever so easily. There was a man on the roof of a house, waving both hands and shouting, "Help! Help me!" I saw another man in a car, hitting the car window and seeking help. *I wish I could do something to help, but I can't do anything.* I felt absolutely powerless.

In a short while, a two-story house that was on fire came, drawn to the east side of the school building on the 3rd-floor level as if being sucked into it, letting out these battering sounds. Window panes of the school were falling to pieces with shattering noises. The smell of something burning was starting to drift about now.

Feeling that I was no longer safe where I was, and with the water starting to recede, I ran around on the third floor. "There it is!" From a window of the 3rd-floor hallway, I found the roof of the 2nd-floor walkway bridging two of the school buildings. "All right, now we can make our escape from there out to the cemetery on the hill in the back!"

I called out to the people to help out and we fetched ten or so desks from classrooms. Some were placed right against the wall in the hallway while the rest were placed on the roof of the walkway, which made it easier for people to climb over the window. Men stood on both inside and outside of the window and took the hand of each elderly person to help them get out.

But we had another challenge to face: how we should go about moving from the roof to the cemetery ground. Younger men would be able to jump over the gap, but that would be impossible for the elderly. The gap was between 1.5 meters and two meters with a drop of about one meter. What should we do?

No sooner had we started wondering than we found two teacher's platforms that were about the right length from the classrooms, which we placed parallel to each other over the gap between the roof and the hill. "O.K. This will do." Again, men guided the elderly and parents with children by the hand, helping all of the people to escape safely. It was a matter of a little more than ten minutes.

We were a bit relieved now, but our fear and the cold remained unchanged. We made our way through a narrow, weedy path in the cemetery and then walked up the steps toward Ishinomaki Municipal Girls' High School.

JUST AS WE STARTED to walk up the hill, we heard a boom from behind. I turned around and saw a fire breaking out. That fire lasted into the next day and devastated the Kadonowaki-cho and Minamihama-cho districts. Although Kadonowaki Elementary School was consumed by the fire, the diplomas were miraculously found intact in the safe, and were handed to the students one month later.

If I had been five minutes early, or late, for that matter, I would definitely have been snatched away by the tsunami. The traffic jam saved my life. I would like to dedicate this life of mine that was allowed to continue for the good of the citizens and the world.

Over 1,000 employees safely evacuated
With bodies buried in rubble, debris was removed with caution

Yoshikatsu Murakami
male, 49, manager of general affairs department
Nippon Paper Industries Ishinomaki Mill

I was attending a meeting at City Hall when the earthquake occurred. The quake was such that I couldn't

Area near Nippon Paper Industries Ishinomaki Mill on the day after the earthquake (photo courtesy of Ishinomaki Mill)

keep standing, which made me think that this was no ordinary event, and I went back to my car to turn on the TV—it was announcing over and over that a major tsunami was on its way.

RUSHING BACK TO THE MILL, I saw that the employees had already started to evacuate by foot to higher ground in the Nanko-cho district, where the company's housing complex as well as its wellness center known as the Mill House was located. There were 1,306 employees at the mill, and, by about 3:10 p.m., all of them had arrived at the high ground. After confirming the evacuation status of the employees, I, too, evacuated.

The tsunami came barreling along from the seaside district of Minamihama-cho to the higher ground of Nanko-cho where I was standing—in a matter of just 20 seconds or so. A white cloud of sandy dust could be seen roiling up in the distance, and in no time a big black mass that was like a wall was engulfing houses and cars with horrendous roaring sounds.

The tsunami was then closing in on the bumper-to-bumper traffic in Kadonowaki-cho, and I was yelling through the loud speaker, "Run away from there!" But one after another, the cars got engulfed in the tsunami.

In one of the houses being washed away, I could see a human shadow. The tsunami now came surging at my feet along with debris, which forced me to back away in fear, and I had to have the employees evacuate to Kadonowaki Junior High School or Ishinomaki Junior High School, both of which were on higher grounds than where we were.

Some of the employees wanted to go and check whether their families and homes were safe. Helplessly torn as I was, I had to plead with them to forgo that urge—secondary disasters had to be prevented.

MY WIFE, 55, AND MY DAUGHTER, 27, had gone to Tokyo to cheer for the company's baseball team—they were playing in the national championship tournament—and we were able to confirm each other's safety by cell phone immediately after the quake hit. And since we lived in a company-owned house on high ground, I was free from worrying about my home as well. I felt I was fortunate that I didn't have to worry about my family and home.

I stayed in Nanko-cho and went around checking to see if anybody was left behind. When it was starting to get dark, I came across a fire breaking out in the Minamihama-cho district. A 30-centimeter flame was starting up from the gas range in a house that had been washed away. *If only I can put it out now,* I thought, but the debris kept me from getting near it. The fire was now spreading and the sounds of propane gas tanks exploding were reverberating. The smell from not only wood but other materials such as rubber and metal burning and scorching was filling the air. It didn't take long before the entire neighborhood was turned into a sea of fire.

I spent the night of the 11th at the job placement office near Kadonowaki Junior High School and Ishinomaki Junior High, both evacuation shelters, and on the 12th I set up our own emergency response headquarters at the Mill House. The first thing to do was to secure food for the 2,000 or so evacuees including our employees and their family members. The Mill House was equipped with a kitchen, a generator, and sleeping accommodations, but only five kilograms of rice were left. Bite-size rice balls were prepared, but only 200 could be made. I had to ask the men to refrain from eating any.

Starting on the 12th, the employees were grouped into teams to be sent to the mill to grasp the conditions the place was in. The entire site was filled with piles of houses, cars, and debris that had been washed up there, two meters in height, leaving no room to step in.

"I CAUGHT SIGHT OF SOMETHING LIKE HUMAN HAIR in the debris," "We could see something like an arm"—when such reports were brought in, it was my role to go out and confirm whether it was a body. A body was to be reported to the Self Defense Forces. The process was a heart-wrenching experience, especially so since I had witnessed people being washed away by the tsunami.

Sometime later, a bereaved family member of someone who was found dead within our premises came to pay a visit from Sendai. She wanted to know where we found the body. For about a week, she could be seen by the mill joining her hands in prayer every day—a sight I will never forget.

It took us until the end of July to clear our premises of the debris. About ten days after the earthquake hit, the Self Defense Forces sent us a unit of about 30 members to help out. Heavy machinery and trucks, three vehicles each, were brought in to make paths that allowed people to walk through, and this took one week. Then we were able to start our own rubble removal effort, mobilizing as many as 1,500 employees on certain days.

Taking into consideration the possibility of the presence of bodies, the removal task was carried out with caution. All the different departments cooperated with one another to remove the rubble by hand. By about the middle of April, enough had been cleared so that vehicles could go through. Meetings were held on a daily basis, where decisions were made as to where to clear next based on the progress being made.

ON AUGUST 10, we were finally able to restart in part the operation of the mill. Seeing the smoke rise from the stack, I was overwhelmed thinking, *Ishinomaki Mill has been revived.*

It is regrettable that five employees who happened to be off duty lost their lives, but all the employees who were inside of the mill were safe. Also, we were able to overcome the chaotic times following the earthquake by the teamwork of our organization, each team assuming responsibility for tasks such as water supply, shopping and patrolling.

Our facilities on the high ground are now stocked with enough emergency food and water supply that would enable our employees to survive three days—this is one example of how we have applied the lessons we learned to disaster preparedness. I believe that it is our mission to pass what we have experienced from this disaster down to future generations to prevent the lessons learned from fading away.

Restored 17th century sailing ship survives tsunami
*Sant Juan Bautista Museum's Dock Hall submerged in waters

Hiroshi Sudo
male, 51, manager at Sant Juan Bautista Museum

The museum was open as usual. It was just another afternoon. There was a tour group of about 30 people from Saitama Prefecture along with some other visitors. There were about a dozen staff members, including those in the office and tour guides.

THE SUDDEN ATTACK OF THE QUAKE made me feel that it equaled the 1978 Miyagi earthquake. The shaking, however, lasted so long that it was beyond comparison. Part of the ceiling panel came apart and TV monitors fell and crashed, but the Observation Deck did not sustain too much damage otherwise. Although we could not watch TV because of the blackout, we received the major tsunami warnings off the radio and the cell phone TV, which was what I had expected.

I first went down the escalator, stopped because of the power outage, to see if any visitors were stranded around the *Sant Juan Bautista* and the Dock Hall, the museum's exhibit space, some 50 meters below the Observation Deck. Fortunately, no visitors were around in that area, so I returned to the Observation Deck with other staff members who had been placed there to attend to visitors. As a precautionary measure, the entire staff guided all the visitors to higher ground in Sant Juan Park. I am grateful that not a single person was hurt and everyone was calm throughout.

As I observed the sea, a dark surface that had suddenly risen was surging over the breakwater that protected Sasuhama Port. The first wave was not so big, but I think the second wave was nearly ten meters high. I instinctively grabbed my cell phone to record this by photo and video.

The *Sant Juan Bautista* was being tossed up and down, side to side like a toy, by the gushing waters that overflowed the dock. The ship's mooring rope had been severed and the Dock Hall sank to the bottom of the dark sea waters. With what had turned into a snow storm, it was a frenzied spectacle. I can still hear the deafening sound of the tempered glass breaking.

THE RECEDING WAVE had such a force that I was gravely worried it would take the ship away with it. What was also astounding was that I could see the very bottom of the entire port that was surrounded by the breakwater. I truly believe that the reason that the restored ship survived all the tossing and turning of the massive waves and escaped being swept away was because the dock with its sturdy doors weighing one thousand tons must have helped to lessen the force of the waves.

As the day turned to late afternoon, we headed for the Buddhist temple Dogen-in up the hill in the back of the museum, an emergency evacuation site designated by the city. There must have been about three hundred evacuees there including those from the nearby coastal communities.

The immediate concern was food. We brought out food and sweets from the museum kiosk and distributed them. We also gathered up and provided anything we could drape over or place under ourselves, such as blankets, cushions or jackets. Dogen-in Temple had some stock of rice and miso paste, which were cooked in the temple's kitchen and served. The best we could do that night for sleep was to huddle together like canned sardines.

The following morning, some of us took the initiative to discuss what needed to be done and assigned the tasks. Some went down to areas where the waters had receded to look for food as well as propane gas tanks and kerosene drums for fuel. A construction company provided a generator which was used sparingly for lighting and charging cell phones. From the museum we brought out supplies of kerosene that were stored in the basement and water from the water receiving tanks. Carpenters constructed makeshift toilets by digging holes in the ground and using whatever material they could find. Nurses took care of the elderly and the sick. Everyone pitched in at this time of crisis.

The following day, about 70 people who had fled to the mountain from the Sasuhama community joined us seeking shelter, and Dogen-in simply ran out of space. We then decided to open up the museum's seminar rooms and meeting rooms, where we asked mostly the museum visitors who came from Saitama to stay.

IT IS NOT CLEAR when all of our staff were finally able to return to their homes. Some had their homes completely or partially destroyed by the tsunami, and some had even lost their loved ones. When I finally returned to my home in Yokokawa of Tsuyama in Tome City, from where I commuted to work, my family was dumbfounded. They thought I had been swept away by the tsunami and had already filed a missing person's report.

Although I was home, I was in no mood to relax. I returned to the museum the next day and, with my fellow staff members, slept in the parking lot office and went about our tasks surveying the damage and doing emergency repair work. I was home for only two days during the month of March after the disaster.

Most of the precious materials relating to the wooden sailing vessel that were exhibited in the Dock Hall were swept away by the tsunami. Fortunately, however, the ship itself remained. This is a legacy for the people of Miyagi Prefecture. October 2013 marks the 400th anniversary of the *Sant Juan Bautista*'s sailing out to sea. I want to see to it that the ship is repaired by then and that it can become a symbol of restoration from this disaster.

*The *Sant Juan Bautista*

The *Sant Juan Bautista* is a fully-replicated 17th century wooden sailing ship. The Sendai feudal lord Date Masamune ordered the ship built in order to send a mission to Spain and the Vatican for the purpose of establishing a direct trade route with Spanish Mexico in exchange for allowing Christian missionary activities in the Sendai Domain. After being built in Ishinomaki, the *Sant Juan Bautista* sailed across the Pacific Ocean to carry Masamune's mission to Mexico, after which she returned to Japan while the mission continued their travel across Mexico and the Atlantic Ocean with Spanish support.

Based on evidence recognized after the disaster of March 2011, the *samurai* mission was most likely organized as part of the recovery effort from a major earthquake and tsunami disaster that befell Tohoku in 1611.

The materials brought back by the mission, including the certificate of Roman Citizenship conferred upon the *samurai* ambassador and his portrait in oil painting, were officially included in the UNESCO's Memory of the World Register, a United Nations program, in 2013.

The Sant Juan Bautista Museum fully reopened in November of 2013 after completing the restoration work.

Kindergarten principal takes children to roof
The tsunami came surging in two layers

Hiroaki Tsuda
male, 71, kindergarten principal

I was on the second floor of our kindergarten located near Ishinomaki Industrial Port, looking out toward the port highway that was in bumper-to-bumper gridlock, when the muddy torrent came gushing in like a waterfall. I had the children go up on the roof in a big rush. There was no escaping. Shivering with cold, I prayed for the water to recede.

WHEN THE EARTHQUAKE STRUCK, I was at Ishinomaki Mizuho Daini Kindergarten in the Shintate district, where I was the principal. The regular kindergarten hours had ended at 1:30 p.m. All children, except for the 13 that were to stay longer waiting to be picked up by their parents, had gone home on the kindergarten bus. Amid the aftershocks, I hurried to the children's hall in the back where we were keeping those children.

The children were huddled in the middle of the room with their teachers. The 11 teachers accompanied them to the second-floor play room. In a short while, two were taken home by their parents.

The radio had fallen down on the floor because of the earthquake, and we couldn't obtain any information. "Tsunami. . ." "3: . . . p.m. . . ." "Ayukawa. . ." "9 meters. . ."—information came in bits and pieces from the cell phone TVs of the staff members, and it was all in fragments.

The kindergarten was just under 300 meters away from the sea. The street that led to the port road and the Okaido district was in a massive jam. There was no way we could evacuate the children in the kindergarten bus. Another parent arrived, but had no choice but to stay.

What would happen if a 9-meter tsunami came

Young children evacuated to the rooftop at Ishinomaki Mizuho Daini Kindergarten (photo courtesy of the kindergarten).

surging. . . ? The second floor is about 3.5 meters. Rooftop is seven meters—is that high enough to survive. . . ? Even then, I had strong doubts. I instructed my staff to prepare two stepladders just in case.

I REMEMBER it was about 3:50 p.m. I looked toward the ocean, and, in between the two port authorities' buildings, a muddy torrent was making its way like a waterfall. It must have been around two meters. I could not believe my eyes—I had always thought that a tsunami came only after the sea water had receded.

The next wave I saw came surging in two layers. Each layer was about three meters high. I remember the bottom layer being a mixture of black and green, and the upper layer as pitch-black.

How could water this high actually come? We moved the children out through the window in the corridor onto the rooftop of the boiler shed, where the ladders had been placed. We then opened up one of the folding ladders flat and propped it against the roof end of the main building. I grabbed the children by the pants, pushed them up the ladder, and two other staff members who were already up on the roof pulled them up. Some children started to cry, but they all eventually made it up to the roof. I was the last to climb, and by then the water was about to reach my feet.

From the rooftop, I could see the muddy waters had spread all around. "We'll be all right," "Don't worry"—I kept calling out to the children, but I was in great fear myself wondering what was going to happen should a higher wave come surging.

In about an hour, the water started to recede little by little. At around 7 p.m., we all went back down to the second floor. Rubble had been washed into the playroom and it was all muddy. The water was about 1.5 meters there. We wiped the mud off of the stage with curtains and other materials, and put down gym mattresses that had escaped being submerged for the children to lie down on. Then we had them put on dress-up play clothes.

As I went halfway down the steps to the first floor, I found by luck some dry bread in plastic bags floating in the water. On the second floor, I found some plastic bottles of water, so I gave them to the children to share.

A member of our staff just happened to get a signal on her cell phone. It said that another tsunami was approaching. We immediately climbed up to the roof again. Mattresses were used to shield ourselves from the wind and the cold. Around two o'clock in the morning, we decided to get back down to the second floor, as we concluded there would be no more high surges.

WHEN DAWN ARRIVED, the water had not receded completely and was still over my height. I attempted to seek help by paddling out in an empty box that I had found floating, but fell into the water and ended up getting soaking wet. The only clothing that was left in the playroom was the Santa Claus outfit that I had worn at the Christmas party. I had no other choice but to put that on.

At around nine o'clock in the morning, members of Japan Coast Guard reached our kindergarten building on two rubber rafts. We were taken to Industrial Port, where we switched to a rescue boat and then we were accommodated onto a Maritime Self-Defense Force escort vessel. All the kindergarteners got to be reunited with their parents by March 15. They held out really well.

We eventually survived this disaster, but I am not really certain if my decision to remain at the kindergarten was the right one. If we had encountered the disaster during the core hours when there were over 100 children, not everybody would have made it to the rooftop. And if the tsunami had come up higher than the rooftop, that surely would have been the end. I can only say that we were fortunate.

Tsunami closes in on police car
Cry for help drew rescue response for mother and child

Takeyuki Kanno
male, 32, police sergeant

The quake hit just after I came back from a patrol to the Chuo Koban police box where I was stationed, located at Chuo 3-chome in Ishinomaki City. I felt such big shakes of the ground as I had never experienced before. The lockers fell to the floor.

TSUNAMI WILL SURELY COME—the thought crossed my mind. I dashed outdoors before the earthquake subsided. There I called out to the people in the neighborhood, "Are you all right? A tsunami might be coming!"

I got in the patrol car with my male colleague, 25, who rode in the passenger seat and drove through town urging the residents to evacuate. While doing so, we received instructions over the police wireless—"We have a case of a gas leakage in the Ekimae-Kitadori district. Go to the Ishinomaki Gas Company in Myojincho—the telephone line went dead there—and take necessary safety measures." We drove over to the company and explained the situation to a staffer.

It seemed to be about an hour after the earthquake, when we were driving north up the prefectural road to return to the police box, that I saw in the rearview mirror a tsunami coming closer and closer from Ishinomaki Fishing Port to the south. The traffic jam was so bad that the cars could hardly go forward now. We turned to the right at a T-junction and went on to National Route 398. I instructed my colleague to get out of the car and conduct evacuation guidance. I could see the impending waters approaching from the direction of the port. I gave up moving by car, got out and called out to people to evacuate. We waved our hands in big motions, urging people to run to higher grounds. There were still people who were not aware of the tsunami.

I COULD NOW SEE a tsunami about waist high approaching from both east and west. *This could be serious*—my mind started to race. The moment I tried to climb over a concrete block fence along the road to avoid the tsunami, I felt water at my ankles. I heard screams around me. I tried to find safety in somebody's yard, but the tsunami had already arrived and I was immersed up to my waist level. Sensing imminent danger, my colleague and I evacuated to a mountain nearby. There were about 50 evacuees gathered up there. They were all drenched to the skin, myself included, and looked frozen. Radio communications were no longer functioning. Cars on the roads were being washed away, making piles here and there.

Around 4 p.m., the water receded somewhat and we walked down to the road, where somebody reported to us, "A mother and child are stuck in a car." We made our way over the piles of cars, straining our ears for the cries, and tried to rush to the site. We found them in a car that was sandwiched in between two houses. The water had seeped into the car, and a woman who I presumed to be the mother was holding the baby up high in the driver's seat, calling for help. We broke the rear window and helped the baby out first and then the mother. She gave no sign of relief, and she was freezing, saying, "I'm cold."

"Somebody, help!" we heard a man crying out. We helped him, an elderly man who had trouble walking, out of his one-story house. We also assisted in the rescue effort of two people who had escaped up in a tree, apparently a father and a child. Though I partly thought I was doing these rescue actions out of a sense of duty, all that I had in mind was that I would do whatever was before me. My body had become stiff because of the cold and I was shivering even while conducting actions. I was at the very limit of my capacity.

It was starting to get dark and the snow was starting to accumulate. When we went back up to the mountain, there were about sixty or so people there. We took up on the kind offer of a family whose house was located at the base of the mountain and suffered no damage, and everybody found shelter there. I carried a child as we moved there.

There weren't enough changes of clothes for all the evacuees, so the children and the elderly were given priority. I spent the night in wet clothes—I will always remember the freezing cold of that night. We endured the night by gathering up close together in one place. Some people became ill because of the freezing conditions, and I gave what care I was able to.

IT WAS AROUND NOON of the 13th that we reported to Ishinomaki Police Station. It took more than three hours, but we were able to walk there. All our colleagues were caught up in disaster response and there was no time to lament. *I finally made it back*—containing this sense of relief inside of me, I rested for one hour, and then had to go to another disaster area. Seeing fires in and around the Kadonowaki-cho district, I felt relentlessly confronted by the menace of an earthquake disaster.

As I look back on those days, although there was a sense of fulfillment in carrying out the duties of a police officer, I remember feeling powerless in the face of the sheer magnitude of that disaster. I don't know whether the series of actions that I took was the best or not. I can't help wondering maybe there were better ways of saving more people, although I don't have any specific idea right now. It's important that we anticipate the possibility of a major tsunami in our daily life and be prepared. I believe that damage in the future can be mitigated if, for instance, more people decide where to evacuate to in advance.

Rescue operation in a sea of debris
Fighting a fire approaching hillside

Rikio Konno
male, 59, chief firefighter, Ishinomaki Fire Department

Off duty on the day of the earthquake, I was spending my afternoon working out in the training room of Ishinomaki City's Kahoku Sogo Community Center, also known as the Big Bang.

WHEN THE TREADMILL STARTED ROCKING and I was unable to run on it, I got off, thinking that there was something wrong with the machine. That's when I noticed for the first time that an earthquake had struck. After making sure that there were neither serious damage to the building nor injured people, I headed for the Chuo Branch Fire Station located in Hiyorigaoka 1-chome.

The radio in the car was alerting people to the major tsunami warning. The Tsujido-bashi Bridge over the Oppa-gawa River had been pushed up as much as 20 centimeters because of the quake, but I managed to just barely get over it. When I passed through the congested intersection of the Ishinomaki Bypass finally, drivers on the opposite lane were waving their arms to try to tell drivers in our lane not to go that way.

I made a turn because I sensed that the tsunami had arrived. I drove back to the bypass, and aimed for the railway crossing that would allow me to get through to the Kokucho district from the north side of Ishinomaki station. But just before I reached the crossing, the road was under water. I gave up the idea of going by car and left it at the parking lot of a DIY store. Wading through the water with my trousers rolled up to the knees, I arrived at the fire station via the Hiyoriyama hills at about five o'clock in the afternoon.

The party on duty had already gone into action to put out the fires that broke out just after the earthquake. When I finished changing into my uniform, information reached us that smoke was seen from beyond the Hiyoriyama hills. Six firefighters including myself and three members of the volunteer fire company split up into two groups, got on the two pumpers that were on stand-by at Fire Brigade Branch No. 1 and headed for the Hiyoriyama hills.

PASSING THROUGH THE JUNCTION of Hiyorigaoka and descending to a point just before Kadonowaki-cho, I was flabbergasted by an unbelievable sight, one that did not seem to be real. The town was not the one I was used to seeing but a sea full of debris, as if bombs had been dropped in a war. Flames were rising about 70 or 80 meters ahead of us.

As soon as we arrived at our destination, some people ran up to us, pleading, "Help us, please!" The nine of us divided ourselves into three parties, and led by one of the people, my party headed for Kadonowaki Elementary School.

On top of the debris that lay in heaps near the west end of the school building were stranded two elderly women, unable to move. The extension ladder we had was not long enough to reach them. We borrowed a ladder from a house on the hill and by using that as well, we managed to reach the women.

The firefighters who were on duty had taken the wireless so we off-duty members didn't have any means to get the latest information or to make contact with others. *Won't another tsunami come?* Although we were scared, we set about rescuing the women. We found a wooden door panel among the debris and sat the women on it. Sliding the panel on the surface of the debris, we brought the women to safety. We asked the people there to take the women to a nearby medical institution and left to go about extinguishing fires.

IT WAS CLEAR that the burning fire was going to spread toward us. We could hear the sound of gas cylinders exploding sometimes. If the fire reached the wooded stretch with miscellaneous trees and bamboos along the edges of Hiyoriyama hills, the houses up on the Hiyorigaoka area would be in danger of catching fire. It was impossible for us to go near the fire. The only thing we could do was to stop the fire from spreading any farther from where we stood.

We connected the hose to a fire-fighting water reservoir and began to spray water on the trees, shrubs and houses. At one point, I went back to the Chuo Branch station to report on the present situation and request them to dispatch firefighters to help us. But the answer was, "Other branches have their hands full. Do your best to hold on." With that, I hurried back to the site and continued spraying water. Then at around 8 p.m., 11 firefighters from the Minami Branch station came to help us, carrying hoses on their shoulders. Connecting ten to 19 hoses together, each piece 20 meters long, we extended them so that we could work in different directions to keep the flames at bay. We continued spraying water on the approaching fires at the foot of the hills; we sprayed from east to west, from the back of Kadonowaki Elementary School to the area near the company housing of Nippon Paper Industries Ishinomaki Mill. The elementary school apparently caught fire while we were working in the west.

The water in the reservoir ran out, so we used water from the swimming pool of Ishinomaki Municipal Girls' Senior High School, and when that ran out we used the water from the swimming pool of Ishinomaki High School. Those hoses that got damaged as a result of the long hours of high-pressure usage were replaced so that we could continue spraying. When the pumpers ran out of fuel, some citizens went ahead and procured fuel from somewhere and filled up the pumpers.

WE HAD THE COOPERATION of so many people—there were those who lent us ladders and those who looked after the elderly women we had saved. We were working so desperately at that time that I don't remember the names or even the faces of the people who helped us. Neither do I know how to express our gratitude to everyone.

The fires burned for a whole night and at the break of dawn they finally died down. In the afternoon of the next day a support group from Niigata Prefecture arrived.

"Help me!"—I heard a lot of cries like this from beyond the darkness and from the areas toward the sea where fires were burning. These voices remain in my ears. All I can think of to say is that I am truly sorry. The force of the earthquake and tsunami were far greater than what we firefighters and our equipment can deal with. I believe this sentiment is shared by all the firefighters, professional and volunteer alike, who were engaged in the work of extinguishing fires.

Examining patients at evacuation centers
Doctor brothers reassured evacuees

Fumihiko Sato
male, 55, physician, Sato Internal Medicine Clinic

I was examining a patient when the earthquake struck. Our clinic was in a 52-year-old building in the Kadonowaki-cho district and, having never experienced an earthquake of that magnitude, I was worried that the clinic would collapse.

THERE WERE SEVEN OR EIGHT PATIENTS in the clinic and I had all of them evacuate immediately to the parking lot with the staff. The pavement had cracked and I thought, *This is no ordinary event.*

My bedridden mother Yoshiko, 88, was in the main house on the same premises. My wife Kaori, 44, and my two older sisters, who also lived at the same site, carried her to the second floor of the medical ward. My second daughter, 7, then a first grader at Kadonowaki Elementary School, was on her way home when the earthquake struck. Our friend found her crying and brought her home by car. At about the same time, our oldest son, 20, a university student, came home in his car. We learned from the television in his car and the community wireless system that a major tsunami warning had been issued. If a six-meter-high tsunami hit, the second floor of the clinic would be flooded. We carried my mother to my son's car and urged all the patients and staff to evacuate the area.

My family and my sisters' families, a total of nine people, got into three cars and started evacuating at around 3:15 p.m. As I was leaving through the gate, I was momentarily undecided which way to go. If I took the right, it would lead us toward Ishinomaki Municipal Hospital, but that was closer to the sea. If I took the left, it would be closer to the river. I figured that the river would be less dangerous and so I cut to the left. As I came across the NTT East Japan building, I remembered a sloping road that would lead to the Hiyoriyama hills, and we took refuge at the parking lot right behind Kashimamiko-jinja, a Shinto shrine.

After we caught our breath, we were saying things like, "Let's go home when the major tsunami warning is lifted." Just then, we saw the tsunami engulfing the Nakaze islet, but we couldn't see the district of Kadonowaki-cho where the clinic was. A friend turned up and said, "The clinic is gone. It was washed away by the tsunami."

WE DECIDED to spend the night in our cars. By chance, I ran into one of my older brothers, 61, on the Hiyoriyama hills. He, too, was a doctor and had been making house calls at the time of the earthquake, fortuitously escaping to the Hiyoriyama hills as we had. Around 10:30 p.m., we became worried about the fire in the Kadonowaki-cho area spreading to the Hiyoriyama hills, so we moved to the Izumi-cho district, where we spent the night in our cars on the street.

On the morning of the 12th, the principal of Ishinomaki Catholic Kindergarten, where my son had once gone, invited us to take shelter at the school. Our family, a total of 20 people, stayed there until April 6. From that day on, patients who found out we were staying at the kindergarten came to see us. My brother had gotten his doctor's bag out of his damaged car and had brought the stethoscope and blood pressure gauge. The two of us used these to examine the patients. Many of them were patients of our clinic, and we hugged each other, sharing our joy in finding each other safe. As doctors, we could only examine the patients and give words of precaution, but they went back feeling reassured, which boosted our spirits in return. After a few days, the devastated pharmacy scraped together what medicine was left and gave it to us, which helped us greatly.

From the 14th on, I followed through on the Ishinomaki Medical Association's decision to open dispensaries in evacuation centers. I started by going to the Ishinomaki Junior High School gym where I staffed shifts alongside my oldest brother, 62, and brother-in-law, 58, who were also doctors. We set up a dispensary in the storage room in the gym and started examining patients, without electricity or water. We shared medicines that the Medical Association had collected. Doctors and staff from the devastated City Hospital had also gathered and we all worked together to take care of patients.

Many of the patients were outpatients of our clinic. It's not like we did anything great, but when they left looking relieved after talking with us, I felt "the power of trust."

Patients also came to the kindergarten. I made rounds at Kadonowaki Junior High School and there was a dispensary in Ishinomaki High School as well. After a while, we agreed that it would be more efficient to centralize, and on the 19th, we decided to integrate our activities to Ishinomaki High School. Three to four doctors saw from a hundred to two hundred patients a day. We also sent doctors to evacuation centers in the surrounding areas. On the 23rd, groups including the Japan Medical Association Disaster Medical Team visited us and opened aid stations in other evacuation centers. Our dispensary in Ishinomaki High School continued running until May 1.

"IF THERE IS A TSUNAMI WARNING, let's evacuate to the Hiyoriyama hills"—that's what my wife and I had always told each other, but when we actually had to do that, I may not have been as calm as I thought I would be. My wife couldn't help but wonder why it was that my first decision was to move my mother up to the second floor of the clinic. Also, it had never crossed my mind to bring my doctor's bag and medical supplies with us as we were evacuating. It appears that I had not really believed a tsunami would ever come.

After the earthquake and tsunami hit, means of communication were severed and we could not ask for ambulances or evacuation helicopters. I keenly realized the importance of communication tools that would work under any circumstances. Our family has another clinic in the Nakaura district of Ishinomaki. The first floor was flooded by the tsunami; however, with some emergency repair work, we were able to reopen on May 16. On the following day, my mother passed away—it was as though she had to see for herself that the clinic would reopen. As it had been for my father, a doctor who had passed away at the age of 58, patients were always her first priority. I am determined to abide by the principles by which my parents lived.

Setting up aid station at school
Cooperating with fellow health professionals

Satoko Tsuda
female, 47, nurse manager at Ishinomaki Red Cross Hospital

After attending the junior high school graduation

ceremony for my second son Fumito, 16, I was relaxing at home in the Watanoha district with my parents-in-law, and that was when the strong quake hit us.

I GOT THE EMERGENCY FOOD, LIGHTS, AND HEATERS ready for my family and next-door neighbor in case I needed to go to Ishinomaki Red Cross Hospital, my workplace. Fumito, who had been at his friend's house, and his older brother Yuto, 18, a high school junior then, both came back home soon.

I heard on the car radio that the tsunami had reached Onagawa Town, but I didn't think it would reach our house. However, the tsunami did come surging in no time, and all of us, including our elderly next-door neighbor, rushed up to the second floor of our house.

In back of our house, we saw an elderly woman on top of a car holding hands with her husband who was next to the car, his body sunk up to his neck. Yuto declared, "I'm going to swim out there to save them," but as the water currents were too strong, I stopped him, saying, "You can't swim out there. Not yet. Keep on shouting words of encouragement."

When we saw that the currents were slowing down, we decided it was time to rescue them. We made a long rope by tying a dozen or so sheets together. Fastening a swimming tube to the rope, we threw it to them, but no matter how many times we tried, it didn't reach them because of the wind. Finally, Yuto said, "I'm going." With that, he entered the cold muddy water grabbing one end of the sheets and the swimming tube.

Later when we saw a photo of the scene, we realized that the distance between our place and the couple was more than ten meters. My son, having swum across that distance, had the woman hold on to the swimming tube that was tied to the rope of sheets and he clutched her husband. Then, those of us in the house yanked at the rope and were able to pull them up to the house. Our neighbor Koichi Takahashi, 54, came to our house to help. As the elderly couple were frozen to their bones, we removed their wet clothes, put them in futon bedding, and massaged them to warm their bodies. The children helped out, too. After a short time, the woman opened her eyes. Her husband, however, passed away just after midnight without regaining consciousness. We administered a heart massage but it did not help.

BY THE MORNING of the following day, the water had receded from the yard. Following a proposal made by Koichi's wife Yoko, 53, we both got out our camping gear and started cooking. We invited neighbors and about 30 people gathered and ate, relieving their hunger. And that was when my husband Yuichi, 46, with whom we had lost touch, showed up drenched to the skin. I felt so relieved.

In the morning of the 13th, we walked along the tracks of the Japan Railway Ishinomaki Line and went to Watanoha Elementary School which was designated as a shelter. There were many evacuees, and among them people who were injured and sick.

Flooded rice fields in the back of Satoko Tsuda's home in the Watanoha district on the day after the earthquake struck. The small car at right is where the elderly couple were stranded.

I said to Yoko, who was the nurse manager at Onagawa Municipal Hospital, "We've had disaster relief training at our hospitals. Let's do what we can to help the people around us." She and I went back to our homes and collected blood-pressure gauges, adhesives, wet packs, digestive medicine and bottles of tea and headed back to the school once again.

When we arrived at the school, the nursing teacher was all alone trying to manage the situation. Together with the PTA steering committee, we set up a first-aid station in the gym. Immediately the injured assembled at the station and we started giving them medical care. When the situation at the first-aid station settled down a bit, we went around the classrooms where people were gathered, giving guidance about preventing deep vein thrombosis, also known as economy class syndrome.

Among the evacuees were colleagues such as Emi Sasaki, 52, nurses from Ishinomaki Municipal Hospital, a nurse from Kobe who had experienced the devastating Great Hanshin-Awaji Earthquake in 1995—all of them offered to help. Later, nursing students such as Emi's daughter pitched in and helped us out tremendously. Our first-aid activity expanded to the point where we went out to neighboring evacuation sites and the homes of victims.

I HANDED OVER a letter to a Self-Defense Forces personnel on the 15th asking him to take it to the Ishinomaki Red Cross Hospital. An orthopedist who had evacuated to Kazuma Elementary School came to help us on that day, and on the sixth day, the 16th, we also were able to receive support from a medical team organized by the Medical Association and a relief squad from the Japan Red Cross. "You can go to work at the Ishinomaki Red Cross Hospital now." Although I was told that, I didn't feel like I could since there were so many people who needed help at the evacuation center in my local neighborhood. I was totally absorbed in the work there.

On the evening of the 8th day, Iwao Kaneda, the deputy director of the Ishinomaki Red Cross Hospital, came with the Japan Red Cross relief squad so I explained the situation we were in and appealed to him to improve the first aid station and the evacuation shelter. I was advised that it would be better if I went to the Ishinomaki Red Cross Hospital and explained the circumstances in person, so I went to the hospital in the relief squad vehicle and asked that appropriate actions be taken.

On the next day, the 19th, the Red Cross Hospital set up an aid station at Watanoha Elementary School. I stayed there until the evening, explaining what we health professionals had done and then transferring the duties to the new staff. Finally my activities at the elementary school came to an end.

Receiving the support of 800 volunteer pharmacists
Coordinating prescriptions and hygiene guidance

Yoshiro Tanno
male, 54, managing director of the Ishinomaki Pharmaceutical Association

About 800 pharmacists from across the nation rushed to the Ishinomaki area in response to the earthquake disaster, and they worked until late August assisting doctors by getting prescriptions filled, distributing over-the-counter drugs, and advising hygiene control at the shelters. As a coordinator for receiving pharmaceutical support, I could reaffirm the collective power of pharmacists.

AT THE TIME OF THE EARTHQUAKE, there were 11 staff members including myself at the combined office of the Ishinomaki Pharmaceutical Association and Ishinomaki Pharmaceutical Products Center pharmacy, located at Kadonowaki-cho 3-chome. When the shaking settled down, the staff went about the task of clearing up. But when the major tsunami warning was released alerting us of a tsunami of over six meters, I instructed all the staff to evacuate. "*Tsunami tendenko* (fend for yourself in case of an expected tsunami)," as the saying goes, I told everybody to decide

Pharmacists at work in the health-care room of Ishinomaki High School, the base for the pharmacists' support team. Otemachi, Ishinomaki City

for themselves where and how to find safety.

A pharmacist trainee from Ayukawa which is at the tip of Oshika Peninsula was unable to go home, so I took him to my house in the Kaihoku district. Following the basic guideline of evacuation, we walked instead of using the car. We arrived home before the tsunami, at 3:40 p.m. At home were three of my family members, plus a neighbor's child. Soon after, the tsunami pushed its way to Kaihoku as well, but because my house was built on a higher plot, the water stopped just short of reaching the floor level. We spent that night at my house.

The Ishinomaki Pharmaceutical Association had made preparations in 2010 on how to dispatch a support team promptly should a major disaster take place outside of Ishinomaki. But we had never thought that a major disaster would ever befall our own community.

THE NEXT DAY, I thought to go to my office, but first plowed through the waist-level water to stop by at the Ishinomaki Fire Department Headquarters to get information. They kept me from going to my office since the surrounding area was dangerous because of the fires that had broken out. I then decided to go to Kaihoku Elementary School since I was their designated pharmacist. I knew about the problems which arose following the Great Hanshin-Awaji Earthquake, such as the dirty floors in shelters because of soiled shoes or the clogged-up toilets becoming unserviceable, so I explained to the principal and the PTA members about how to deal with such situations.

On the third day, I looked for such roads as would allow me to walk, and with the use of a bicycle as well, I went to Ishinomaki High School. As I was their designated pharmacist there as well, I asked that the sanitary conditions be maintained properly. A temporary clinic had been set up at the school, where a pharmacist was working very hard.

On the 14th, I went to the Ishinomaki Red Cross Hospital which was the designated disaster base hospital. I had expected that the concentration of patients at that hospital would necessitate the support of the Pharmaceutical Association. I borrowed a satellite phone from the hospital, got a hold of an acquaintance at the Japan Pharmaceutical Association, and requested support. On the same day, I came across a taxi from Sendai at Kaihoku Elementary School during my daily visit there, and asked the driver to deliver a note to the Prefectural Pharmaceutical Association requesting their support.

On the 16th, the sixth day from the disaster, Takashi Kodama, chairman of the Japan Pharmaceutical Association, visited Ishinomaki and reassured me saying that he would send in volunteer pharmacists. We agreed that I would serve as the coordinator at the receiving end. From then on, my cell phone was the office of the Ishinomaki chapter of the Pharmaceutical Association.

On the 17th, the first team of three pharmacists arrived. We decided to use the health-care room of Ishinomaki High School as the base for the support team as well as for supplies, and from there necessary personnel and supplies were to be dispatched to the specific shelters. Some of the volunteers took part in the joint medical team which was based at the Ishinomaki Red Cross Hospital. Alcohol sanitizers and toilet deodorizers were distributed to the shelters first, followed by cold medicines. Later, we had to supply medicine for people whose skin got damaged from using the sanitizers.

TWENTY OR SO VOLUNTEER PHARMACISTS arrived every day, scheduled to stay three nights and four days on average. The base at Ishinomaki High School was where they slept at and where they worked out of. Later a pharmaceutical distributor offered some space in their branch office in Kadonowaki Ichibanyachi, which we used as the frontline base, and the base at the high school was closed on May 3.

The warming temperatures brought about a huge outbreak of flies. In cooperation with the Hygienic Insecticide Industrial Association of Japan, insecticides were applied at such places as shelter toilets and garbage disposal areas.

From September, the Ishinomaki Pharmaceutical Association was the only organization left to respond to medicinal needs. In order to provide medicine to the patients staying at home, a pharmacy had to be in place. The Prefectural Pharmaceutical Association responded to this by setting up a temporary pharmacy at Suimeikita 2-chome, which opened on October 1.

THE ISHINOMAKI PHARMACEUTICAL ASSOCIATION comprises about 160 members. This is something I learned about later, but some 20 pharmacies had been devastated with nine pharmacists dead or missing. The number of casualties will be much greater if family members and pharmacy staff are included in these figures. Each time such bad news reached me, I was devastated.

I kept at my work going between the Pharmaceutical Association's base and Ishinomaki Red Cross Hospital. With the area of Ishinomaki being expansive, I had to struggle to obtain information that was necessary for pharmaceutical actions. The Ishinomaki Red Cross Hospital was where I gathered information primarily. Although negotiating with various organizations and groups was demanding at times, I believe I was able to gain the know-how required of those at the receiving end of disaster support.

Attacked by tsunami in the dark
Candlelight saved my life

Sadao Owada
male, 79, retired

I had lost contact with my wife, 75, and was out looking for her when, in the darkness, I was engulfed by the tsunami. What saved my life was a candlelight that emerged out of total darkness.

I WAS ENJOYING A GAME OF MAH-JONG held twice a week by an NPO at Yamashita Kaikan Hall in the Nishiyama-cho district of Ishinomaki. The intense quake struck all too suddenly. My body got tossed up, and the mah-jong tiles were flung away. The place, filled with dozens of people, was thrown into an uproar.

I had graduated from a fisheries school in Rikuzen-Takata City, worked aboard fishing boats and had been in some dangerous circumstances in both domestic and overseas waters until I retired at the age of 57. But this was the first time I had ever experienced such an intense earthquake. I was in a panic.

Our house may have fallen apart—the thought crossed my mind. I rushed up the hill from Yamashita and headed for home which was near Ishinomaki City General Gymnasium. The power was out at the house, so the TV was no use. We didn't have a radio, which meant that I wasn't able to get any information.

I was concerned about my wife—she had left

home earlier saying, "I'm going to Minato." Before it got dark, I went out to buy some supplies including candles. Just after 6 p.m., I put on high rubber boots and left for the Minato district to look for my wife, flashlight in hand. I wasn't aware of the arrival of the tsunami then. As I went down the hill in front of the city library and came near Ishinomaki Elementary School, there was a car left sideways in the middle of the street. Nobody was out walking, and I felt something was wrong.

When I got to the street where the city hall used to be, I saw quite a few cars scattered around on the street along with what looked like wreckage. That was when I finally realized that the town had been attacked by a tsunami. *Is what I'm seeing real?* I wanted to disbelieve my own eyes.

MY CONCERN ABOUT THE WHEREABOUTS of my wife was heightened. From the old city hall street, I took a right and headed for Kyu-Kitakami-gawa River down Hirokoji Street. Shortly after turning left at the river bank, I could hear strange sounds from behind. I believe it was about 6:30 p.m.

"Gha, gha, gha, gha"—they were the most eerie kind of sounds. As I looked back, a wall of water that was over twice my height was closing in. *I'm not going to die here.* I impulsively held on to the guardrail that was between Kyu- Kitakami-gawa River and the street.

The next thing I knew was that I had been carried some 100 meters along the street up to the western end of the Utsumi-bashi Bridge. If I had been swept into the river, I would never have made it to land. It was a blessing within my misfortune.

Surrounded by water all around, the range of my actions was limited. Two boats were stranded on top of the bridge side by side. I thought that it would be safer if I went on one of them. But there was no ladder around to go up on. My right leg had been injured when I got washed away by the tsunami, and I was at a loss as to what to do.

In a short while I was obsessed with this notion—*If I just stand around here, the next tsunami could come surging.* Withstanding the pain in my leg, I piled up pieces of rubble and, using them as a stepstool, managed to roll into the boat.

After a moment of relief, however, my soaking wet body was overtaken by the cold. I was afraid that I could freeze to death. Hoping that my body would be recovered quickly even if the ship got swept away, I tied myself to the boat with a rope, allowing about five meters of play which enabled me to move around a little.

ABOUT 10:30 P.M., I could see a small light from the second floor of a house just before the Chuo-Koban police box. It was candlelight. Feeling certain that somebody was there, I called out repeatedly in a loud voice, "Help me out!" Then a reply came from inside the house, "Come on up the stairs!"

I thought that I was finally able to make an escape. I wrung out what strength that was left in me and set out for the house. The house was a few dozen

Stranded boats blocking the bridge. Sadao Owada found temporary shelter on the upright boat, to which he tied himself with a rope. West end of the Utsumi-bashi Bridge, March 16, 2011

meters away. The water came up to my neck, which made the trek very long. When I finally reached the house and climbed up the stairs, I passed out.

When I came to, I found two men and three women taking shelter in the room. It was extremely cold. We covered our legs with one futon and waited for dawn.

I noted my name, address and phone number on a piece of paper, left it with the owner of the house, and headed for home, my eyes taking in the devastation of the town. I just barely made it home.

Although I had survived, my wife's whereabouts remained unknown even after three or four days. I even went to check the list of casualties at City Hall. Not being able to find her name on any list, I was starting to consider filing her death report, when I got word from a neighbor that my wife had evacuated to Monou-cho. I hurried to go over and get her. When I saw my wife's face, tears came flowing out, and I couldn't stop them. It was ten days after the disaster that we were finally reunited.

Golden wall of water closes in
Aitopia Street turns into sea of sludge

Kiyoko Abe
female, 50, owner of Japanese restaurant Yahataya

The lunch hour at my restaurant had finished, and after closing the place for the afternoon, I was back in my room on the second floor and was taking a rest. I was sitting on the bed, then put on my jacket and was about to stand up when the intense shaking of the earthquake made me land on my bottom on the floor.

THE CUPBOARD that was near the door and a carpet that was propped up against the side of the cupboard had fallen over, blocking the door. I shoved the carpet aside to make enough room to get out. What was in the hallway—the washing machine, microwave, etc.—had all been overturned and the glass doors were broken. I put on slippers so I could step over these and escaped outside of the restaurant.

The roof tiles had fallen off from the restaurant and the wooden window frames had come off. Some of our neighbors had come outside as well. I got some disaster information there, and went back inside the restaurant for my radio and flashlight so as to secure safety for after it got dark. However, there was no way I could find them since everything had been flung all over because of the intense shaking of the earthquake. The large cooking equipment had overturned. I closed the main valve of the gas.

I got into my car which was parked in the space in front of the restaurant, turned on the radio and learned that a tsunami of six meters was expected. Worried about an employee who had gone back to her apartment near Sumiyoshi Elementary School after the lunch hour, I went to pick her up. The water level in the Kyu-Kitakami-gawa River had dropped, and I knew intuitively that a tsunami would come.

The street leading to Nakasato and the one connecting Tachimachi to the Utsumi-bashi Bridge were jammed. As soon as I got to a parking spot by her apartment, I had the employee get in my car and drove right back to my restaurant. I got all the coats and clothes I could find, handed them to my father, 76, and mother, 71, who were waiting on the first floor, and went outside.

I called on a neighbor, 70, who lived alone to get her to evacuate with me, and was about to return to my restaurant, when I saw a golden wall of water in the direction of the river. It was high enough to hide the view of the hill behind the river.

RATHER THAN BEING SCARED, I was overcome with a sense of shock—the shock of having seen what was impossible. *The force of the tsunami is rather strong now, so it won't come into little alleys for now, but once it slows down, it can flood the alleys as well*—that was what I thought, and the five of us went up to the second floor to take shelter.

Looking down at our alley from the second-floor

Kiyoko Abe stands in the alley in front of her restaurant in Chuo 2-chome and points toward the Kyu-Kitakami-gawa River, where she saw the golden wall of water.

window, we saw jet-black water with white foaming waves come flooding in. In a short while, various objects such as chairs, televisions, and tables came by, carried by the current. Once the current stopped, those objects that had flowed in went back out. What the tsunami carried went back and forth along the alley.

As the water level rose, the glass panes of the store across the street broke and the water flooded into the store. The display window of our restaurant was smashed, too, and the water came rushing in. It rose quickly, and, afraid that the second floor was no longer safe, we got a stepladder and chairs ready so we could escape to the roof.

Fortunately, the water stopped rising just before reaching the first-floor ceiling, but it rose to about three meters in height. My mother, who was watching Hashi-dori Street from another window, said, "Cars are being carried away. Is our car all right?"

I opened the window facing our parking space to check outside: the water was making a whirlpool and cars were drifting close to buildings; a signboard that had been carried away was spinning around in the whirlpool. Our car had been washed away.

As we were low on candles, I wanted to find some more before it got dark. I remembered that there were six wedding candles, which I found in the tatami* room. There was nothing to eat, but we had a bottle of juice to share. We lined up futon cushions, on which we lay down in our coats, wrapping ourselves in three or four tablecloths.

IN THE EVENING, the sound of the surging water could be heard; it would cease and then it could be heard again, and this happened repeatedly. I could not get a connection on my cell phone, and there was nothing we could do but wait for the water to recede. As dawn came and the water receded, I went outside. The front entrance was full of sludge with carpets and other things mixed in it. The wall of concrete blocks next door had fallen over.

Looking over the debris toward the river, I could see the bow of a boat that had been washed up onto the street. Aitopia Street had turned into a sea of sludge with mounds of debris. I was devastated by the overwhelmingly terrible condition.

I can only look ahead and keep on walking believing that happiness will follow. I was able to re-open the restaurant on July 15. The year 2013 will mark the restaurant's one hundredth anniversary. I would like to make this an opportunity to meet once again the people who had supported us.

*tatami: See note on p. 078

Water almost reaches ceiling
Helping elderly parents dive under doorway

Yoshihide Okumura
male, 53, director of kimono store

On March 11, I was planning to deliver a kimono to one of our long-term customers in Onagawa Town and was going to leave about 2 p.m. However, some customers came to visit the store, and the earthquake happened while I was attending to them.

AN INTENSE SHAKING CONTINUED, making the kimonos and accessories on display fall down and breaking light fittings. After the quake settled, I went outside to find that the sidewalk had cracked and become uneven. Passing neighbors said, "A big tsunami is coming—we are running to the Hiyoriyama hills." My father, 80, locked up the front entrance while I, somewhat in disbelief about this, carried the kimonos upstairs.

I was looking out at the Aitopia shopping street when I saw a café signboard streaming away, and I could hear the surging sound of tsunami. When I saw the black swirling water was about 50 centimeters high, I said to my father and mother, 80, "We're not safe here. Let's go upstairs now."

At that very moment, the glass window facing the garden on the east side broke with a booming sound, and the tsunami came rushing into the store in a single burst, almost reaching the ceiling. The three of us floated up, our struggling bodies submerged up to our necks and our feet thrashing about in the water. A wall-mounted mirror was close to us, so I said to my parents, "Grab the edge of the mirror!" We all managed to reach it, our bodies floating in the water. I quickly thought about what to do next. I figured that escaping to the stairs at the back of the store was the only way. To get there, squeezing through the doorway that was one meter away was the only option.

BY THEN, however, the water had risen up to just below the top of the doorway. *The only way to survive is to dive under it,* I thought. When I swam over by the doorway, however, a square wooden box used as the computer stand was blocking the passage. I managed to push it away by hitting on it with my hand. The three of us then dove through the doorway and got to the other side, where our heads came up out of the water. There was a sink there, and there was another doorway ahead of the sink, and we had to swim under it before we could get to the backstairs.

We all stood on the sink. I first swam through the doorway and reached the stairs, where I confirmed where to pop our heads up out of the water. I swam back to stand on top of the sink and said to my parents, "Hold your breath a bit longer when we go under." We took several deep breaths for practice, then I pulled my mother's hand forcibly to go underwater, and swam to reach the stairs. It was about two meters from the doorway to the stairs. She had swallowed some muddy water. I went back to help my father. I pulled him by his hand and we went underwater, but perhaps he was too cold to put any energy into it and that first attempt was a failure. For a brief moment I couldn't hear his voice and thought this was no good. I said to him, "Dad, hang in there!" and pulled him by his hand, and we made it the second time.

Soaking wet, we climbed up to the third floor which was our living quarters. Because of the severe quake, broken dishes were scattered all over the floor with nowhere to step. As it was cold, we changed our clothes, and my parents just stayed by the kerosene heater. I had pieces of broken glass stuck in my right foot. I pulled them out, and put lots of bandages around my foot. During the night we could hear these creepy sounds of tsunami surging and receding dozens of times, and from out the south window we could see red blazes rising from the areas beyond the Hiyoriyama hills.

NEXT MORNING, inside of the store was all sludge after the water receded, with the tatami* mats curled up high and everything knocked down. Walls and windows were broken by the rubble that had bumped into them. It was a total wreck that left us at a complete loss as to what to do. On the Aitopia shopping street, cars that had been caught up in the tsunami were piled one on top of the other, and the empty store across the street from ours had a car jutting into it. I was just dumbfounded at this ghastly sight.

When the tsunami came invading our store with its ferocious intensity and I was struggling to keep afloat, I thought, *Why should the tsunami be coming way out this way?* I still can't believe what had happened, but I have come to terms with the fact that, after experiencing the terror of the tsunami, "the unexpected" can actually happen. If, by chance, the front entrance had been destroyed when the tsunami attacked, all three of us would have been swept out of the store and our lives would have been in greater jeopardy. It's a dreadful thought.

The tsunami had made a monster out of the Kyu-Kitakami-gawa River, making me painfully aware of the fearfulness of nature. Assumptions are dangerous. "Run no matter what"—this is the only way to respond in an emergency.

*tatami: See note on p. 078

Ships knock down electric power poles
The gushing water was like a horizontal waterfall

Nanae Onodera
female, 36, clothing store owner

A powerful shaking with wide swinging motions lasted for a long time during that earthquake. Hanger racks on wheels were moving in unison with the shaking, and, with all the merchandise that had fallen down from the shelves, the floor of the store was left with no room to step.

IF I WERE TO DESCRIBE the feel of the shaking, I would say it was so powerful that I had to hold on to something to keep myself from getting flung away. It was as if I was riding on a flying carpet in an amusement park. In a little while, the school bus of the private kindergarten where my only son, 7, attended arrived in front of the store some ten minutes later than the scheduled arrival time of 2:46 p.m. The bus had stopped in front of a restaurant near my store and they waited there until the quake settled down. I get the shivers when I imagine what could have happened if the bus had gotten stuck in a traffic jam of evacuating cars.

My mother, 75, was listening to the disaster prevention wireless system that was announcing the major tsunami warning, and said, "A 6-meter tsunami is coming." I was half in doubt about it and was hesitant about evacuating. I wasn't fully aware of the danger of the tsunami.

"Let's evacuate," my mother said. We remembered to follow my late father's advice to run to Shoei Parking next door in case of an earthquake or tsunami, and we decided to run. I put on a coat and changed shoes, put my father's Buddhist spirit tablet into my son's kindergarten bag, grabbed my mother's medicines, and then we set off. I didn't take any food or drink as I was expecting to come back in the evening.

We couldn't climb the stairs—my son was too scared of the shaking of the earthquake, while my mother said her legs were shaking too much—so we all walked up the ramp to get to the roof terrace of the 6-story Shoei Parking Building. When we got there, there were already about ten people, and they were saying, "The tsunami has just come." We made it in the nick of time. When I saw the tsunami from the roof terrace, I felt that something extraordinary was happening.

THE OKADA THEATER was swept off all too easily by the first tsunami. Since I had never actually seen a tsunami before then, I was astounded by the fragility of the buildings in the face of the ferocity of tsunami. The Utsumi-bashi Bridge had bunches of cars and lumber lodged around its columns—they

The torrential waters of tsunami flooded Chuo 2-chome in central Ishinomaki, sweeping boats down the street. Photo by Nanae Onodera, March 11, 2011

had been carried up the Kyu-Kitakami-gawa River in one great surge of the waters. I could see cars stuck in traffic on the bridge, and the tsunami was now going over them. I was worried about the safety of the people who were in those cars.

All sorts of things had been carried to the street that our store faced, with the water flowing with such a force that it was like a horizontal waterfall. Sailboats and other ships that had been moored along the Kyu-Kitakami-gawa River were also being carried away—they sped past in front of us as if we were watching white-water rafting.

A large ship came streaming down the street, coming to a stop only after knocking down some electricity power poles. The whole street was attacked by the muddy torrent—if one were to get caught in it, it seemed hard to crawl out of it. The third tsunami that I saw at 4:52 p.m. on the Kyu-Kitakami-gawa River was flowing with black overlapping waves.

Across the street from Shoei Parking was the credit union Ishinomaki Shoko Shinyo-kumiai's headquarters, where on the first floor two staff workers were left behind—they were holding on to curtains and resisting the water. When the water showed signs of receding, the young master of the Japanese restaurant Hamacho who was also on the roof terrace with us put on his wetsuit and took the plunge to rescue the two men at the risk of his own life. I was moved when I saw him submerged in the water up to his chest and successfully bring the older clerk to safety on his surf board.

I heard later that the younger clerk requested that the older clerk be rescued first. We lost sight of the younger clerk a while later and were worried, but the next morning we were relieved to see him safe and sound on the roof terrace of the credit union's building.

IT WAS QUITE COLD on the roof as there was nothing to block the wind. On the night of the earthquake, the 18 of us evacuees split into two groups and spent the whole night in the two cars of Hamacho's young master and his wife, turning the heater off and on. We were so grateful to the couple. In the late evening we could see the burning red of fire in the direction of the Hiyoriyama hills. What with those booming sounds of explosions as well as the sound of siren urging people to evacuate, I couldn't sleep at all. I prayed that the night would be over soon.

Around noon of the following day, we went down from the roof terrace, got out on the external staircase on the second floor, went over the tops of two cars which had drifted in and finally managed to come out. Holding each other's hands, we all walked over the debris and went to find shelter at Ishinomaki Chuo Kominkan, a community hall.

I didn't have a sense of danger about the tsunami and had forgotten about its terror. In a natural disaster, security and safety aren't guaranteed. The lesson I learned from this disaster is to keep it in mind to get away immediately.

First floor of school: Sea of sludge

Staff immediately respond to needs of students and evacuees

Toshiyuki Fukuhara
male, 60, former principal of Ishinomaki Elementary School

It was absolutely no time to indulge in reminiscing over my teaching career which was about to be concluded—concentrating all my energies on how to respond to the disaster was what the last three weeks of my career was all about. I feel most happy that all our pupils were safe.

WHEN THE EARTHQUAKE happened, I was in the principal's office at Ishinomaki Elementary School. The shaking was so intense that I couldn't keep standing. It continued for about two minutes. Most of the framed portraits of the past principals fell to the floor while the drawers of the desk came sliding out. The fluorescent lights went out after flashing and the power went down.

A tsunami will definitely come—I thought intuitively. The first and second graders had finished their classes and were preparing to go home. The third and fourth grades were having classes, while the fifth and sixth grades were practicing the graduation ceremony procedures in the auditorium. I gave instructions to the assistant principal about evacuation actions, and, after the shaking settled down, I had the children go to the school yard for safety.

Worried parents who lived near the school were gathering in groups of twos and threes. Those students whose parents were confirmed were sent home while the rest were instructed to return to their classrooms for the time being since the school building had withstood that intense quake. I discussed measures with the assistant principal and head teacher in the school yard, and we came to the conclusion that all students be sent home. Text messages were sent to the parents requesting them to come and pick up their children.

A major tsunami warning was issued, and residents of the Chuo, Aitopia and Kadonowaki-cho districts came to our school to seek safety one after another, including some elderly people with walking disabilities. "Please come in the auditorium"—the assistant principal and I together guided the evacuees. The classroom teachers handed over students to their parents at the entrance hall. Guiding the evacuees and handing over students to parents had to be conducted simultaneously.

"DON'T GO IN THAT DIRECTION! Head for the hills for safety!"—we called out to those parents who were trying to go back toward the areas along the Kyu-Kitakami-gawa River since a major tsunami warning had already been issued.

Seeing that the arrival of people seeking refuge had ceased, I thought to just go and see what it was like outside the school gate. I had just gone outside the gate and was looking toward the intersection from the sidewalk, when I witnessed a muddy stream of water crossing the intersection at a frightening speed like a river, flowing from the direction of Kadonowaki-cho 1-chome along the Kyu-Kitakami-gawa River to the east.

The tsunami was about three meters high. The muddy torrent sped past the Buddhist temple Eigan-ji just on the north of the school, and down Kotobu-kicho-dori Street to the northeast. At that moment, I thought, *Oh! We're in for it!* I rushed back to the school yard, shouting at the top of my voice, "The tsunami has come! Don't stay here, go up higher!" Thinking that the evacuees would be exposed to the danger of tsunami, I instructed the assistant principal and other staff to have everyone go up to the second and third floors of the school building for safety.

I went back to my office, and then ordered the teachers to open the fire-resistant safe and move important documents such as student records to the second floor. I myself got out important documents from the bottom drawer of my desk and carried them to the second floor.

When I went back down to the first floor, the water had already reached the corridor. It was rising gradually. In the principal's office, it had come up to above ankle height. Up on the second floor, from out the window I could see this black water making its way toward us as I observed the school yard. Vending machines, old tires and rubble came flowing our way.

Cars in the staff parking area floated up in the water and drifted, turning and bumping, and piled up one on top of another. I was just staring at those cars—the hazard lamps were flashing and the horns kept blaring relentlessly—the flooding and the resultant short-circuiting had triggered them on.

THE TOP PRIORITY FOR THE SCHOOL is to protect the lives of students. The children remaining at school were taken to the third floor for safety while the evacuees were directed to the second floor. The first floor had become a sea of sludge.

Snow started to fall and it became much colder after dusk. Because of the blackout, the fan heaters in the classrooms could not be used. What blankets and futon bedding we had at school were hardly enough. Male teachers went to get blankets from the Chuo Kominkan, a community center, enough for the approximately 130 people at the school including the children, evacuees and school staff.

Because it was so cold, I wore a stadium jacket and jersey pants over my regular suit, wrapped myself up in a blanket, head and all, and spent the night shivering badly and listening to the radio. The teachers looked after the children and the evacuees all through the night.

The next morning, there was snow outside. I had some teachers go and check the situation in the central part of town. They reported to me and that was how I first learned about the devastation there. I went outside by the front entrance and, using a handheld microphone, called out to the neighborhood for help. "This is Ishinomaki Elementary School! There are 30 pupils here, plus people evacuating. We have no food or water. We're running out of candles also. . . ."

This was a prologue to the long struggle to get the school restarted.

Wall of white wave behind us
Desperate getaway with family in car

Chika Unakami
female, 46, part-time worker

I had just bought my lunch at Supermarket Ainoya, the Kadonowaki-cho 5-chome branch, where I worked part time. I was walking upstairs to the employee lounge on the second floor when I was overtaken by a sudden, strong earthquake.

THE LOCKER IN THE ROOM was about to fall over. I asked two part-time workers, a high school student and a woman in her 20s, both of whom had just come in to work their shift, to help me hold it up. When the shaking settled down, I said to them, "I'll go and have a look at the liquor department," and went downstairs.

The store was completely dark and I realized that the power was down due to the earthquake. Goods had fallen off the shelves and were scattered on the floor, and the glass above the cash register had also fallen on the floor, its shards also scattered.

The staff and the customers had gone outside the store, but a few people were still inside the store and said to me, "We want some food." The cash register did not work due to the power outage. Taking into account the amount of damage I saw, I thought, *This is nothing like any we'd experienced before*. I went out of the store, too.

It was the store manager's day off, so I asked the thirty-something man who ranked next to the manager for instructions about what to do. He said, "Our employees can either go up on the Hiyoriyama hills, or go home if they are able to do so," and we split up at that point.

I was concerned about my mother-in-law, 79, and two sons who were at home so I immediately drove my car home. When I arrived after a few minutes, my boys opened the window of the living room on the first floor, leaned their bodies outside the window and said to me, "The shoe shelf has fallen over; you can't come in from the front door!" So I went in the house from the front yard.

MY MOTHER-IN-LAW was at a loss as to what to do. A friend of my second son was there as well. We had made it a family rule to evacuate to my parents' house in the Hebita district by car whenever tsunami warnings were announced, and that's what we had done in the past when there was an earthquake.

I went upstairs and found that the chests, bookshelves and storage boxes had fallen over in the room. I instantly thought to evacuate to my parents' house and said to everyone, "Hurry, hurry up! Get in the car!" At that point, however, I did not expect that a tsunami would really come. I was only thinking, *There would be a lot of cleaning work to do when I returned home after the shaking had settled down.*

But, as my house was located in the Minamihama-cho district which was near the sea, the notion that an earthquake meant a tsunami had been implanted in me by my husband, 54, ever since we got married.

I grabbed the bag that had my wallet in it, and without changing out of my store uniform, jumped in my car. My first son sat in the passenger seat in the front. In the back seat sat my second son and his friend, still in their school uniforms, and my mother-in-law, who was holding her husband's Buddhist spirit tablet.

FROM MY HOUSE I soon reached Prefectural Route 240, the Ishinomaki-Onagawa road. Making a left at the pastry shop in the Nanko-cho district, I then went on to the road in front of the north gate of Nippon Paper Industries Ishinomaki Mill. I drove west on the road. *Should I continue to go straight ahead? Or should I turn left to the port road that runs along the Ishinomaki Industrial Port?*

Thinking that cars would be moving faster on the port road, I decided to take that route. That was the route I usually took when I went to my parents' home. At the time, I visualized traffic congestion on Route 398, the main road running through the Okaido district and so taking the port road was the only option that came to mind. The port road runs parallel to the sea and so now, when I look back at what I did, I am horror-stricken.

In the beginning, we proceeded smoothly but the road was becoming crowded as we went on, forcing us to inch along. When we made a right at the crossing of the National Port Bureau building and went on to the city road, it was congested. There were people who looked like workmen on the sidewalk and I said to myself, *Don't these guys have to run away?*

As there were five people in the car, it was getting hot and the windows were turning foggy, so I opened the front windows of the driver's and passenger's sides slightly. That action turned out to be a lifesaver. Suddenly, a truck came from behind and overtook my car, followed by a car which also overtook my car. I thought it was rude of them since we were all standing in the traffic. Then, a man's loud roar reached me. As I opened the window on my side of the car and looked back, though it was just for an instant, I saw a white wave that looked just like a wall.

A tsunami is coming!—I instantly thought that we had to run away. I overtook the cars in front of me just before the Abekatsu Auto branch shop in the Nakaura district, and returned to the proper lane I should have been in just before the crossing near Kitamura Camera shop. I do not remember how many cars I overtook as I was desperate to escape. The cars that did not escape in time may have been swept away by the tsunami.

The traffic lights were not working due to the power outage and the Nakaura-bashi Bridge was heavily congested. It was not until after I had gone past Route 45 and was heading straight toward Hebita that I thought—*Ah, we have escaped death.* My heart was pounding loudly.

Murky water shooting out between houses
Running for dear life to Hiyoriyama hills

Hiroyuki Suda
male, 39, ornamental fish breeder

Before the earthquake, I was in the business of breeding ornamental freshwater fish. When the earthquake hit, I was on the second floor of my house.

A BOX OF BOOKS overturned because of the intense shaking, and after a few seconds, the computer screen went out. It was a power failure. I rushed downstairs to go to my workshop behind the house, and saw that the cupboard had fallen over and the door of the refrigerator was open.

The quake of lower six on the seven-stage Japanese seismic scale continued for about two minutes. When I entered the workshop, I was worried about the aquariums, 40 altogether, on the steel racks, and I was desperate to hold them so they would not be overturned. But six of them fell down, while the rest lost about half of the water due to the splashing caused by the shaking. When the shaking ceased, the water was cloudy. The room was cold, there were no heaters, and I thought, *The fish aren't going to make it*.

In the meantime, the emergency warning siren started blaring, and I learned a major tsunami warning had been issued. I had experienced tsunami warnings many times, and I did not feel I was at serious risk at that point.

As a stopgap measure, I placed bars against the racks as to keep the aquariums from falling over in hopes of preventing further damage. I expected the tsunami to come above floor level, so I took my work equipment to the second floor of the house.

Quite some time had passed since the earthquake started. When I went outside of the front door with my three dogs, the tsunami had not arrived yet. That was two to three minutes before I took off to escape.

I WAS WAVERING as to whether I should take a bag or the cell phone battery charger. My bedroom was on the second floor, so I thought that I could come back for them later when the earthquake and tsunami had subsided—that's how lightly I thought of the situation. Another reason I wasn't worried too much was because I had been told that the Kadonowaki-cho district did not experience flooding from the tsunamis that accompanied the Great Chilean Earthquake in 1960.

I headed to the bottom of the steps that led up to the Hiyoriyama hills. I was walking at the beginning of my escape. But then I heard the earth rumble, and birds took off all at once—it was an extraordinary spectacle. After that, a snapping sound followed. Not knowing what the sound was, I kept walking along the road from my house.

When I was about to reach the street in front of the Buddhist temple Saiko-ji, I noticed that the sound was getting closer and closer. I could see some people chatting on the street and others evacuating to Kadonowaki Elementary School on bicycles. I was now so scared I ran for dear life. Before long, I saw murky black water shooting out furiously from between houses.

MY LIFE'S IN DANGER!—I knew intuitively, and ran my best on the mild slope to the steps leading up to the Hiyoriyama hills. I am not a good runner but I ran desperately, chased by the muddy waters. The dry surface of the road turned into a murky black ocean in a matter of a few seconds. The force of the water was fierce.

When I arrived at the steps and ran up four or five meters, I felt that I had made it safely. During my run to safety, I passed at least six people. I was the last one to reach the steps in time. An elderly man who had arrived there earlier said to me, "You barely made it!"

While climbing further up the steps, I looked back to find only the third and fourth floors of the Ishinomaki's city hospital above the water. The water there must have been about ten meters high. I saw houses being washed away and fires here and there. I looked in the direction of the area where my house was located, but it wasn't there.

When I finally reached the top of the Hiyoriyama hills, I was by the *torii* gate of the Shinto shrine there and looked toward the Minamihama-cho district. The tsunami that had surged there was spinning around in a whirlpool. It was a dreadful sight.

I WAS CONCERNED about the safety of my parents: my mother, 60, who worked at a supermarket in the Kadonowaki-cho district and my father, 60, who worked at a fish shop in the Chuo district. Luckily, both had arrived at the Hiyoriyama hills earlier and we were overjoyed that we were safe.

We evacuated to Ishinomaki Municipal Girls' Senior High School, the closest site from the Hiyoriyama hills. There was a fire by the foot of the hills, and I was afraid that the fire might come up toward us.

As I stood by the corporate housing compound of Nippon Paper Industries Ishinomaki Mill and looked all around, I heard from various directions voices beseeching rescue, "Help! Help me!" Propane gas tanks were exploding, and big fire balls were shooting up almost 40 meters into the sky.

At 2:30 a.m. the next morning, we moved to Ishinomaki Junior High School. It was extremely cold and we spent the entire night without sleeping.

What was this big earthquake all about? I think it will take some time before I come to terms emotionally with the tremendous damage that we suffered.

Bookshelf becomes lifeboat

Evacuee gives birth to baby at school

Nobutaka Shoji
male, 39, teacher at Kama Elementary School

I was in charge of Grade 6 and was in the middle of the sixth class period of the day. We were sorting out the works of the entire year as our homeroom class activity when we were hit by a tremendous earthquake, the likes of which we had never experienced before.

"GET UNDER YOUR DESK!"—I immediately told my pupils. Shortly afterwards, the TV set next to the blackboard fell down, but no one was injured. "Yikes!" "I'm scared!"—our classroom which was on the fourth floor was abuzz with anxiety, but I also heard voices encouraging each other, "We'll be fine!" and "It'll be OK!" I stood in the middle of the classroom and told the children to calm down.

The glass in the windows had cracked. When the shaking ceased, I told the pupils to get in line in the corridor and had them trot down to the schoolyard. The corridor was scattered with study materials that had fallen down from the shelves along the corridor and we had to push them aside on our way to escape.

In the schoolyard, children of the other grades were lined up and their teachers were taking roll call. I asked my pupils to sit down and took roll call as well. Before long, there were some aftershocks and after that, as I recall, the major tsunami warning was announced through the emergency wireless system.

While we were in the schoolyard, the guardians of some of the pupils came to pick up their children so we let them leave. As we had undergone emergency drills, I thought that things went along smoothly. In a little while, we moved into the gymnasium. During this time, more parents came to pick up their children.

Later, the school principal told us to go back into the school building, so we started moving into the classrooms on the second floor and higher. On our way from the gymnasium to the school building, I saw a wave approaching gradually from both the west side of the building and from the front gate.

IT WAS HARD FOR ME TO BELIEVE that the wave actually reached our school that is located far away from the beach, but the water level started to rise very quickly. I suggested to a male teacher who was in charge of another sixth grade class, "Let's go up to the third floor," and we decided to do so.

When I looked out from the veranda of the third floor, I could hear voices crying, "Help!" and "There's a person over there!" I looked out over the scene before me, but could not find anybody. However, another teacher found a person near the main gate pleading for help, shouting, "There's someone in the car!"

I have to do something—I jumped outside into the water. Although I am 174 centimeters tall, the water came up to my neck. I was so cold and scared that I was forced to return to the building. Then some other teachers departed, using a bookshelf about 2 meters by 80 centimeters from the library as a "lifeboat." There were two men trapped in the car. One by one these men were helped onto the bookshelf, and the teachers waded across the water, towing the boat for about 30 to 40 meters to the school building. Winding the hoses of fire extinguishers around the rescued men, about ten of us school staff members hauled them one by one up to the veranda of the second floor. We were so desperate in our effort that I don't remember how long this actually took, but my recollection of this is that it took a very long time.

The two men were shaking with cold and could not even voice a word. We quickly took them to the infirmary, put them in the futon bedding which was laid on the floor, and rubbed their bodies to warm them up. There was one oil heater there and we barely managed to save their lives.

THE INFIRMARY AND THE REST OF THE SCHOOL BUILDING were filling up with many injured people and evacuees from the neighboring area. The total number of evacuees was more than one thousand. There were many pupils who had remained at school as well. During the night, I walked around the building, visiting each room and asking the evacuees, "Are you okay?" It was during this time that I heard someone say, "A pregnant woman's waters have broken!"

I immediately carried the woman to the infirmary. There happened to be two nurses among the evacuees. Working together with the school nurse, they took care of the woman. By the time the date changed, a healthy baby was born. In the middle of the turmoil, the happy event of a new birth was heartwarming to the school staff and the evacuees.

Later when I found out that two of my pupils, a boy and a girl, had become victims of the tsunami, tears came overflowing.

The waters receded on the following day, and we school staff members helped to remove the dead bodies from the area around the front gate of the school. "March 11"—I witnessed life and death at close range. I will never ever be able to forget that day.

Restaurant owner and staff brace up to rescue people
Seventy people took shelter at Chinese restaurant

Yuko Yamamoto
female, 67, restaurant owner

I was on the first floor of our Chinese restaurant Peking Daihanten that my eldest son Kazuhiro, 42, managed, chatting with some customers when we were suddenly hit by this fierce shaking.

THIS ONE MIGHT BE A BIT BIGGER than the one two days ago—that was the extent of my initial reaction. I didn't take it very seriously, but since the lateral shaking grew stronger, I rushed to the checkout counter by the front entrance. In the earthquake that hit several years ago, the cash register, the cable broadcast equipment and lots of bottles of liquor from the shelves fell down, so I wanted to keep them from falling this time. The customers, in the meantime, were about to run outside in haste, but I stopped them, shouting, "Stay inside until the shaking stops!"

I was astounded when I saw the tables which had been affixed to the wall moving around. From the second and third floors, I could hear the horrible sounds of dishes and glassware breaking. I had never experienced anything like that before.

After checking the damage inside the restaurant, I went outside to see the customers off. Seeing that roof tiles were scattered all over the parking lot of our restaurant and the convenience store next door, I went about cleaning them with our staff.

At that point, I didn't have the slightest inkling that a major tsunami would come. And that was in part because, with the electricity down, there were no TV or warnings from the emergency wireless system. My son wanted to check on the safety of his two sons and his wife and headed home two minutes away by bicycle. About ten minutes later, while the staff and I were cleaning up the second floor of the restaurant, I heard my son, who had just got back, yelling out from the first floor lobby, "A tsunami is coming!"

FOR A MOMENT, I thought it was a joke, but when I looked out from the veranda on the second floor, I faced an unbelievable sight. From my left, lots and lots of debris and cars came gushing at a breakneck speed in a muddy stream. I felt my blood freeze when a propane gas tank came streaming past, releasing smoke as it sped along like a jet plane.

The water level gradually rose, and more and more debris and cars were coming. It was like a scene from a movie. I was just glancing around the area, when a man in a minivan caught my eye.

I called out, "Try and get over here!" At first he stuck his head out of the window and said, "I'm all right." But the rising water forced him to climb up onto the roof of the minivan. I then called out, "Get over here before it gets dark." And he replied, "There's an elderly couple in the back!"

I remembered that there was a rope, so after tying it to a post as a lifeline three of our employees went out to rescue them. They managed to save the three people, and we were taking a little breather, but then I noticed my son was not around. He had jumped into the water to rescue a young woman who was clinging to a nearby fence.

Although he had taken swimming lessons until junior high school and was a confident swimmer, I was awfully worried. It was fortunate that he was able to rescue the woman, but as a mother, I could not help feeling that it was a reckless act.

INSIDE THE RESTAURANT, the three rescued and our three employees were soaking wet so I had them change out of their clothes and into white uniforms or casual jackets. Unfortunately, it was snowing then. I placed cushions on the second floor lobby, where we sat and withstood the cold by using tablecloths and things like that as blankets, and by making a fire with cardboard boxes and disposable wooden chopsticks. There was food, but, because of the distressed state we were in, we couldn't take more than a few bites.

We weren't able to get any sleep for that matter either. The sound of roaring helicopters and boat engines echoed in that extraordinary atmosphere. My staff and I looked outside and could see fierce red flames of fire from three spots to the southeast. It was a night of beautiful stars, and I will never forget that for the rest of my life.

As we were preparing to evacuate at the crack of dawn, a man came running into our place seeking shelter. The situation being what it was, I allowed him to join us. And in the end, about 70 people took shelter at our place at one point.

By any measure this earthquake disaster was dreadful. Although I was not swallowed up in the tsunami, our restaurant was flooded up to 1.5 meters, and we had to spend much time and money before we could reopen. What I can do as someone who survived would be to pass on what I saw and experienced down through the generations.

Battle for life on top of car
Each time I fell I thought *This is the end*

Shota Ito
male, 22, university student

I was swept off by the tsunami near the intersection of the port road and National Route 398. Repeatedly falling into water, I fought a "battle for life" on top of a car that had been washed to the Miyagi Nissan Ishinomaki dealership.

AFTER THE EARTHQUAKE, I was with my family and some neighbors evacuating by car, but was caught in a traffic jam while being chased by the tsunami. The murky black sea water was already crawling on the street. *The streets are going to turn into pathways of tsunami.* I turned into the south parking lot of the Nissan dealer. I got out of the car first. Looking at the port road, cars and wreckage were being washed away thick and fast. The water at the parking lot was rising as well.

I was helping the people in the car—my mother, 48, my brother, 18, a woman in the neighborhood, 71, and her granddaughter, 20—to get out, when a big tsunami came surging and washed all of us away. The fence that stood between the parking lot and Miyagi Nissan got overturned. My mother, brother, and the neighbor were holding on to the steel post of an outdoor lamp by the fence. The granddaughter, hampered by the two dogs she was carrying, was swept away and had disappeared.

While I was being carried away, another man, 21, came by, also being carried away by the current. Both of us were brought to a spot where cars had piled up in the car dealer's yard, and we climbed up on the roof of one of the cars. "Let's stick it out together," I said to him. I was worried about my family and the neighbors—they had gone out of my sight, but I couldn't do anything.

From the second-floor office of Miyagi Nissan, an employee was calling out to us. It was about ten meters to the entrance to the office, but not knowing the depth of the water, I could not muster enough courage to head out. I asked them to look for a rope, but was told that they didn't have any. "Hang in there! Rescue should be arriving in a bit," the staff encouraged us. The two of us made small talk as we waited for the rescue.

A REFRIGERATOR TRUCK came toward us after a little while, being carried away from the south. If it hit the steel pole, it would endanger my family and the neighbor. Fortunately, the truck went past the steel pole and crashed into the shutter at the center of the car workshop.

But my relief didn't last long. My mother and the two others got swept away now, and all three were sucked into the workshop. "Are you all right?" I called out, and to my relief, my brother responded,

The water still remained two days after the tsunami on Route 398 in Tsukiyama 1-chome. Shota Ito fought the tsunami at a Nissan car dealership located 300 meters ahead.

"We are OK." I couldn't see the inside of the workshop, but they told me later that they had climbed up on the roof of a car that was on a car hoist.

I had lost sense of time. It was freezing. *How long do we have to stay up here?* I wondered. Then the water receded gradually and I began to see some hope.

Around 9 p.m., however, another big tsunami came. The front part of the car we were on went under water and we were thrown into it. *Is this the end?* I lost hope, and was overcome with dread.

Somehow I was able to get up on a car again, and then helped the other guy get up on another car. Then it was my turn to climb up higher. There was a roof rack on the car, so I tried to grab it and climb up, but I was too exhausted and my body wouldn't move the way I wanted it to because of the cold. I tried to jump up with what little momentum I could build, but failed and fell in the water. I tried this several times. *This is the end,* I thought each time I fell. But then again, I switched my thinking mode, telling myself, *There's no way I'm going to die.* I don't remember exactly, but I was somehow able to get my foot hooked on the roof rack and made it up onto the roof.

In the middle of the night, I asked the Miyagi Nissan staff the time, and was told that it was just about past 12:00 a.m. on March 12. I could tell that my body was getting weak. *I won't be able to make it if I stay here any longer. We have to move into the building, even if we have to swim.* Both of us got down from the car. The water came up to my chin, so it was probably about 1.5 meters deep. We had no idea what could be at the bottom, but we started to wade.

WE MADE IT to the door of the first-floor office safely. An employee lit our path with a flashlight, which was helpful. When we went up to the second floor, there was the neighbor's granddaughter—she had gone out of our sight—with the two dogs, and I was relieved.

The two of us and a man who came into the office after us took off our clothes in a back room and kept our bodies warm with what was available including newspapers, cardboard boxes and sales promotion banners. That was when it hit me—*I have survived.* However, there was nothing I could do for the rest of my family who were inside the workshop. After a long while, I finally fell asleep.

When I woke up, it was already bright outside. The Nissan dealer staff were making a raft from tires and wooden boards. A male employee pushed the raft across the water, and rescued my family members and the neighbor.

Tsunami rushes in at breakneck speed
House struck second floor of office building

Maki Shiratori
female, 37, corporate employee

I encountered the tsunami at my workplace which was located in Mitsumata 4-chome. It engulfed everything in no time at all and the first floor of our company was submerged in water. Isolated on the second floor and enduring the cold, we spent one night terrified beyond all reason.

OUR COMPANY faced the four-lane main road connecting the Ishinomaki Industrial Port to the south and Okaido Street to the north. It was diagonally across the street from the Buddhist temple Fusei-ji and was in the neighborhood of Mizuho Daini Kindergarten. The area was bustling with traffic and businesses including a convenience store and a restaurant in the neighborhood.

I was on my way back to the office after handling some business at the 77 Bank Kokucho Branch and the Okaido Post Office. As I was driving near York Benimaru supermarket chain's Okaido store, my car suddenly started to bounce up and down. It was a very long and strong quake, and I was overwhelmed with terror. I held the steering wheel firmly and applied full force on the brake pedal while I endured the shaking.

The window panes breaking in the houses and businesses in the area resounded, and I could tell that the electricity had gone out. Once the shaking settled down, cars and people began moving all at once, causing an extremely heavy traffic jam.

Are my company and home all right? It so happened that my home in the Okaido-Higashi district was on the way back to the office, so I headed there first. When I arrived, I found my mother-in-law standing in the snow, holding her dog in her arms and looking dazed. My husband came home shortly after. I didn't have much time to talk with them, so I hurried back to my company. Concrete block walls along residential lots had totally collapsed.

ALL MY COLLEAGUES were outside waiting for me when I arrived at the company. Seeing them there, the tension within me snapped and tears welled up in my eyes. Inside the office, the personal computers had overturned, and papers were scattered all over. There was no space left to step. The street in front of the company was heavily congested, and many people were out walking home. *What's going to happen now?*—gripped with anxiety, I turned on the TV on my cell phone, which showed that a major tsunami warning had been issued.

The conditions then did not allow us to continue to work, so we were all dismissed immediately. As we set out to lock up the office, however, we couldn't pull down the shutter because of the power outage. We decided to quickly cover that space with a blue tarpaulin.

At that point, a colleague screamed at the top of his voice, "The tsunami's come!" No sooner had he yelled than a tsunami came rushing toward us at a tremendous speed from the south, the direction of the Ishinomaki Industrial Port. We dashed up the stairs to the second floor. What I saw from the window was nothing less than a scene from hell. The main street had turned into what seemed like a torrent, where cars and houses were being washed away one after another.

I was still composed enough to take some photos with my cell phone. In a short while, however, a house that came surging from the direction of the industrial port struck the windows on the second floor of the company building head on. That moment, the word "death" crossed my mind.

I opened the window and thought really hard. *How am I to handle myself when the wave comes? Isn't there a way to strike open the ceiling before the tsunami gets here and go up higher?* There was no more time left, and the situation was intimidating.

There were six men and three women left at the company. As we went up on top of the table on the second floor and kept watch on the situation, the force of the waves ceased. The water, however, had reached the table legs, so we still couldn't let down our guard. When the tsunami came to a lull, we moved to the warehouse since it stood at a place that was a little higher than where the office building was.

SNOW WAS FALLING as evening came, and it was

Torrential waters flooded the main street in front of Maki Shiratori's workplace in the Mitsumata district, 3:50 p.m., March 11, 2011 (photograph by Shiratori).

hard to see things anymore. But the tsunami was losing its force, and after getting my composure back somewhat, I sent text messages to my husband and to my parents.

My husband replied at 5:47 p.m., "On top of roof now and can't move. Cold. How about you?" And my mother replied from her home in Nakazato 2-chome at 6:50 p.m., "Water almost at our house. . . ," followed at 7:08 p.m. by "Street by house turned into river. Missed chance to evacuate to school. Tatami* mats floating."

During the night, text messaging was totally out of service. In the darkness, strong aftershocks continued intermittently and the waves surged from the beach over and over. I was also worried about whether I could endure the cold for a long time. I covered myself with a blue tarpaulin which I found at the company and tried to bear the cold. I had never had and will never have such a night when I waited so eagerly for the break of dawn.

A little after 10:00 a.m. the next morning, I saw a rescue team on the main street. "There are nine people here!" I called out repeatedly. Then a reply came saying, "We're handling the rescue at the kindergarten first. We'll come back for you. Don't worry, we will!" It's hard to express how much those words encouraged me. After 2:00 p.m., they came to our rescue as promised.

On my way home, the devastation I saw was horrendous, and there was absolutely no telling how far that wretched sight had extended.

*tatami: See note on p. 078

Tsunami engulfs tide barrier pine trees
Large cargo ship under construction slides into ocean

Mamoru Onuma
male, 56, director of waste incineration plant

The Ishinomaki Koiki Clean Center, the region's waste management center where I work, is located to the west of the Ishinomaki Industrial Port in the Shigeyoshi-cho district. It is an incineration plant that handles the general waste of the Greater Ishinomaki Region and is also equipped to generate electricity using the heat from the plant.

UNTIL THE EARTHQUAKE occurred, March 11 was just another Friday. The amount of waste brought in that day was about 250 tons. The temperature inside the melting furnace where the waste is burned was around 1300°C, normal readings.

2:46 p.m.—I was at work in the office on the first floor when suddenly the quake struck. The shaking grew gradually stronger in intensity and it seemed as if it was challenging us to test how much more we could take. The power went out, and then the emergency power generator came on automatically. However, we only had 400 liters of light oil for fuel which would only last for a few hours. We did our best to limit the output power in order to save fuel.

Although I was concerned about possible casualties, I was also worried about the melting furnace, the heart of the plant. It was structurally explosion proof. However, the risk of fire would increase if it collapsed—it had the capacity to melt metals and glass. I tensed up at the thought. Fortunately the emergency stop circuit was activated, and there was no abnormality in the gas emissions, drainage water or various other functions. Our center staff, the sub-contractors, and the construction company workers who were working there at the time were all safe, and I was relieved.

But this feeling didn't last for long. The news that the major tsunami warning had been issued reached us. We decided to go up to the third floor for safety. Some 20 workers from the adjacent Amagasaki Seikan's canning factory and Nanko Clean Center came over seeking refuge, and altogether there were 62 people at our center.

AROUND 3:25 P.M., the first wave of the tsunami came over the quay. The streets around the Center flooded up to over half a meter. An apprehension that a larger tsunami might follow crossed my mind when I saw that the first wave was bigger than the ones triggered by the 2010 Chile earthquake. We thought it might be dangerous even on the third floor, so we moved up to the visitors' hall on the fourth floor, the top floor which was nearly 40 meters above ground level. I believe that all the evacuees shared this sense of security—*We'll be safe as long as the center doesn't collapse.*

From the south window we had an entire view of the ocean. As I was watching the coastline about a kilometer away, suddenly there appeared something I could not make anything out of—somewhat like water vapor or a mist. I remember that it was about 3:45 p.m. It was the spray that was being released from the second wave of the tsunami. It easily went over the tide barrier of pine trees, reaching over five meters in height, and it seemed to be moving at the speed of 50 or 60 kilometers per hour. It broke through the dockyard of Yamanishi Corporation with an astounding force. A 24,000-ton cargo ship which was under construction at the dock slid into the ocean as in a launching ceremony and went adrift. Another ship of the same class which was being outfitted at the quay shook its bow to the east once, then swung it back in a large curve to the west, and went up the Jo-gawa River, eventually running aground in the Omagari district in Higashi-Matsushima City.

On the east side of Yamanishi, piles of logs were washed away from the storage yard of the plywood manufacturing company Seihoku. The second wave, having scraped out the mud from the seabed, was now a muddy torrent of a wave surging toward the Center with full force. The first floor was flooded and the dozens of cars that had been in the parking lot were washed away to join all the other objects that were drifting.

THE TSUNAMI CAME AND WENT, back and forth, repeating the same pattern over and over again. When the tsunami went out, it receded so much that the bottom of the Jo-gawa River was exposed. It went out at an astounding speed, and when it came back, it pushed its way back up the river, with miscellaneous things including logs being scattered all over the surface.

On the first floor of the Center, water had risen about two meters from the floor so it was impossible to take even one step outside. Everyone was to spend the night in the Center. We went back down to the third floor, where a television was brought in to the central control room and all the men stayed there to gather information and to get some rest. Meanwhile ten or so women that were there rested in the night duty officers' sleeping quarters next to the control room.

Television and radio programs were reporting about the devastation along coastal regions over and over again. However, there was very little information about the situation in Ishinomaki, Higashi-Matsushima, or Onagawa. Telephones went out of service right after the earthquake occurred, so we couldn't get the information we needed.

Each and every one of us was worried whether our family members were safe and if our houses had survived the disaster, but no one dared to voice that concern. I myself went about silently checking all the machinery, flashlight in hand, awaiting daybreak without gettig any sleep.

Disaster victims out in street scattered with rubble and washed-up cars. Photo taken around 10:45 a.m., March 14, 2011, Watanoha, Ishinomaki City

Heading for shelter with invalid family
Escaping disaster with help of many

Hideki Saito
male, 43, home care worker

I was at home watching television on the second floor when the earthquake occurred. I was supposed to go and see a relative at 3:00 p.m. Suddenly the earthquake alert* buzzed on my cell phone.

I WENT DOWN THE STAIRS right away and said to my father, 75, who was disabled by a stroke and my mother, 74, who was suffering from complications of diabetes, "A big earthquake is going to strike now." I put my bedridden grandmother, 95, in the wheelchair, covered her head with a floor cushion with my hand holding it for protection, and waited until the shaking ceased. Once it stopped, my father said, "Let's get away from here." The man living next door, 68, who had once before offered to support us in any emergency, came to our home as promised.

I was worried whether my family and our neighbor could manage to get to Minato Elementary School, the designated evacuation site, so I rushed out to National Route 398 which ran in front of our home, held my arms high, gestured and stopped a police car patrolling in our neighborhood. The road was jammed. I saw people walking down the middle of the street not caring about the cars. I pleaded with the police officer, "My family members are physically disabled. Please help us." The officer got out of the car and directed the traffic so we could go on safely. Some firefighters who were on duty also helped us. I pushed my grandmother in the wheelchair, my mother carried my grandmother's medicine and we hurried on. My father, using a cane, walked with our neighbor assisting him and headed for the shelter.

We arrived at the evacuation site at Minato Elementary School just before 3:00 p.m. It was a miracle that all four members of our family, including the physically-challenged and the sick, survived. There was only a fine line between life and death. We evacuated to the second floor of the school building, but we were sent up to the third floor by the school staff who said, "Water might come up to the second floor. Please go up to the third floor."

WE WENT INTO A CLASSROOM where people who required nursing care stayed, and there I was looking out of the window. Around 3:25 p.m., the first waves came flowing into the school yard, but they were only swirling ripples. The water was just below the knee level. I saw about 20 people in the school yard. "Waves are coming right behind you! Run quick!" called out the people who were already inside through open windows. I, too, yelled out loud.

The first waves were not that strong, so about 20 people went back home. Many people tried to stop them saying, "It's too dangerous to go back now." It seemed that they did not come back to the school again in the end.

Before long, the tsunami came from three directions—Fudocho to the north, Sakanamachi to the south, and the Kyu-Kitakami-gawa River to the west. The water was a dark, black, muddy torrent. Some people were engulfed by it even though they had managed to reach the school yard. The groans for help could be heard from all directions, "Help!' Help me!"

There were cars that had been washed away on each and every street. At the intersection in front of Minato Elementary School, some 15 cars that had been carried at a terrible speed had piled up altogether and had turned into heaps of rubble. A few cars had also been carried into the school yard. It was dreadful to see several cars that had plunged into the swimming pool.

I WAS REALLY FRIGHTENED and unnerved by how destructive the tsunami was. A *torii* gate torn off its foundation from some Shinto shrine could be seen knocking down houses, a flower shop and a rice store while swirling around. It was like a bulldozer. My house was completely destroyed. I was truly dumbfounded to see someone's house that had landed in a parking lot near our house.

The water rose up almost to the first-floor ceiling at Minato Elementary School. On the day the earthquake happened, about 1,600 people had sought refuge in the school. About a hundred of them required nursing care. I am a certified home care worker and a certified social worker, so I worked alongside the students from the Ishinomaki Red Cross Nursing School and helped the evacuees to stay warm by all possible means including massages. I also changed diapers for the people who required it.

On February 11, one month before the earthquake, I had a dream that several relatives who had already died stood by my bed and said to me, "Watch out. Something dangerous is going to happen." One week before the earthquake, I heard dogs barking and cats meowing in strange manners around midnight, and the clouds in the sky at sunset looked dark red which was different from normal. They might have been some sort of a sign.

I am wondering if this is a case of mental stress after the disaster—I am scared of driving over the Utsumi-bashi Bridge to go into the Hachiman-cho district. It makes me recall the devastation. My mother tells me that she never wants to go back to see our severely damaged house.

Currently we are living in a temporary housing in Hirobuchi, which is in a district inland. I am worried when I think about our future. However, all I can do is to be positive and live every single day of my life with hope.

*Earthquake alert
Most cell phones in Japan are equipped with an automated earthquake alert system. The alert is expected to reach the phone several seconds before the arrival of the main shock, allowing the owner to take the most essential actions for safety.

First floor submerged in sea
The river turned into a black writhing horizon
Katsuhiro Suzuki
male, 63, barber

I encountered the earthquake at my own house where I ran a barber shop in Minato-cho 1-chome, some 70 meters east of the left bank of the Kyu-Kitakami-gawa River. After I had my family evacuate to Minato Elementary School, I stayed on at home, however, and witnessed the process in which my neighborhood was devastated by the tsunami and how people left on rooftops were carried away along the river.

I WAS RELAXING in the living room with my family during a short break between customers. The quake that struck was so intense that we could hardly keep standing. It felt so long that you couldn't tell if it would ever end. When the shaking finally settled down, I found pieces of furniture scattered all over but no major damage to the house could be found.

Is our neighborhood all right?—I was worried and went outside to check. My wife's parents' house which was close to my home had some windows broken and the broken pieces were scattered on the road. I cleaned up the glass and quickly went back home, and tried to turn on the TV but there was no electricity. I searched for the radio and turned it on. At that very instant, this shocking announcement was being aired—"A 10-meter tsunami is coming."

Nothing could be heard from the community emergency wireless system. There were no emergency vehicles from the fire department or the municipality going around urging people to evacuate. *Something could be wrong*—was one thought. Another thought was that, even if a tsunami came, based on my experience from the tsunami that was caused by the Great Chilean Earthquake of May 1960, the highest it would get would be just above the floor level on the first floor.

This earthquake, however, was so much stronger. If a 10-meter tsunami did come, this area would definitely be submerged. Assuming the worst-case scenario, I urged my family saying, "Hurry up and evacuate!" and had all five members of my family, including my 4-year-old grandchild and my 88-year-old mother, rush to Minato Elementary school, 400 meters away, for safety.

It took a bit of time for my family to prepare blankets and medicine to take to the shelter, but I received a call later on that they were able to evacuate safely before the tsunami reached the area.

I STAYED in my living room alone. I do not remember the time precisely as I was bustling around. Suddenly, I heard these great ripping sounds—they sounded as if 10 or 20 heavy equipment vehicles were tearing down different buildings all at once. I could hear no sound of water, so I was thinking to myself—*What is this? Is this what a tsunami is?*

I ran upstairs to the second floor—still incredulous—and looking out from the laundry-drying platform toward the Kyu-Kitakami-gawa River to the west, I saw water that had risen three to four meters higher than normal was flowing back up the river. It was like what one might call "a black writhing horizon."

Roofs of houses that were afloat were speeding up the river at 50 to 60 kilometers per hour toward the Utsumi-bashi Bridge. I counted at least 30 houses. Some people were clinging to the TV antennas on their rooftops and others were lying flat on the roof holding onto it desperately trying not to fall into the river. I thought if they kept on going that way, they would surely hit the bridge and be thrown into the river, but I couldn't do anything, as they were more than 100 meters away from where I was. All I could do was simply pray that they would survive.

The tsunami now surged to where I was standing on the laundry platform on the second floor of my house. The first floor of my house was already submerged and the surrounding area had turned into a sea. The houses in my neighborhood were already being washed away, blocking the roads and breaking the fence of the house across from us. Then in a short while I heard this great tearing noise. It was the sound of an electric cable that got severed when the houses being carried away knocked down some of the electric power poles.

Darkness gradually set in. The contour of the Hiyoriyama hills in the west had turned red. I could easily tell that it was fire. I prayed with all my heart that it would not spread any further.

I WAS ISOLATED on the second floor with no drinking water, electricity or food. My house was tilting now with the tsunami having lifted it partially.

The bedroom my wife and I used was submerged, but only a small part of the children's room was wet. Thanks to this, I could rest on a dry bed. This sense of relief lasted for only brief moments, since the tsunami came invading again around 7:30

Katsuhiro Suzuki stands on the laundry hanging veranda at his home in Minato-cho 1-chome, pointing to the direction where he witnessed "a black writhing horizon."

p.m., 10:30 p.m. and then at 3:30 a.m. the following morning. I could not see anything in the dark, but I could tell that it had come with the now familiar ripping and tearing sounds.

The long and cold night had ended. Around 10:00 a.m., I could see the asphalt of National Route 398. *This condition will allow me to go to Minato Elementary School*—I convinced myself. I tried to go down the stairs but they were full of debris. I found instead a safe evacuation route along my roof. I had to climb over houses that were blocking the road, but finally I was able to meet my family again at the shelter. Nakadori Street to the west of Route 398 in the Minato district was completely blocked with debris and it would be over a month before it would again be open for vehicle or pedestrian traffic.

My soon-to-be-born baby must wait for help!
Enduring the pain

Yukako Sasaki
female, 35, stained glass artist

I kept talking to the baby inside of me—the baby who was ready to come into this world at any moment—while I waited for help in the storage room on the third floor of my sister's house.

JUST THAT MORNING, I had been to the Ishinomaki Red Cross Hospital for the last regular pre-natal checkup. I was only 15 days away from my due date. "The baby is ready to come any time," the doctor told me. As I was nervous about delivering my first baby, the words had brought comfort to me.

I had heard from my 32-year-old sister, married to a priest of Tafuku-in, a temple located to the east of Minato Elementary School, that she was alone at home with her six-month-old daughter. So I visited them with my husband, 36, and had lunch together at her house in the temple compound.

My husband then went to work and I was having a relaxing time with my sister and niece in the living room on the second floor, when suddenly the violent shaking started. I was unable to stand up. My sister and I held on to each other. Due to the unexpected shock, I started to feel a sharp pain in my stomach.

A short time later, we heard the emergency wireless system telling us that a major tsunami was on the way. We agreed to evacuate to our parent's home in the Sengoku-cho district of Ishinomaki City. While I was preparing to evacuate, I looked out of the window and saw a massive traffic jam on National Route 398, the road along the southern side of the temple. I recalled my father's words, "If a tsunami warning is issued, you should always evacuate on foot." But it was too painful to walk, so I decided to stay where I was, telling myself—*Since we are in a temple, Buddha will save us.*

MY SISTER set about collecting all the drinking water, food, blankets and other items we might need in the house. Then she was talking on the phone with her husband, 34, who was the assistant priest of the temple and was away on business in Shikoku, an island region in the southwestern part of the country, when she suddenly screamed, "The gate!" I looked over and saw a black wave flowing into the temple compound, engulfing many cars and trucks from the direction of Route 398. The gate at the entrance of the temple was leveled to the ground and loads of cars crashed into the main sanctuary of the temple. The door of my sister's home was destroyed by the muddy stream, and making a roaring noise like a waterfall, the waters flowed into the first floor. Soon the house was filled with a combination of the smell of mud, oil and fish. "The second wave is larger than the first wave." My father's words drifted through my mind. *Water could come up to where we are.* My heart was filled with fear.

I saw a man in the driver's seat of a van that had been swept into the cemetery of the temple compound. He was struggling desperately as the water level rose in the car but soon he slumped over the

Yukako Sasaki with Reita standing on the spot where the gate to the temple used to be. Tafuku-in Temple in Yoshino-cho 1-chome

steering wheel. I became distraught from the blaring of the horn and my stomach started to hurt even more. "What are you going to do if your water breaks?" My sister's voice brought me back to reality. I realized that it was my mission to keep my water from breaking. I said to my baby, "You are not allowed to come out yet. Do you understand?" Taking my niece with me, I climbed up to the third floor, where a storage room that had a height about 1.5 meters was located. I was prepared to put my niece in a clothing storage case and let her float in the waves if the water reached us. In the meantime, my sister stayed on the second floor gathering up such things as diapers, baby milk, and blankets. I was told later that the second wave did not reach as high as the second floor and the water level gradually lowered.

After the water level receded enough to walk, about 20 people who had evacuated to the main sanctuary came over to the house. They were soaking wet. My sister provided them with clothes and food. When she explained my condition to them, one woman said that her daughter worked as a midwife in Tokyo. She got in touch with her daughter and scribbled down the necessary steps I should take in case the baby was born. *Warm the baby on your belly without cutting the umbilical cord. Wrap the baby with a dry towel. Wrap the placenta with newspaper and keep it near the baby.* I chanted this repeatedly until I had it memorized. Before the earthquake, I was so scared of the labor pains but after experiencing this tragedy involving so many deaths, including the one of the man in the van, my fear turned into an awareness of my duty as a mother to safely give birth to a new life. I said to the baby in my stomach, "If you want to come out now, you will be welcomed."

AFTER A SLEEPLESS NIGHT, the piled-up cars and the people who had most likely lost their lives were visible from the window. I could tell that something really awful had happened, but if I looked outside, my pains would appear so I waited inside the storage room to be rescued.

On March 13, two days after the earthquake, a student of Ishinomaki Red Cross Nursing School came to see me. She had evacuated to Minato Elementary School. She encouraged me by saying, "If your water breaks, yell toward the direction of Minato Elementary School." In the evening, an ambulance came and I was taken to Ishinomaki Red Cross Hospital. The hospital was packed with people and I slept on a bench for three days in the outpatient waiting room.

Finally at 9:25 p.m. on March 17, after 17 hours of hard labor, I was able to give birth to my baby. It was a healthy baby boy weighing 3,166 grams. "Finally, I get to see you!" I gave him a big cuddle. Thanks to the support of so many people, I am able to live a merry life with my son Reita.

House stabbed by fishing vessel in Watanoha, Ishinomaki City. Photo taken about 11:55 a.m., April 24, 2011

Seafood processing cooperative near Watanoha Beach suffered great damage in Matsubara-cho, Ishinomaki City. Photo taken about 6:50 a.m., March 22, 2011

Escaping to a slope, just in the nick of time
The tsunami swallowed up a line of cars

Yoshietsu Sasaki
male, 57, real estate business

When the earthquake happened, I was at my office-cum-factory in 1-chome of the Matsunami district of Ishinomaki City. I could not get outside because the shaking was too strong.

EVERYTHING ON THE SHELVES fell down. I was worried about my family and eight elderly people who lived in rental houses near my house in the Yoshino-cho district, so I jumped into my minivan and headed to my house. The roads were not yet crowded, so I managed to drive home pretty easily. The eight elderly people had been outside buying groceries from a travelling fruit-and-vegetable truck at the time of the earthquake, but they were all safe. My wife, 60, and oldest daughter, 34, were at home, but two grandchildren, who went to Minato Second Elementary School, had not yet returned home. I had my daughter go to the school to look for her children.

From my experience of the major earthquake that occurred in 1978 in the sea off the coast of Miyagi Prefecture Miyagi Prefecture, I was aware of the possibility of both a blackout and a water cutoff, so I asked my wife to go with the elderly neighbors to get some food from a nearby convenience store. I drove back to my factory to get generators and kerosene heaters.

National Route 398 running toward Watanoha had no traffic. Shortly after making a right turn heading toward the fish market, a middle-aged man came running toward me, and with both arms up in the air shouted, "Go back! A tsunami has reached that area over there!" In the distance, I saw a car facing sideways coming toward me being pushed by the tsunami. The man who had warned me ran toward the hills. I put my car in reverse gear and changed my direction heading back toward Route 398. However, there was a big truck and a car in front of me blocking my way. The tsunami was coming behind me. I felt impatient. When I looked to the right, there was a slightly elevated vacant lot. *If I can just get past this place I can reach the highway!* I put my minivan into four-wheel drive and drove up onto and through the vacant lot.

When I managed to get to the highway, luckily there was space for one vehicle on the lane going west and I was able to squeeze my car into it. But once I got onto the highway, the line of vehicles I was in did not move at all.

THE DRIVERS ON ROUTE 398 probably had not yet noticed that the tsunami was already close by, but I had no time to tell everyone about that. There was no traffic in the opposite lane so I drove down that side a little. Then, I turned right and headed toward the two-storied parking lot of a pachinko hall at the base of the hills. I could only think about going up the slope there.

I stopped my car, got out and ran to the side overlooking Route 398, and saw the tsunami had engulfed all the roads I had just taken and the cars on the roads. If I had waited five seconds more, I would have been swept up in the water, too. There had been lots of cars on the highway when I was there, but now all I could see was moving water. I did not see a single person around. Houses and cars were hitting against each other, making a hair-raising metallic screech at times, but I heard nobody's voice. It was very quiet and ominous.

There were more than a hundred people in the parking lot on the second story of the pachinko hall. It started snowing. Then we began to hear a woman's voice from the debris underneath the parking lot. I heard her cry, "Help! I have a child here." The cries were coming from a young mother with a small boy. Several men on the roof looked around for something to save them with like a rope. One man climbed down while clinging to the mountain slope behind the pachinko hall and bravely went into the water and was able to reach out to the woman and her child. First the young boy was carried and handed over to people in the parking lot, and then the mother was saved.

It was very cold and we couldn't stand it, so we all went to the scrapyard that was on the side of the slope to look for something to make a fire with. We found three oil drums. We made firewood out of the boards and other debris that had been swept up by the tsunami. However, my back was cold from the wind. I remembered that there was a big tarpaulin sheet in my car, so I went back to my car to get it. When spread out, it made a windbreak for the women who were shivering from the cold. There were about ten women gathered together sharing the sheet to cover their backs. Workers from the pachinko hall found three or four boxes of juices and snacks—prizes for pachinko customers—in the store which was damaged by the tsunami, and distributed the goods to us evacuees. I was very thankful.

NIGHTTIME CAME. The fire from the nearby Kadonowaki-cho district turned the western sky red. Nobody talked; it seemed that everyone was engrossed in their own thoughts. I myself could not stop thinking about my family. After a while, I finally received a text message from my wife, and finding out that my daughter and grandchildren were all safe, I was very relieved.

I decided to go back home the next morning. The city streets were still flooded and full of debris. I was wearing sneakers, so I took out the plastic supermarket bags that I found in my car, covered my stocking feet with them, put my sneakers back on and set off, going along the side of the hill.

Passing over the cemetery, I took a route from the panoramic view spot of Daimonzaki Park that is known only to residents of the area. I reached the rear of Ichioji-gu Shrine. I had no choice but to wade in the water from the front of the shrine office to make my way home. The water came up to my stomach. I felt the water was as cold as ice. I moved forward frantically, pushing away pieces of debris with my hands. *Ah, I'm getting closer to home at last.* Then I saw my wife standing at the terrace of the second floor. I called out to her, "I'm home!"

Water gushing out at front approach to Makiyama

"A tsunami is approaching!" I yelled to a line of cars

Hitomi Chiba
female, 70, homemaker

My house was near the Ishinomaki Fish Market. It was located in a residential area on flat ground about 500 meters from the ocean. When the big earthquake happened, I had been waiting at home for two women to whom I taught knitting.

THE SUDDEN SHAKING was so tremendous that I could only shout, "What is this!?" I could not move at all during the quake. I was near a window, so I tried to open the window to get out of my house, but the shaking from the earthquake was so strong that I could not even stand up. When the shaking stopped, my next-door neighbors—an elderly couple and a young couple—came to my yard and said, "Mrs. Chiba, quick! Let's evacuate together!" Soon, there was a blackout. I could hear a warning outside being announced quite firmly: "A big tsunami is coming."

I was a little bit confused by what had just happened, but I put my seal, bank books, some chocolate, rice crackers and other snacks into my bag. The street in front of my house was becoming packed with cars, so I walked with my neighbors to the funeral hall Hotaru along National Route 398, which was the designated emergency shelter for our community. On our way, we crossed paths with a group of people who were heading to Minato Junior High School and Minato Second Elementary School. They told us, "Schools are bigger and better," but I didn't change my mind because I had always had it in my head that Hotaru was where I would evacuate to if there was an emergency. Further on, we came across the site of an accident between a crane truck and a woman on a bicycle. The woman and her bicycle were under the truck. After we saw that someone had called for an ambulance, we started walking again. I found out at a later date that the woman had narrowly escaped death.

To avoid crowds, we walked on a back street. The street was so badly damaged that it seemed like no car could drive on it. We managed to get to Hotaru. I was standing in front of the entrance with the scores of people who had gathered there when we heard someone shout, "Fire!" When I looked around, I saw a dense cloud of black smoke coming from the direction of the area where the Red Cross Hospital used to be before it moved to its present location. I became worried about my close friend who lived near there. I told the people I was with, "I'm going to check on my friend, and then I'll come right back." I headed west on Route 398 alone.

THE HIGHWAY was packed with cars. To avoid the congestion, I took a turn near Ichioji-gu Shrine to a back street that ran on the north side of Route 398 and continued heading west. I crossed at the front approach to the Makiyama hills. I saw that water had started to cover the street a couple meters ahead of me. I decided that I had no choice but to escape by climbing up the front approach to Makiyama and go into the mountain.

The approach to Makiyama was still dry but water began spurting out of the holes of the drainage ditches alongside it, making a gurgling sound. *This is terrible. I'm sure that this is a sign that a big tsunami is coming.* The traffic heading up the hills all the way to the shrine at the top was not moving at all. I shouted at people in the cars, "A tsunami is coming! What are you doing? You have to leave your car and run!"

However, it seemed like they could not hear my voice. As I ran up the slope, I knocked on car windows and shouted, "A tsunami is coming! Run! Run! Quickly! Quickly!" When I looked at my hands, I noticed my fingernails had broken and were bleeding from pounding on the windows. Despite my earnest pounding, most people did not come out of their cars. Most likely everyone thought, "Some strange old lady is saying something." Only a few people noticed how serious the situation really was.

WHEN I REACHED the electric substation where houses were sparse and looked back, I saw that the tsunami had swept away the whole town and there were cars just floating buoyantly. There were people who had gotten out of their cars and were holding on to telephone poles. There were people who had climbed on top of the fences around their houses. I will never forget the cries of people shouting, "Help me. . . ."

After the tsunami receded, it started snowing and got very cold. *Where should I evacuate to?* The streets were full of cars lying on top of each other; they were also covered with water and mountains of debris, which made it impossible for me to go ahead, so I walked along the edge of the hills.

I managed to reach Makiyama-Sando-Kaikan Hall, and was able to take refuge there. When I arrived, there were no one there, but soon an 86-year-old woman arrived. She had evacuated from the Inai district, which is in the north along the Kyu-Kitakami-gawa River. She had two blankets, and kindly let me use one.

As the two of us sat in the middle of the room wrapped up in the blankets, more and more people began to arrive and there were about thirty of us by midnight. The two blankets encompassed one more person, and then another, and yet another until eleven of us were rolled up in the two blankets. I shared the chocolate and rice crackers I had with me with everyone. I could not stretch my body, so I spent the entire night in a sitting position.

Traffic jam hampers evacuation
Water comes to chest on 2nd floor

Kenichi Abe
male, 44, company employee

The earthquake occurred when I was at my work-

Standing inside his company's warehouse in Sakana-machi 2-chome, Kenichi Abe explains that the tsunami went above the brail net with its long pole running across on the warehouse wall over his head.

place right behind the Ishinomaki Fish Market. The shake was the biggest and the longest I had ever experienced, so I immediately thought, *A tsunami is coming. We're in danger.*

OUR BOSS WAS AWAY on a business trip to Tokyo, but it was decided that all seven employees should go home quickly. I headed toward the Hiyori-ohashi Bridge first to go home in the Hebita district, but the street was already filled up with cars. So I changed the destination and turned around to go up to the hills in Makiyama, but that street was also packed with cars.

A major tsunami warning was continuously being broadcasted on the car radio as well as on the local disaster prevention radio. *I wouldn't make it through the traffic jam. I wouldn't make it in time before the tsunami comes,* I thought.

Because of my line of work, the next thing that immediately came to mind was to put on a life jacket in store at the company's warehouse. That way I might be able to float if the tsunami swept me away, or in the event I died, the chances of my remains being found would be higher.

But when I got back to the Sakana-machi district and entered the warehouse, I found it in such a mess from the fierce quake, with fishing tools and equipment scattered all over the place, that I could not find a life jacket.

I wondered then how our business partner in the neighborhood was doing, and headed to the fishing boat engine dealer, located a few hundred meters away. The president of the company remained there alone. As we stood there discussing what to do, we heard a report on the radio, "A tsunami of over ten meters reached Onagawa." The president told me that he was going to stay in their two-story building. I decided to go back to my own company building, which was also a two-story building but was relatively high and solidly built with reinforced concrete.

I LEFT MY CAR in front of the company building and rushed up to the second floor. I wrapped my cell phone tightly in a plastic bag to keep it dry, and then looked out of a window on the south side overlooking the fish market. A tsunami of about 50 centimeters had already flooded the area. To my surprise, that level of water was enough to lift trucks and make them drift away. Soon after, a big wave of four to five meters rushed toward me, destroying the roof of the fish market on its way, making a scrunching noise. The broken roofs and uprooted buildings were approaching the window I was standing at.

I ran into a tatami* room on the northern side of the building. Then a tremendous noise of something cracking echoed behind me, and water came gushing into the room. In a blink of an eye, the water came up to my knees and then to my waist. In order to secure my way out, I smashed a window with what I found around there and stood on the window's frame. The water level continued to rise and finally came up to my chest. When I thought that I had no choice but to swim out of the room, the water stopped rising.

133

I could see the hills in Makiyama on the north side from the window and the Kadonowaki-cho district on the west side. I saw the tsunami was flowing back and forth many times toward Makiyama and smoke was coming up from the Kadonowaki-cho district.

After a while, the water went down but it stayed, fluctuating just above the floor level of the second floor. *I have no choice but to spend the night here.* I found a dry towel from a locker and wiped my wet body. I also found a sailor's rain jacket and put it on over my clothes which were still dripping wet. There were some snacks and cans of coffee scattered around the floor, and I could ease my hunger with them. I thought there must be some people like me left in the surrounding buildings which had not been taken away by the tsunami because I could see flickers from flashlights.

Aftershocks continued to occur, causing a number of small tsunamis throughout the night. I didn't feel like I was alive. After a night without any sleep, the morning came at last. I saw a few people walking around outside. So I went out myself and walked to a three-story building nearby. There I was able to join a group of more than ten people who had been left there. It was at this moment that I finally felt I had survived.

I STAYED ANOTHER NIGHT in that building. On the third day from the earthquake, I came across a fishing boat that had entered the port. I borrowed a satellite-based cell phone on the boat to contact our president who was in Tokyo on business. All I could tell him was that I was safe. I couldn't find any words to express the devastating states of the port and the town. At that point, the whereabouts of two of our colleagues were unknown, but later both of them were confirmed safe.

That day I headed back to my house in the Hebita district on foot. I found it difficult to walk straight along the streets. I lost words at the sight of the town which had been completely destroyed. There was smoke from fires rising and helicopters were flying about. I belong to a generation without any experience of war, but I imagined what I was seeing then was something similar to the aftermath of an air raid.

Did the tsunami reach Hebita? How's my family? I was so anxious. After walking for six hours, I came home to find that my house was intact and my wife and children were all safe. I felt relieved at last.

WE HAVE SET UP a temporary office in the Yamashita district and have resumed business with our four ships—all of them were undamaged. I can tell this story now because I was able to survive. I don't know how we will recover from all this. I know that it would require tremendous effort. I just want to hang on and do my best.

*tatami: See note on p. 078

Getting washed away in car

With no time to escape, my car floated in the water and started drifting

Ryuji Hayashi
male, 35 years old, *soroban* teacher

I was going to teach my soroban *(Japanese abacus) class from 3 p.m. and arrived at Doba School in the Kazuma-Minami district of Ishinomaki City 20 minutes early. There was a second-grade girl waiting to get into the classroom, so I invited her to go in with me.*

JUST AS WE WERE ABOUT TO enter the classroom, we were overtaken by a horrifying shake like I had never experienced before. Wrapping my arms around the pupil to protect her, I was stuck there, unable to move. She did not cry, but turned pale and was shaking. "It's okay. It's going to be okay. Don't worry," I said, trying to comfort her.

When the shaking stopped, I went back to my car and turned on the radio—it was reporting, "A tsunami in Onagawa." I also heard a major tsunami warning being announced on a local disaster prevention radio system.

We must evacuate to higher ground. Quickly, I took the girl in my car and hurried to the Makiyama tunnels. The traffic was not as bad as I thought it would be, and we were able to get there quite smoothly. "We will be okay here," I told the girl. I stopped my car in a parking area between the two tunnels in Makiyama and called the home of the girl. Fortunately, I got through. It was decided that one of her parents would pick her up at the abacus school. So we headed back there quickly and I handed the girl to her father.

A MAJOR TSUNAMI WARNING was continuously being aired from the disaster radio system, and the car radio repeatedly alerted of a six-meter tsunami in Onagawa. *It will be dangerous around here too*, I thought and decided to evacuate to Kazuma Elementary School, which was near the abacus school.

As I was driving, the tsunami gradually came rolling in from the east side over the main road that was near the elementary school, so I pulled my car up over the curb. Then in a blink of an eye, the level of water rose and I saw a fast-moving torrent carrying cars and refrigerators toward me, making big cracking sounds. It was like a scene from a movie and I just couldn't believe what I was seeing.

With no time to escape, my car floated in the water and started drifting. *Oh, no! No!* There was nothing I could do but let the car move with the flow. After drifting for some tens of meters, the car crashed into the rooftop of the garage of a house with a thud and stopped.

Trying desperately to get out of the car, I cracked open a window using whatever I could find and managed to get out. Then I jumped onto the rooftop of the garage, barely escaping death.

As I looked in front of me, there was a man on the rooftop of the opposite house waiting for help, trembling. Then I saw a light pick-up truck crashing into my car. A young driver, maybe in his early 20s, held out his hand from the driver's seat, asking for help.

I must help him. Reacting instantly, I pulled the man out of the truck. Probably because of the frantic state I was in, I remember being able to do this more easily than I would have thought. He was all wet and trembling badly. Then, I saw my car flip and sink.

IT HAD GOTTEN COMPLETELY DARK by this time. *It would be the end of us if we stayed here like this.* The young man and I decided to evacuate to Kazuma Elementary School which was about one hundred meters away in a straight line. Seeing that the level of water started to go down from its peak of about two meters, I jumped off the rooftop. I sprained my left ankle as I did so.

The young man followed me, also jumping off the rooftop, and we set off for the destination. I made my way tolerating the pain in my ankle and shivering in the cold water. On our way, we came across a man probably in his 50s who told us that his wife had been swept away, and the three of us headed for the elementary school together.

We approached the school gate, but could not get in because of the dozens of cars that had piled up there. So we entered the school by climbing over a nearby fence. The school was packed with people, but I was let in the school infirmary and had my sprained ankle bandaged. I could also warm myself by a heater.

There was, however, nothing to eat or drink. On top of the hunger, I was anxious about the safety of my family. With a feeling of despair coming over me, I spent a sleepless night. I still wasn't able to go to my home in the Okaido district, or to the Futaba-cho district where the headquarters of my abacus school and my parents' house were located any time soon, because the roads to those areas were flooded. I spent the next night at Sumiyoshi Junior High School. It was around 2:30 p.m. on the third day that I finally made it to my parents' home dragging my sprained foot.

MY FAMILY, my parents and brothers had almost given up hope for me because I had been out of touch for that long.

"I'm home," I called out as I entered the house in muddy clothes. My wife, two kids and parents were overjoyed and in tears. "You're alive! Good. Great."

We held each other in joy as we were reunited.

Helping 20 escape to station rooftop
Rescuing people trapped in flooded cars

Kaichi Nishino
male, 59, company employee

I had just finished a task at the ice-making factory where I worked in the Watanoha district of Ishinomaki City. I had gone over to the office section of the company where I was about to take an afternoon break when the earthquake struck.

HMMM, this earthquake is a bit bigger and the shaking is continuing longer than usual. That was what I thought at first. I didn't take it very seriously. I remembered the 1978 Miyagi earthquake where it was impossible to keep standing, but this one was not as bad.

However, as I went outside the office and looked around, I realized that we had lost power all around the area. So I went back to the factory and followed emergency procedures such as closing all the valves. While I was doing this, our president issued an order, "Evacuate right away!" At this point, however, I didn't know the extent of the damage done to the whole Ishinomaki area.

I drove over to Watanoha Station on Japan Railway's Ishinomaki Line, parked by the public phone booth and stayed there for the time being. I thought I would go back to work again if the damage was minor.

I think it was around 3:30 p.m. that I heard something unbelievable on the car radio—"A three-meter tsunami hit Ayukawa at the tip of Oshika Peninsula." I wondered if the Watanoha district, which is close to the sea, was all right and got out of the car, and right at that very moment, my eyes caught an astounding scene.

From the direction of the Daiichi-Negishi-Kaido railway crossing some 100 meters away, cars that were washed away by the tsunami were heading toward me one after another. It was as if I was watching a scene from a TV program or a movie. *How could the wave reach here?* I was dumbfounded and at the same time felt overwhelmed by the fierce power of nature.

DOZENS OF CARS filled up the street in front of the station in no time at all, with great amounts of debris scattered all about. I spotted a ladder just in front of the waiting room of the station. "Go up to the rooftop of the station with this!" I urged the children and young people in front of the station, guiding them to evacuate along with some adults.

I think it was after I had had about 20 people go up to the rooftop when I happened to look toward the back of the station and saw muddy waters coming toward us from the direction of the Kazuma district.

I was in danger now. I moved to the public lavatory nearby and started to get ready to go up to the roof. A young man, probably a university student, helped me by setting up a makeshift ladder by putting two bicycles on top of the guard rail by the lavatory.

Luckily cars and debris piled up in one place and acted as a seawall, slowing down the force of the tsunami. It looked like I did not have to go up to the rooftop to escape from the tsunami after all. So I perched on the guard rail that enclosed the lavatory and the bicycle parking lot, observing what might happen for about half an hour.

I FELT SAFE NOW and got down to the ground. I was worried there could be some people still left in the cars that had been washed up. With the water up to my stomach, I searched for survivors together with some other people. We found some elderly people and others in their 40s and 50s with the water up to their necks in the driver's or passenger seats.

The elderly, probably out of shock, were in a daze and unable to move. The car doors opened when I yanked at them with all my might, and I was able to rescue those people one after another. It started to snow and it was so freezing that the elderly were trembling. We worked in pairs to help them to move to the station building, supporting each person on both sides. I was so desperate then and I'm not sure how many we saved even now. It was as if my body was moving on its own before I even started thinking what to do. As I look back now, that exertion of power was probably something similar to the "fight or flight response."

The station's waiting room had filled up with people in a short while. We had the people who had been saved from their cars change into the clothes that were offered from the clothing store nearby.

Then a big bus came and parked in front of the station. About 100 of us spent the night either in the station's waiting room or in the bus. Food and water were secured surprisingly smoothly as the local residents who were in charge of disaster response had made arrangements with supermarkets and convenience stores around the area.

Fortunately, I was able to confirm the safety of my family through an acquaintance, so I devoted myself to helping out around the station for five days. It was indeed a terrible disaster. I still wish it had been a bad dream.

Big black waves wash away neighbor's house
Three children rescued from rooftop

Yasuhiro Kikuchi
male, 46, study support business owner

I was walking down a street in the Minato district in Ishinomaki. The shaking was extremely terrifying. It was so intense that trucks were bouncing up and down, and I could barely manage to keep standing. An elderly woman was crouching on the ground trembling with fear, so I called out to her, "Are you all right?"

AFTER THE SHAKING stopped, I said to her, "Please be careful on your way home" and saw her off. I got my car out of the parking lot nearby and drove back home to the Watanoha district where my wife and parents were. On the way I heard the major tsunami warning on the radio, but it never came home to me that a tsunami was really coming.

At a crossing in Ibaratsu, a policeman was directing traffic by hand signals. Since it looked like a congestion was starting, I took a shortcut and was able to get home smoothly. I had my parents evacuate with only the barest necessities to Watanoha Kominkan Community Center, and then went to pick up my aunt—she lived in the neighborhood alone and had difficulty walking—so that she could join my parents at the community center.

After that, I headed to my parents-in-law who lived about one kilometer away in Koganehama. They were busy cleaning up shattered dishes on the floor. Just as I called out to my father-in-law asking him to move his car out of the way so I could park my car, he looked at me and shouted, "Look, here it comes!" I turned around to find a small wave of water a few centimeters high by my feet. My wife standing nearby screamed at the top of her voice, "We have to run!" A car ahead of us started to float and a huge black wave came surging toward us. We rushed up the stairs to the second floor. I brought up the rear and ran up the stairs without taking my shoes off. The view from the veranda was just horrific. The roaring, surging wave almost reached the veranda. My car and my father-in-law's floated up in no time and were carried away.

I HEARD A WOMAN'S VOICE calling out from the veranda two houses away from us, "Where am I?" She seemed to be in her 20s. Apparently she was swept away while driving down National Route 398 before reaching the unfamiliar house. I went over the roof to the next door neighbor's roof, where I called out to her and suggested she break the window pane and go inside that house. She then used some object

Yasuhiro Kikuchi points to the roof of the house where the three children were calling for help. Koganehama in the Watanoha district

that came floating by and set out to break the glass. In a short while, the house I was standing on was hit by a floating car and started to move. I hurried back to my father-in-law's and in no time the house I had been at was swept away. I could also see a man in a drifting car clinging to the steering wheel, but soon the car was swept out of sight.

And now a large truck could be seen drifting toward us together with all sorts of floating objects like refrigerators and washing machines. With a big crashing sound, my father-in-law's house got partially destroyed. I found a square cork board under the bed and shoved it to my parents-in-law, saying, "Never let go of it!"

LOOKING OUT FROM THE VERANDA, I spotted two children on the rooftop of a house about 200 meters away calling out for help. I called out, "I'm coming to rescue you so hang in there." The sun had already set and it was starting to snow. The water level had lowered to my neck. Driven by the idea that I had to do something, I headed toward them in the cold water. The water, in fact, was not too cold, but it was difficult to walk in it while pushing away floating objects. After about ten minutes I reached the house where the children were. To my surprise, there were three children instead of two. They were sixth-grade and third-grade girls and a preschool boy. They were not crying, but were trembling with cold and fear. I stretched my arms over to the roof to bring each of them down, and with one girl in each of my arms and the boy riding on my shoulders, I waded back to my in-law's house. I encouraged them saying, "You be my engine and get me going" and with their feet kicking water, I kept on wading in the water desperately.

It was dark and I could not see my path, but I managed to keep on walking by following the faint light of the cell phone the woman two houses down from us was holding. I was greatly relieved to finally reach my in-law's house. The children showed no emotion but they were constantly worrying about their mother saying, "Mom was swept away." I kept saying, "You will see her tomorrow, it'll be all right." We spent the night with the curtains as our bedding.

The next morning, I carried each of them, one at a time, by piggyback to Watanoha Elementary School, a designated evacuation shelter. When I visited the shelter later that afternoon, I found the mother and the children smiling together in the corner of a classroom. Their smiles brought tears to my eyes—I was so happy.

Massive wave fended off by skillful boat maneuvering
Split-second decision saves life

Shuichi Utsumi
male, 38, fisherman

I was fishing on my boat offshore from Ohara when I heard a noise like the earth rumbling even though I was at sea. My boat swung fiercely with the bow and the stern alternately crashing to the sea surface, the center of the boat working like the fulcrum point.

WHEN I LOOKED OVER toward the land, the sky was a yellow fog of pollen flying up from the cedar forests. I immediately called my wife, 42, at home in the Nakasato district, and told her to pick up our two children from kindergarten and school.

Soon after turning my boat toward Watanoha Port, I heard a radio bulletin from the Japan Coast Guard announcing a major tsunami warning. Sailing at full throttle, I reached the breakwater at Watanoha Port in twenty minutes. From the dock at Shinkama, I saw my parents' house across the bank at Shiotomicho. It was leaning steeply and the stone walls had collapsed. It was clear that the house was now uninhabitable.

My father, 68, and my uncle, 65, were picking up oyster farming ropes that had fallen into the sea due to the earthquake. They told me that my mother, 63, was on her way to our newly-built house in Shinsei 3-chome with my grandmother, 90. Just then, my wife called on her cell phone, saying that she had picked up our children and they had no injuries. I had confirmed, at least, that my family was all right.

NOW I WANTED to save my boats next. With the help of my father and uncle, I moved them—one for oyster farming management and two for bay sailing—as far up onshore at the Mangoku-ura Sea as possible. Just on the way back from anchoring the boats to oyster rafts, I saw a receding tide, a possible precursor of a tsunami. Rafts near the entrance of the bay began to be carried along by the tide. I dropped off the two men by the oyster processing site at Shinmei in Watanoha because it was close to higher ground, and made sure that they started walking away. Just then, I saw that the water had begun to repeatedly rise and fall in a fierce manner, turning the seawater muddy black.

While I was wondering where to leave this boat I was on, a swollen wave, about one meter high, obviously a tsunami, was approaching, passing under the Mangoku-bashi Bridge. The boats anchored along the wharf were hit side on by the wave, and were capsized easily. Although small, the wave had an overwhelming power. I had quickly turned the bow toward the wave and had successfully ridden over it, when I heard this great roaring sound—I

Shuichi Utsumi fended off the massive tsunami near the oyster processing plant shown in the background. Shinkama, Watanoha district

thought it was another quake but it wasn't. It was a massive wave making its way, engulfing both sides of the Mangoku-bashi Bridge. I tried to escape by turning at a right angle to the course of the wave, but could not go forward—dodging the debris the receding waves were carrying was the best I could manage. The big wave was now engulfing these receding waves as it kept rolling and closing in. *Can't get away now,* I thought. I turned my boat around, setting the bow toward the wave almost at a right angle. Just when the boat was about to go over the wave, the white crest of the wave appeared, and then it came crashing down over my boat.

I clung to the steering wheel hard so as not to get swept off the boat. The one moment that my head was out of the water, I looked ahead to find that the bow had swung up high and was out of the wave. *I can make it,* I thought and revved up the engine, and I was able to come out of it.

The boat was full of water inside and was just barely staying afloat. However, the continuous running of the engine helped the water to drain, and the buoyancy of the boat was gradually recovered. But then, another wave that was higher still came surging. I could now hear my own screaming voice, but a split-second decision had me set my boat diagonally toward the wave this time, and this eventually enabled me to go over the wave and fend it off.

After that, small waves of less than a meter repeatedly came and went. I saw a drifting car with people inside, but there was nothing I could do to save them. I anchored my boat near the wharf of the oyster processing site, leaving the searchlight and engine on. Then I tied the boat up alongside a big ship that had been anchored and saved from being swept away. The wharf was ten meters away. I caught a capsized boat that came drifting near me and straddled over it. Rowing with a hooked pole used for pulling in oyster farming ropes, I reached the wharf.

THE WATER ON LAND was about the same level as tall rubber boots. However, it might have been deeper in places. So, keeping a life vest on and testing the water depth with the hooked pole, I headed toward the JR Watanoha railway station. I think it was almost 9:00 p.m. The station was lit by generators, and there were many people in the station building as well as on a bus nearby. It seemed that no more people could be accommodated there.

Then I heard a woman calling me from a nearby house, "Could you please help me?" Inside the house, an old woman was trapped under a fallen refrigerator and a cupboard. The woman who had called out to me seemed to be her daughter. I helped her to rescue her mother. Fortunately, she was not injured. The floor was not wet, and they said to me, "Why don't you stay here tonight?" So, I got to spend the night there, keeping warm next to the kerosene heater.

The sea did a good job of messing us up, but no fisherman would speak badly of it. I still want to continue fishing, and I'm sure the sea will reward us again.

Inundated areas in Oshika Region

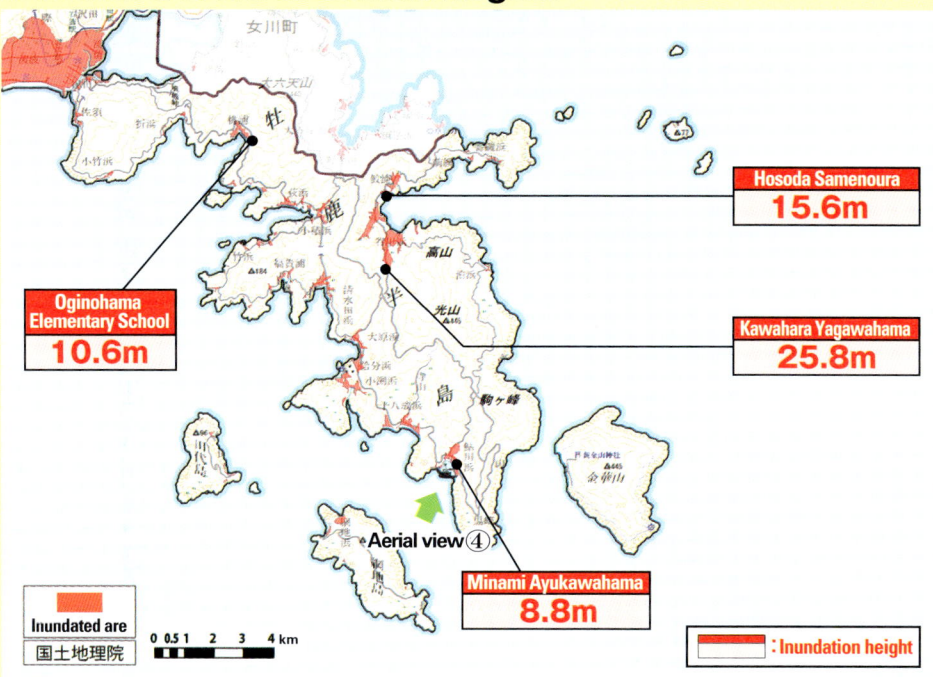

- Hosoda Samenoura **15.6m**
- Oginohama Elementary School **10.6m**
- Kawahara Yagawahama **25.8m**
- Minami Ayukawahama **8.8m**

Inundated areas in Kahoku, Kitakami, Ogatsu Regions

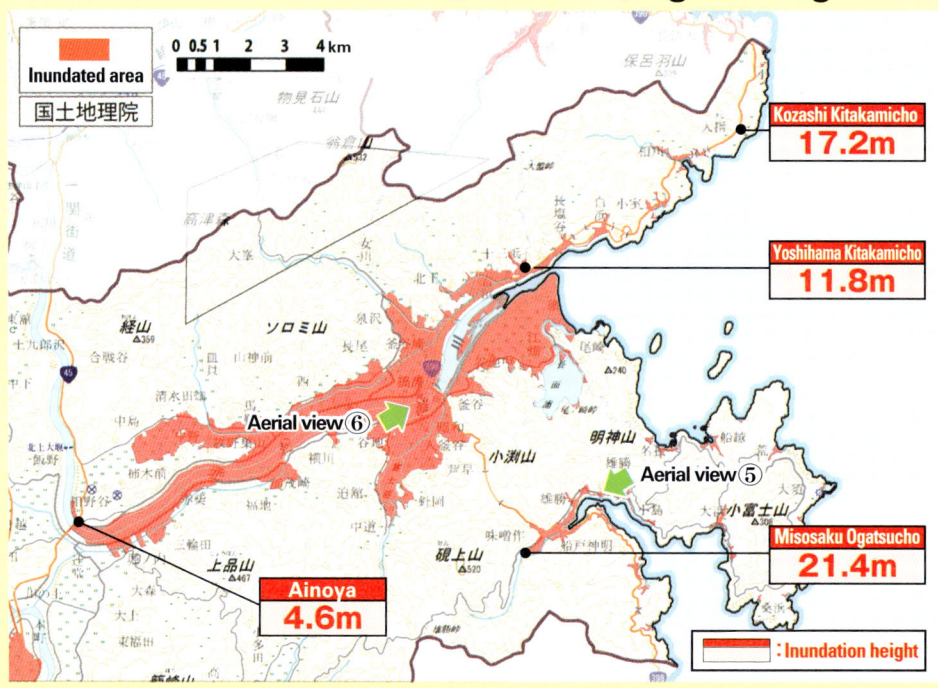

- Kozashi Kitakamicho **17.2m**
- Yoshihama Kitakamicho **11.8m**
- Misosaku Ogatsucho **21.4m**
- Ainoya **4.6m**

Aerial view ④
Ayukawa District

Town of Ayukawa, gateway to Kinkasan Island, is known for whaling. On right near deep end of breakwater is tourist facility Oshika Whale Land. (Photos Top: May 2002 Bottom: June 15, 2011)

Aerial view ⑤
Misosaku Ogatsucho

In pre-disaster photo, Ogatsu Junior High School with its large square yard stands on left side of small river flowing into Ogatsu-wan Bay. Behind is museum of inkstone for which the area is known. Large building at bottom right is Ogatsu Branch Office of Ishinomaki City Hall. In post-disaster photo, L-shaped building at bottom right is Ogatsu Hospital. (Photos Top: August, 2003 Bottom: April 5, 2011)

Aerial view ⑥
Area around Shin-Kitakami-ohashi Bridge

Community to right of Shin-Kitakami-ohashi Bridge is Kamaya district. Large building with brown roof in pre-disaster photo is Okawa Elementary School. (Photos Top: November 1985 Bottom: April 17, 2011))

Oshika Region

- Mangokuura
- Onagawa Bay
- Watanoha
- Ishinomaki-Ayukawa Road
- Oginohama
- Yoriisohama
- Enoshima Island
- Ashijima Island
- Oginohama Port
- Samenoura Bay
- Ishinomaki Bay
- Kitsunezakihama
- Yagawahama
- Makurohama Fishing Port
- Kitsunezaki Fishing Port
- Koamikurahama
- Kobuchihama
- Kugunarihama
- Tashirojima Island
- Oshika Junior High School
- Kiyosaki
- Ayukawa Port
- Ayukawahama
- Kinkasan Island
- Ajishima Island
- Kurosaki

Kahoku, Kitakami, Ogatsu Regions

- Minamisanriku Town
- Kumano Shrine
- Aikawa Elementary School
- Aikawa Fishing Port
- Tome City
- Kitakamicho-Jusanhama
- Yoshihama Elementary School
- Kitakami Municipal Branch Office
- Kitakamigawa River (Oppagawa River)
- Nikkori Sun Park
- Oppa Bay
- Hashiura Elementary School
- Kaizoan Temple
- kitakamicho-Hashiura
- Okawa Elementary School
- Onosaki
- Health Care and Medical Center
- Shin-Kitakami-ohashi Bridge
- Nagatsuraura
- Okawa Junior High School
- Nagatsura
- Kamaya
- Ogatsu Municipal Branch Office
- Ogatsu Hospital
- Iinokawa
- Fujinuma Lake
- Ogatsucho-Ojima
- Kahoku Municipal Branch Office
- Harioka
- Ogatsucho-Ogatsu
- Ogatsu Funeral Hall
- Ogatsucho-Tachihama
- Ogatsu Bay
- Ogatsucho-Kuwahama
- Shiroganezaki Lighthouse

Boat out of control
Fellow fishermen support via wireless

Satoru Watanabe
male, 48, fisherman

I was fishing for sea cucumbers on my 1.2-ton boat Kaishinmaru *at Oginohama Bay. The moment the quake struck, I felt a great force as if the bottom of the boat was suddenly uplifted.*

IT WAS a very unnerving sensation. *This one's no ordinary quake*—the sensation seemed to be shared by all my colleagues who were also fishing for sea cucumbers (known in Japan as *namako*). Hurrying back to port, I saw the cliff to the west of the lighthouse on the levee had collapsed extensively. The mountains looked as if they were enveloped in yellow flames. All the cedar trees that were shaken up by the earthquake were releasing tons of pollen. I was sure that a tsunami was coming. The wharf was also seriously damaged. The concrete had broken apart, the ground had shifted and become uneven—the wharf had been torn to pieces.

I managed to anchor my boat and climbed up to the wharf, where I found my oldest son, 22, and my father, 73—they had been doing preparation work for oyster farming—and my wife, 46, who had just rushed there to join them.

I told my wife to evacuate to a higher place with her parents who were at home, and I left the wharf on my other boat, *No. 7 Kaishin-maru*, 9.7 tons. However, my anxiety was growing stronger—*Is it all right to move offshore?* The rocking motion I felt was extraordinary enough to make me feel that it was not. I turned the boat around just before getting out of the port, and dropped off my son. Though I briefly wondered whether I should run to higher ground on land as well, the desire to protect the boat outweighed the other choice since a boat is a fisherman's life itself. I left the wharf again, but the boat would not move as fast as I wanted it to. The tsunami was already encroaching bit by bit.

FIFTEEN MINUTES after leaving the wharf, I had come near an oyster farm some five to six kilometers off the coast, when I heard my colleague's screams on the wireless radio, "It's coming! It's coming!" Just then, an abnormality happened to my boat—ropes from the oyster rafts got tangled in the propeller. I couldn't maneuver my boat. The boat turned itself around and now its bow was directed toward the shore. It was in such a dangerous condition that my mind went completely blank. Immediately after that, a big wave came from the stern and flooded the bridge of my boat with a big crash. My boat almost got capsized. "Leave your boat!"—wireless calls from my colleagues' boats came in one after another. I got on the small tow boat with an outboard motor, undid the rope, and headed frantically for my

Satoru Watanabe with fellow fishermen points to the bay where they took shelter. Oginohama Beach

brother's boat that happened to be the nearest one and got onto it.

I was soaking wet from the tsunami wave and the falling snow, and could not stop shivering from the cold and the fear. I was lucky to be able to warm myself and to dry my wet clothes with the heat of the engine, but my hands and feet would not stop shaking for a long time even though my body got warmed up.

My brother's boat had a wireless device, but not a regular radio. Frightening pieces of information could be heard off the wireless from the boats that were at nearby beaches—"All houses wiped out in Momonoura village," "Omotehama got devastated, too. Every cove's the same." Seeing the red sky in the direction of Sendai City and Ishinomaki City, I immediately sensed that big fires had broken out. On the other hand, the sky toward Oginohama Port was completely dark. Unable to see where the wreckage of fish farms was, we couldn't move. All we could do was just wait until morning. *Is my family all right?*—without any access to communication, I was frustrated with impatience.

THE NEXT MORNING, the boat of a younger fisherman got entangled with the ropes and buoys of oyster rafts, then drifted in the sea, and ended up being stranded by Tashirojima Island. As it was quite a dangerous situation, my colleagues went in their boats to his rescue. It was a touching moment when those fellow fishermen successfully rescued him.

It was after ten o'clock in the morning that we got back to our port. There was wreckage of fish farms scattered everywhere, and as we got closer to the port, we could see all the rubble that was floating. Almost all the homes in the seaside community where I was born and brought up were gone. I got a ride on a small pickup truck by the beach to go to Oginohama Junior High School, where many people had evacuated to. Fortunately, everyone in my family, including my parents, was safe. I will always remember the sense of relief I felt then.

When I went back to the seaside village later, an unbelievable scene was spread out before me. *Is this for real?*—I found myself murmuring over and over.

As for our house, only the skeleton remained, and just about everything got washed away by the tsunami. All I could find was a few photos that I had kept in my photo albums.

We are still living in an evacuation center. Demolition and clearance work as well as consolidation of communities has just been started in the village. I think all we can do is to just go step by step on the strength of the bonds of our seaside village.

Boat suspended from six-meter wave
Battered by sprays of flotsam

Tsutomu Hiratsuka
male, 61, oyster farmer

On March 11, I was gathering in hijiki seaweed with fellow fishermen at a rocky beach close to Kitsunezaki Fishing Port. The earthquake struck when I was getting ready to take a short rest at home after finishing the harvest.

EARTHQUAKES ARE OFTEN SAID to be either a "vertical shake" or a "lateral shake," but this time it was neither of the two. If I were to use words to describe the shaking, I'd say that it felt like "a very strong shake with both the vertical and lateral shake combined." It was a kind of quake I had never experienced. The outer walls of my house fell and the roof was severely damaged. Right after the long quake came to a halt, I knew intuitively that a big tsunami was coming.

I let my cat go outside, turned off the main tap of the gas and moved my forklift and small pickup truck to higher ground. Next, I needed to decide what to do with my boats, a 6-ton fishing boat and a smaller 1.5-ton boat with an outboard motor, both moored at the pier at Kitsunezaki Port. I tied the boat with the outboard motor to the fishing boat with a rope and decided to move them to the neighboring fishing port of Makurohama where the waves were always calm. On the way I noticed a mountain landslide along the coast and I was shocked to see that the familiar landscape that I had seen for decades had undergone a complete change.

When I got to the Makurohama Port, I saw the waves heaving back into the ocean. It might have been the drawback of the first tsunami. I knew that the second and third tsunami waves definitely would be larger. I knew that it would do no good to leave the boats there so I instantly decided to take shelter by heading out to the open sea.

THE ESCAPE TO THE OFFSHORE, however, was a succession of horror. Oyster farm rafts, barrels, ropes and logs came hurling toward me one after another at great speed. The barrels created sprays of water; it was as if they were water skis. If any of the flotsam got caught in the propeller, the boat would come to a stop. I tried with all my might to dodge the debris. To make things worse, I was subjected to the further onslaught of the high waves that came. When a wave of about six meters came, it felt as if the boat almost stood upright on its stern and, to tell the truth, I was beside myself with fear.

I remember that it was about 4 p.m. when I finally reached the calm sea, about three kilometers offshore, and could breathe a sigh of relief. I couldn't believe all these events had happened in just over one hour since the earthquake struck. When I looked around, the sea was full of many small fishing boats that had escaped like me. I guess there were about 200 boats.

Although I had on clothing geared for cold weather, it didn't feel like it was enough. It was snowing and it was a really freezing day. I wrapped a shirt that I happened to have left in the boat around my head and endured the cold. Needless to say, I had nothing to eat or drink, but I didn't feel hungry or thirsty at all, probably because I was so absorbed in fighting for my life. After a while, oyster-raising friends who were out in the open sea as well handed me some juice and snacks.

It became dark as I continued dodging the floating debris, and then pillars of fire caught my eyes. The coast was pitch-dark from the blackout but there were three places several kilometers ahead, red in flames. It was so vivid, like a scene from a movie. Flames could be seen until dawn. Later I learned that the fires had been in the districts of Minamihama-cho and Kadonowaki-cho.

I RETURNED to Kitsunezaki Port at dawn. The waves were rough in the bay, probably from the after-effects of the tsunami. An astounding amount of logs were drifting into the bay, which made it impossible for me to secure the boat at the pier. I had no choice but to make a U-turn, heading back out to sea, and came back to the port on the boat that had the outboard motor.

There was a fishing boat washed ashore—probably one from another port as I was unfamiliar with the name of the boat. The port was filled with so much wreckage that it was almost impossible to find a spot to place my foot. My house is several hundred meters away from the port but there was a barrel that had been washed up into the garage. I was horrified to know that the tsunami had reached my house and at the same time I really understood the ferocity of nature.

Fortunately, my mother, 86, was away at a rest home in Ayukawa and my wife, 51, away on a women's fire prevention club's training session in Iwate Prefecture. For me their safety was more important than anything else. It was indeed an extremely huge earthquake disaster, and I still wish that it had only been a bad dream.

A devastated seaside community
Working for our "Large Catch"

Hidenori Abe
male, 48, fisherman

The earthquake came when I was shopping at a hardware store in the Watanoha district of Ishinomaki City. It gradually intensified into a ferocious shaking, and by then I had dashed out of the store and jumped into my car.

THAT'S BECAUSE I knew a tsunami was coming and I wanted to get back to Koamikura and move my boat offshore to safety if possible. I drove home as fast as possible on the prefectural road which had cracks here and there from the earthquake.

The drive was probably more than 20 minutes. When I got home, about 40 women and elderly people were in front of the community center right behind my house. It was seven to eight meters above sea level. My father, 83, mother, 77, and wife, 44, were there.

I headed to the fishing port. I thought I might not have enough time to take the boats out to sea, but at the very least I wanted to move the new forklift which I had just bought and some materials that I had left on the quay to a place somewhere behind the seawall.

About ten fellow fishermen had finished bringing in their loads and were watching the sea from around the oyster processing factory. From behind, I heard them shout, "No, Hidenori! It's too dangerous! Come back!" The sea level was gradually rising over the quay. It was the first wave of the tsunami. I got onto the forklift and drove as fast as possible. I don't remember the details of some of the things that happened after that very clearly. Caught up by the wave, I climbed onto the roof of the forklift. Once the water rose up to my waist, it stopped rising and then started to draw back.

When I climbed down to the submerged ground, I saw an elderly woman, 90, who lived by herself stuck in the middle of the nearby debris. I helped her out and left her with an elderly couple who managed to survive the first wave on the second floor of their house.

I WENT OUT AGAIN and this was when the second wave came. It was monstrous. I managed to survive by running up to higher ground, but since it was a long way from where my family had evacuated to, I walked on the hillside to join them. The community center where they had first taken shelter had been swept away and they escaped by moving to a house that was located in an even higher area. Fortunately, both the elderly woman I had saved earlier and the elderly couple were safe as well.

I noticed that some of my fisherman friends were nowhere to be seen. I had thought that they had all run away from the waves. From what my wife had seen, not everyone had run to the higher ground. Three to four men climbed onto the roof of the oyster processing factory. They climbed onto the even taller seawater tank but they were all swept away by the second wave.

I was worried about my daughters. I figured my third daughter, an eighth grader, would be safe because her school Oshika Junior High School was high up on the hills. My second daughter, a junior at Ishinomaki Municipal Girls' Senior High School, was in Sendai and was supposed to come home in the afternoon. On the radio there was news about a train on Japan Railway's Senseki Line that runs between Sendai and Ishinomaki having been swept away. *What if she had been on that train...?* A few days later, I was told that she had not been on the train and was safe. Around the same time, a teacher visited me to inform that my third daughter was safe as well.

About 50 houses stood in my community before the earthquake but many of them were swept away; out of the roughly 100 people who lived there, 14 died, and three are still missing.

We had had an earthquake and tsunami just two

Hidenori Abe works out of this temporary fisherman's hut, built at the former site of his home, aiming to reconstruct the seaside community.

days earlier on March 9. Because of this, we might have underestimated the March 11 earthquake and the tsunami, telling ourselves, "This is no big deal. It's just like the last one." The community center where people took shelter was built at a place considered safe because the area had survived the 1933 Showa Great Sanriku Tsunami. Many elderly people who lived in houses on higher ground lost their lives because they did not move from their homes, thinking that a tsunami would never reach them.

IT IS IN THE FISHERMAN'S NATURE to keep looking for friends lost at sea until they are found. This time there were more than ten missing comrades, but we just could not summon up the energy to move at all. I don't really know how to express this properly but we were overcome by a sense of loss, and became lethargic and numb. For one or two months since that day, I had lacked a sense of reality as if I had been in a dream.

In spite of this, we all worked together to find the remains of two persons. They were of a fellow fisherman's family: his elderly mother who had a bad leg and his wife who went back to the house to help the mother escape. My friend had also run after his wife to help, but the tsunami came just as he jumped into the house. He was the only survivor. He could not be persuaded to leave the ruins of his house. Even though we told him, "You have to eat," he wouldn't eat. Unable to stand idly by any longer, we all worked together to find his mother and wife under the wreckage and took them to the morgue at Ayukawa. After that he seemed to have found some peace.

My fellow fisherman and I are now working for a recovery of our community in a fund-raising project called "Large Catch" (大漁プロジェクト=tairyo-project.com), in which small-unit contributions can be made to support the reconstruction of our community. The sea took just about everything from us, but it is the same sea that had continuously given us blessings up until now. The gifts from the sea—it'll be good to receive them again. With my family safe from harm, that is how I feel right now.

Steering frantically in turbulent waves
A village that disappeared without a trace

Fumio Kimura
male, 57, fisherman

The earthquake came when I was securing my 2-ton outboard motorboat to the quay. I had just come back from fishing for sea cucumbers about one kilometer off the coast from Kobuchihama on Oshika Peninsula, a part of Ishinomaki City.

A HUGE VERTICAL QUAKE continued for a long time. The boat rose and fell from 50 centimeters to nearly one meter and the undulations made me fall over. When the earthquake finally stopped, I hurried home past the seawall. When I got to my house a few hundred meters away, Naomi, the 23-year-old wife of my eldest son Hiroki, also 23, was in front of the house entrance, holding my then 18-month-old grandchild in her arms and curling into a ball. At that time, Naomi was pregnant with their second child.

Of course it was the first time for me to experience such a huge earthquake. My intuition told me that a big tsunami would follow, so I yelled, "Run away to higher ground!" and urged them to evacuate. Hiroki had just returned from work, and so I watched the three of them as they made it up to higher ground.

Next, I had to decide what to do with my outboard motorboat. I took a container of 25 liters of gasoline with me and got onto the boat. Then I hurried offshore near Tashiro-jima Island. I don't remember clearly, but I think that by this time 30 to 40 minutes had passed since the earthquake.

While I was waiting offshore, I saw a small island that we locals call Usagi-jima going under the waves in a split second. An island 200 to 300 meters wide and 30 meters high suddenly vanished. Needless to say, I was in shock. After that, the waves immediately started to draw back and I could see the seafloor bedrock which should have been at least 25 meters under the sea. The same familiar scenery I had seen for decades changed instantaneously. I could not believe it. *Is this a dream?*—I could not help but think that.

I SHOULDN'T BE HERE! I thought that the best strategy for me would be to go farther offshore and sped off in the boat. Behind me was the tsunami coming to overtake me. *I'll lose my life if I'm tossed out of the boat.* I held tightly on to the steering handle as numerous waves rose and fell on me. When I looked around, I saw that there were about ten outboard motorboats and small fishing boats that had fled just as I had.

Just when I finally felt safe and the tsunami was coming to a halt, driftwood and other objects started to come toward me one after another. *If any of the floating objects gets caught in the motor, the motor will stop.* So, I had to concentrate on dodging the debris. This continued until midnight. With strong winds and snow, it was cold even with a raincoat and a life vest on. Moreover, there was nothing to drink or eat. Though I had not eaten since my breakfast at 6 a.m., I did not feel any hunger. That was probably because I was fighting for my life with all my might.

As it drew close to midnight, I casually looked in the direction of Ishinomaki and noticed in the pitch darkness where there was no electricity, bright red flames some kilometers away. The flames continued until dawn. I later learned that the fires were in the districts of Minamihama-cho and Kadonowaki-cho.

To avoid the strong winds I moved close to an island near Fukkiura and after that I returned to Kobuchihama at dawn. There I again could not believe

Fumio Kimura reflecting on the days following the disaster at Kobuchihama Port

my eyes when I saw the horrific scene in front of me. The community around the Oshika Omotehama Center and the Omotehama branch of the Prefectural Fisheries Cooperative where there had been clusters of homes had vanished without a trace. It was all covered with sea water and great amounts of wreckage. Because of this, there was no place to secure my boat. I was forced to make a U-turn.

I attached my boat to a raft for oyster farming nearby, and spent the second day from the disaster with other fellow fishermen. I ate some instant noodles given to me by relatives. I was thankful for the first meal I had had in a long time.

ALTHOUGH THE LAND was filled with wreckage with hardly any space to walk and the sea water was still up to my waist, I went ashore because I was worried about my family. My house which stood on a relatively high plot was flooded. Not only was I surprised that the tsunami had reached the house, but I truly realized how violent and fierce a tsunami could be.

We were lucky that Hiroki, Naomi and their child who had escaped to higher ground, as well as my wife Kumiko, 51, who had been in the central part of Ishinomaki City when the earthquake struck, were all safe. We were able to meet again in the afternoon of the third day after the earthquake, that is, on March 13.

It is now close to a year since the disaster occurred. My grandchild is now two years and five months old and the second grandchild was born last June. Since our house was damaged, my wife and I now live in a temporary housing unit with my mother Miyoko, 85, and our dog. My son and his family have moved to Wakuya Town. The after-effects of the disaster on our family life are not small.

Presently, I am dealing with liver cancer. In spite of this, my enthusiasm about going out to sea and fishing once again has not waned. In the days ahead, I intend to live life to its fullest, encouraging my family and being encouraged by them. This I will do as someone who was allowed to live when so many of my acquaintances lost their lives in the disaster.

Houses washed away into ocean
First wave engulfs cars

Fumiko Toda
female, 75, homemaker

I encountered the tsunami at Kugunarihama on my way home to Ayukawahama from the Aeon shopping center in the Nagaru district of Ishinomaki City. When I witnessed the horrific scene of houses by the sea being washed away into the ocean, I could do nothing but put my palms together and pray—Please may there be no victims.

THAT AFTERNOON, my art teacher, 89-year-old Kikunosuke Kudo who was also a resident of Ayukawahama, drove me to the Aeon shopping center. Without any sign, an uplifting jolt, the kind I had never experienced before, came from underneath the floor and shot through my body.

I instantly held on to the store shelves. The floor and the ceiling moved in opposite directions, and it seemed that the building was being twisted. The power was so enormous that I was rather surprised that the pillars didn't break. There were people running out of the store. Mr. Kudo said, "Let's run outside," but I stopped him saying, "It's better to wait a while." We went to the parking lot after the quake ceased.

Things were rather calm outside and there were only three or four cars ahead of us when we left the parking lot. We went west on National Route 398 and entered the prefectural road connecting Ishinomaki and Ayukawa. The traffic lights at the crossing in front of Watanoha Station were working and a blackout had not occurred yet.

Soon afterwards Mr. Kudo, who was listening to the news on the radio, exclaimed in an extremely tense voice, "A 6-meter tsunami is coming!" Although we knew that the coastline would be dangerous, we headed for Ayukawa. There were cracks here and there on the road. In some parts, landslides and fallen trees were in our way.

I was worried about the tsunami and was looking only at the sea from the car window. There was no change as we passed by the beaches of Tsukinoura, Momonoura and Oginohama. We drove through the Kozumi tunnel and went past Koamikura safely. As we were driving through Shimizuda to Ohara, Kyubun and Kobuchi, several men tried to stop us but we were so worried about our homes we kept on going.

AS WE WERE GETTING QUITE CLOSE to Ayukawa and approaching the bend before Kugunarihama, I noticed the surface of the sea ahead of us on the right off Cape Kiyosaki had swollen, and the wave came sweeping the mountainside and into the bay. It was the tsunami. The distance between the tsunami and our car was one or two kilometers. Since it was impossible to pass through Kugunarihama, we parked the car on high ground just before the bend.

Again, there were some men trying to stop other cars, but two or three cars ignored them and sped through. When those cars were passing by the pine trees several hundred meters ahead, the tsunami went surging over them. I screamed out loud, feeling as if it was happening to me. That scene is imprinted on my mind.

That was the first wave. I don't remember the exact time of its arrival, but it was over five or six meters high. The tsunami easily reached the shore, entered deep into the Kugunarihama village, and easily lifted up the houses, sending them adrift. The whole scene was like a miniature model set used for making movies. I did not want to believe what was happening in front of my eyes was real.

In a while the tsunami started to draw back. It made creepy and bizarre sounds as it toppled heavy things like power poles and rocks, dragging them to the very rim of the bay. The second and the third waves came and drew back as well.

The fifth wave collided with the fourth that was drawing back and became incredibly high. And when that started to draw back, a group of about ten people who were looking at the sea from high ground sensed danger and ran away in fear. The backwash was so powerful that it swept blocks of the broken seawalls away into the ocean and then revealed the bottom of the bay.

With each wave of the tsunami, the houses afloat in the bay gradually lost their shapes and eventually sank into the sea. *Please, let there be no one left in those homes.* I could only implore as I witnessed that scene.

WE SPENT the night nearby at the home of my former classmate Kimio Goto, 75, which was on high ground. It was too dark to tell what was going on but I kept on looking out to the sea from a window. There were rolls of thunder at times and I was not able to fall asleep.

I woke up at 5 a.m. the next morning. Because the roads around Kugunarihama were scattered with debris, it was impossible for cars to pass through. The alternative would be walking to Ayukawahama, but I had seen on the previous day that a big house was blocking the road. Climbing over it to walk home would have been very difficult.

But Mr. Kudo and I made up our mind to walk and left my classmate's house. The big house was gone. More waves must have come and washed it away to the sea during the night. It was about 8 a.m. when I arrived home. More than anything, I was so happy to be able to see my son, who was also safe.

Barber shop washed away by second tsunami
Restarting as barber at shelter

Tadao Takeda
male, 63, barber shop owner

I was at my barber shop, Barber Takeda, when the enormous earthquake hit. I was putting things away after a customer had left. At the first jolt, I rushed to hold up the shelf where I kept my barber tools with both hands.

MY WIFE, 60, crawled out of the shop. The shaking, instead of settling down, grew even more violent in the middle. *Oh, no!* I thought as I stumbled out the door. I heard the glass break as the shelf that I had been holding fell to the floor.

Things looked ghastly outside. The power poles were shaking and the sidewalks were moving like rolling waves. Because the sidewalks were laid with red bricks, the wiggly movements were even more conspicuous and bizarre. The hard concrete blocks that separated the sidewalk and the road were bent like soft candy and there was a deep crack forming between the sidewalk and the road, which heaved up and down. My wife and I just stood there in disbelief.

My eldest son, 33, also a barber, had been out at Ayukawa Port that day, helping locals with the task of boiling cultivated *wakame* seaweeds. He rushed into our shop with an alarmed look on his face, shouting, "A tsunami is coming! We must get out of here right now."

I had experienced the tsunami from the Great Chilean Earthquake when I was a junior high school student. It flooded our old house up to ten centimeters from the floor. From that experience, I presumed that even if a tsunami of a larger scale ever came, it would be safe if we just went upstairs to the second floor.

My son didn't agree with me. He had seen the waves draw back with such enormous power that it almost revealed the sea bottom. He told us that fishermen who had observed the sight with him had declared emphatically, "The color of the ocean is different. A huge tsunami is coming." My son urged us to go up to higher ground immediately.

We took our cars and left. Just before we left, my son asked what we should do with our family's Buddhist spirit tablets. I answered, "It should be all right to leave them behind." Now, there is nothing more that I regret than the fact that we didn't take them with us.

As we were leaving, our next-door neighbors, a couple who were in their 70s, were getting ready to leave. The husband had started the engine and was waiting for his wife. I said to him, "It seems like we should all hurry!"

IT DIDN'T TAKE more than a minute to get to Oshika Municipal Branch Office on higher ground. We made it there at around 3:20 p.m. Evacuees there were all looking anxiously at the sea beyond Ayukawa Port. It was past 3:30 p.m. We saw a straight white horizontal line on the sea surface between Kurosaki at the tip of Oshika Peninsula and Ajishima Island which is located off the peninsula. "Here it comes!" The screams were very tense.

The white waves approached the shore in no time and went over the seawalls of the port. There was still a long line of cars trying to evacuate to the

Tadao Takeda stands at the site of his former house and shop in Ayukawahama, pointing toward Ayukawa Port from which the tsunami came.

branch office. Among them was the car of our next-door neighbors. Soon the tsunami reached the uphill road to the office, engulfing several cars including our neighbor's.

Later their car was found by the community center to the east of the branch office. Their bodies were found near the car. The car key was found in the husband's pants pocket. They must have gotten out of the car to run when they were swept away. It was indeed a great shock to lose someone you had known for a long time.

The second tsunami wave that came was much bigger—it was beyond comparison. It obliterated the lighthouse. I saw it sweep away my house and shop, which came drifting toward us. Other houses and shops were also drifting in black water, a dark color I had never seen before.

About 100 of us stood motionless, shivering in the cold snow which had just started to fall. At times there were low moans of "Ah. . . ." No one was crying or screaming. We all shared the same sense of helplessness as we witnessed the tsunami destroying everything.

The whirls from the tsunami collided here and there, making complex movements. The drawback started. The houses were falling into pieces as they were carried out to sea.

IT WAS FOUR DAYS LATER when we were able to go back to where our house and shop had stood. There was no trace of the house. Everything was gone, except for my barber chair which was anchored firmly.

When we fled, my son took the minimum necessary tools for barbers with him. I started to hear such requests among evacuees: "I want to get a haircut" and "I need a shave." Some volunteers brought my barber chair to the branch office. I cleaned the chair and on March 23, I opened a temporary barber shop in the lobby on the first floor of the office.

"Oh, it's the smell of a barber shop!" People would say, smiling. I realized that it was so important for us to have some means of getting back to our normal everyday life. It was free of charge, but the work brought back some energy to me. In September, I was able to open a makeshift shop near the branch office.

Drawback of tsunami reveals sea bottom
It reminded me of a scene from the movie *The Ten Commandments*

Toru Sasaki
male, 67, welfare center administrator

On March 11, I climbed Mt. Kinkasan (445 meters), which itself is an island off Oshika Peninsula, with a group of old high school classmates. Thirteen of us had gathered to go on that hike. It was on our way back that we witnessed an incredible and furious power of nature, which had me want to disbelieve my eyes. I feared that the tsunami would engulf the whole island of Kinkasan. I even felt my life was in danger.

HAVING FINISHED our hike safely, we were in the shop by the pier, waiting for a ship to return to Ayukawa Port. Suddenly, we were hit by a violent shaking. Expecting the quake to subside soon, we remained seated in the waiting room, but it grew stronger and stronger. We ran outside as we felt we could be crushed, building and all.

We had to try hard to keep our balance. As I was facing the mountainside, I could see deer running up the slope while the rocks were falling down. With the intensity of the quake what it was, wild animals must have been extremely surprised as well.

My friends said that the shaking had lasted for more than five minutes or nearly ten minutes. In any case, the strength as well as the duration of the quake was something I had never experienced before, and that's probably why I didn't even have the composure of mind to try to listen to the radio.

About 15 minutes after the earthquake started, two of the group members left the port on board a ship returning to Ayukawa Port. The eleven of us who remained on the island, standing near the pier, were thinking about what to do next. Then we heard a loud speaker blaring this announcement: "A 6-meter tsunami is expected to arrive shortly. Please evacuate to higher ground immediately."

WE DETERMINED that we would inevitably be engulfed by the tsunami if we stayed around the pier. We all agreed to evacuate to Koganeyama-jinja Shrine. The asphalt hill road leading up to the shrine had turned into horrible shape.

While going up the hill, a big rock of around two meters in diameter suddenly came falling down. I felt that if we took too much time, aftershocks could trigger more rocks to fall and we could be crushed. The members who were leading the group kindly guided the rest of us, checking the safety of the mountainside and the paths we were taking.

We made our way cautiously, taking a detour around big rocks or going under fallen trees. The left side of the road was a steep cliff facing the sea. At some points, we were forced to move along the edge of the road bordering the cliff. The distance of a few hundred meters to the shrine felt very long.

We managed to go half way up to a point, about 40 meters above sea level, where there was a gently sloping stretch of land covered with grass, commanding an open view. Across the sea on the opposite side was Yamadori-Watashi, the very tip of Oshika Peninsula.

I was able to feel somewhat safe there. We were then looking down at the sea, wondering what kind of tsunami would be coming, when an unbelievable spectacle began. Between the peninsula and Kinkasan, the water gradually started to recede into two different directions, one toward Onagawa and the other toward Ayukawa. We could see the bedrock of the sea bottom. It was rather flat, and now the few hundred meters connecting Kinkasan and the peninsula were only land.

This reminded me of a scene from the movie *The Ten Commandments*, in which Moses guided many people to walk through the sea after it split in two. Is what's happening now for real? I had to disbelieve my eyes.

SHORTLY AFTER THE WITHDRAWAL of the water, gigantic waves, maybe over twenty meters, came surging in from both sides. The two waves with white crests crashed fiercely against each other, producing a huge booming sound. At that moment, the waves turned into a 30-meter-tall partition, completely blocking our view of the opposite shore.

Part of this combined tsnami wave pushed its way to Kinkasan Island as well. Overcome with dread that this force that was beyond imagination could engulf the entire island, we rushed to a spot that was higher still.

The red roof of the waiting room in front of the pier was submerged in water now. The rocky beach nearby was being hit hard by the tsunami waves again and again. Clouds had gathered in the sky—a sign that it would start snowing very soon—turning the surrounding area into a gray world.

WE SPENT THE NIGHT in the office of Koganeyama-jinja Shrine. Snow was blowing hard and the cold was intense. The rumbling from the deep bowels of the earth and the intense aftershocks continued throughout the night, causing the trees to shake. The shrine, however, built in the Meiji period with attention to details, stood firm.

We were provided with plenty of food and drink by the shrine. When the sky cleared, I went outside to see that the stars were like fireflies, shining in the heavens above.

Something like being in awe of nature, if you will, or the smallness of human actions—these were the things that struck me. I spent the night feeling devastated, thinking that outside of this island, too, awful things must be happening.

In the evening of the 12th, we went back to Ayukawa Port on a boat that had been dispatched to pick us up. We spent the night at Oshika Municipal Branch Office. At 6 a.m. on the 13th, four of us started to walk from Ayukawa to Ishinomaki. Every seaside community we passed had practically all the houses completely destroyed. *How many people were killed?* I was in deep despair thinking along the way.

Tsunami walls close in on fishermen
Devastation leaves seaside village in despair

Katsuyuki Atsumi
male, 53, fisherman

When the earthquake hit, I was on my boat in Yagawa-wan Bay. Suddenly, I felt a shock with a powerful uplift, and my body jumped up 30 centimeters. There were landslides everywhere and the high-tension power lines were scattering sparks.

A HUGE TSUNAMI will come.... I went back to the port right away, but the wharf was damaged heavily. At the wharf, my wife Misako, 52, was cleaning up another boat that we owned. I asked her to take care of her father, 76, and hurried offshore to protect the boat.

My house was on high ground on a gentle slope away from the port, about six meters above sea level. *There's no way a tsunami would come up to that level*—that was my assumption.

At three o'clock in the afternoon, I left the port. There were about 50 boats coming out from various ports, one after another. "The further offshore the better." We were traversing the waters between Kinkasan Island to the south and Ashijima Island to the north, and hurried at maximum speed out to the Pacific Ocean. When we almost reached a point midway between the two islands, one tsunami appeared to the north of Kinkasan and another to the south of Ashijima. The two tsunamis came closing in on us, the distance between the two getting narrower and narrower. *We're done for if the two waves meet.*

It was a race against time. My boat was the first to go through the gap between the two tsunamis and the other ships followed, one by one, each clearing the walls of the tsunamis—except for the last two boats; they were engulfed in that great wave that swelled up high when the two tsunamis came together. Later I found out that the owners of those boats were killed. It was truly a hair's-breadth difference between life and death.

ALL THE OTHER BOATS had now reached the open sea off Kinkasan and stayed in groups according to their home port, sailing in circles and trying to survive the second and third waves. There were eight fellows from Yagawahama protecting their boats. My boat's fuel tank had just been filled, and the fresh water tank was also full. I had loaded two dozen cans of juice. I had always thought that I needed to be prepared in case the engine failed and the boat went adrift. We went into the engine room in shifts, where we tried to warm up and dried our wet clothes.

After midnight on the 12th, we went back near the port. All sorts of debris were drifting from the direction of the village. There was no doubt that the tsunami had attacked the village. We all had been calling out to one another trying to hold out against fear, but now all of us had become quieter: everybody was concerned about the whereabouts of their family. My daughter was in Sendai. My son was in downtown Ishinomaki on an errand. At home were my wife and father-in-law.

I sent two young men to the seaside village in complete darkness, and after a while they came back to the boat—both disheartened. "There's nothing. There's nobody." There was despair in the air.

After a long night, we went to the village at six in the morning. There I saw the tragedy that had befallen my hometown. Everything was gone. I found out later that the disaster had claimed more lives in our village than in any other village in the entire Oshika Peninsula. There were 167 residents before the earthquake, and the tsunami had claimed 24 lives. Out of 62 houses, only one house that stood on a hill remained.

"Hey, is anyone out there?" I called out in a loud voice. Then, a few people appeared on the hill, and women followed one by one. But neither my wife nor her father was there. Then a friend of mine appeared and said, "Misako's all right—I saved her." He mentioned her by name. *She is alive?*—I couldn't believe it then.

MY WIFE AND HER FATHER were at home when they were swallowed up in the tsunami. My wife clung to some tree and held out against the strong receding tide, but then she got stuck in rubble and couldn't move her body. She called out for help over and over again. But nobody heard her, and her strength, both physical and mental, was dwindling. She mustered the small bit of strength left in her to call out, "Help me!" thinking that that might be her very last call.

My friend explained that her call was heard by some villagers who were passing that spot in a car. She was pulled out from the rubble by four men. Her leg was injured and she received first-aid treatment in an indoor facility in the neighboring village.

Her father was washed away offshore, and his body was found 50 days after the disaster. My wife had witnessed him being swept away by the tsunami, and the scars in her heart are yet to be healed. I met my son—he walked back. I was relieved from the depth of my heart when my wife's safety was confirmed, but at the same time I felt how ruthless it was that her father had been swept away by the tsunami.

Onagawa Town Hospital had lost its medical instruments when the tsunami reached its first floor, even though it was located on a high hill. So I took her to Ishinomaki Red Cross Hospital, where she had to have 30 stitches on her left foot. It was a serious injury.

Before the earthquake, I made my living by cultivating scallops and *hoya*, also known as sea pineapples. Currently, I am working to make a comeback. There's nothing left in Yagawahama now, but we can't live without the sea. And I earnestly wish to have my home on a high hill.

Muddy tsunami hit rooftop
Diving into torrent to swim for life

Noriko Watanabe
female, 48, fisheries cooperative branch manager

The water kept rising higher and higher, and it was getting closer to the rooftop of the branch office of the Fisheries Cooperative where we had run up to for safety. It seemed that escaping by swimming was the only way we would survive. "You guys don't wanna die here, do you?" Following the former branch manager, we dived into the muddy torrent and swam frantically toward the slope that was about 50 meters away.

WHEN THE EARTHQUAKE HIT on March 11, I was at the Yoriiso branch office of the Prefectural Fisheries Cooperative. The vertical rocking with a powerful uplift turned into big horizontal shaking motions. It was so intense that I would have fallen down if I hadn't been holding on to something. I believe there were a few vistors, but I don't remember how they made their way out. The cooperative members who were in the reception room escaped outside from the front entrance. The former branch manager of the Yoriiso office Yutaka Hayasaka, 52, and my colleague Morinobu Aizu, 28, went back into the office after going outside once, and were going about putting things like the small safe back to where they had been. Hiroaki Suzuki, 30, in the meantime, went out to the wharf to take our office's patrol boat *Azuma* (5.2 tons) out to the open sea.

The siren was blaring, the major tsunami warning had been announced, and I learned that a 6-meter tsunami was expected. I moved my car that I had parked near the office to my home in the village. After I confirmed that my husband, 50, and mother, 70, were safe, I went back to the office, where Yutaka urged me to evacuate to the village's designated evacuation center. After talking for a while with the women in the neighborhood, I became anxious about the office, so I walked back there.

Yutaka and Morinobu were on the second floor of the branch office, and were calling out to the people who were working by the wharf to evacuate. There were still about ten people remaining there. Some people were trying to take their small boats they used for fish farming out to sea, but we stopped them because it was too dangerous.

THE WATER, in the meantime, was rising higher and higher. I remembered that there were some life jackets on the first floor, so I fetched three of them and brought them to the second floor where we put them on. The horns on the cars that were submerged in water kept blaring because they had short-circuited. The tsunami was now hitting the branch office building with the water splashing up high like a water fountain.

We went up to the top of the roof using the emergency ladder. Although I'm acrophobic, I couldn't afford to feel fear of heights at the time. All the houses around us were flowing away making these tearing and splitting sounds. It looked like one of the boats that went out offshore was higher than where we were on the rooftop. The water was about to reach my feet now. A roof that was being carried away landed on the rooftop of our office.

Maybe this is the end—I was about to give up right then and there, but at the same time I was remembering how I had *Azuma*, the co-op's boat, taken out offshore. I regretted what I had done, thinking, *Maybe I have sent Hiroaki to his death*. Later on when I confirmed that he was all right, my tears just wouldn't stop.

With Yutaka and Morinobu supporting me, we made it up onto the edge of the rooftop which was about one meter higher. There was no further escape. "You guys don't wanna die here, do you?" said Yutaka, and we agreed. "We're gonna swim and make for that wooded hill over there."

In the Yoriiso village, the houses were built in such a way that they looked like they were pasted on the steep slopes. There was a wooded slope behind the branch office, and that was where we aimed to swim to. Without any hesitation, I dived into the pitch-black water after Yutaka.

The waves had become calm. I didn't feel the coldness of the water. It was about 50 meters to the slope. I grew up surrounded by the sea and so I should have been good at swimming. But even so, I could hardly move forward. The life jacket that I had put on was under my jacket and had slid somewhat, making it hard for me to swim. I tried to hold on to some floating buoys, but that didn't work. Then Yutaka knocked down some bamboos and other trees, and I could hold on to them and manage to touch the ground with my feet. Morinobu was having a hard time, too. "Noriko, I can't get there!" This time, it was me who found some bamboos to thrust over to Morinobu, and Yutaka and I were able to pull him up out of the water. When we all got up out of the water, we could see the water swirling around by the spots where we had swum across.

Noriko Watanabe and her colleagues on the rooftop of the Yoriiso branch office building of the Miyagi Prefectural Fisheries Cooperative. Photo taken around 3:15 p.m., March 11, 2011

"We made it!"—we stood there stunned, but then the next moment, the cliff right next to where we were came tumbling down. If we had been a few minutes later, we would have been caught in the landslide and killed.

THE THREE OF US walked to the house of Morinobu, who is also my cousin, and we got out whatever clothes we could find and changed into them. Just when we were heading to the evacuation center at the elementary school, I could see my own house breaking apart and getting carried away by the tsunami. Along the way we met an elderly woman from the neighborhood and took her with us to the school.

The wife of the chief of the local fishery co-op's steering committee found me and said, "We need to prepare meals now!" This helped me to remember that I was also the head of the women's association of Yoriiso. I set about the task of preparing food with the help of the other people who had evacuated to that place.

Family carried away offshore, house and all
Spending night on drifting boat

Kyuetsu Abe
male, 57, electric appliance shop owner

I was heading to an auto garage in Ogatsu-cho in Ishinomaki to have my car checked. The jolt came with a powerful uplift, and I knew instinctively—a tsunami will be coming. *I turned around to go back home while the shaking continued.*

AT THE TIME, there were six members of my family at home—residence and shop combined—my wife, 57, oldest son, 24, and second son, 22, both of whom worked for the family shop, daughter, 18, who was in high school, third son, 16, also in high school, and my mother, 83. We decided to split up and move the truck and cars up by the mountain. We parked a few of our vehicles in the front yard of the home of our friend Hisashi Sugiyama, 57, since it was closer to the mountain than Wakaba-Yochien Kindergarten, a designated evacuation center. All our family met up at the Sugiyama home.

The volunteer fire company's vehicle was going around announcing, "A 10-meter tsunami is coming!" My oldest son, a member of the fire company, had just come back from closing the floodgate by Ogatsu Hospital, and said, "I could see the seabed out toward the open sea when the water receded."

Standing just outside of the entrance to the Sugiyama home, I was looking out toward the bay, and heard this roaring sound from far away. The sound increasingly became louder, and then down below by the residential section of the town, a spray of water rose.

"Run to the mountain now!" shouted Sugiyama, and he started to run. The mountain was about 100 meters away. That was impossible for my old mother. So I said, "Go up to the second floor!" and all seven of us rushed to the staircase in the Sugiyama home. There was a woman from the neighborhood walking nearby, and our second son took her by the arm and brought her upstairs, too. When we got out onto the terrace which faced the bay, we saw houses being swept away in a continuous stream, making creaking sounds. The water had risen so much that it almost reached the balustrade of the terrace.

I yelled, "Go inside!" but in just a few seconds the water rose up nearly reaching the ceiling of the second floor. My two older sons climbed up on the roof and didn't get wet, but the rest of us were all swallowed up in the water. I was frantically struggling to help the others, but then the house floated up gently, and my feet touched the floor. I helped my daughter and the youngest son to go up on the roof, while the rest of us—my wife, my mother, the neighborhood woman and I—stood on the terrace where the water covered us up to our stomachs.

THE HOUSE was getting swept away now. When it got out in the bay, there were lots of house roofs and lumber floating there, covering over half of the surface of the water. Each time an aftershock hit, there were ominous rumblings from the bottom of the sea, but I wasn't afraid as I had confidence that we would survive.

The house was slowly rotating as it headed out to the open sea at the speed of about 20 kilometers per hour, keeping a distance of about 100 meters from the Karakuwa and Mizuhama districts on the opposite shore. I saw some people on land. I could hear my second son on the roof exchanging words with them—"Do you have any ropes?" "Try and jump onto the boat there!"

Ahead of us I could see a child—perhaps elementary school age—riding on a refrigerator that was floating. I wanted to rescue him, but he was too far. My wife was calling out to him, saying, "You try and hang in there!" when a muddy torrent came smashing into the house we were in, together with a heavy piece of square timber, 50 by 50 centimeters. That was another of the tsunami attacks. Those of us who were out on the terrace got shoved into the house, where we struggled desperately for our lives. When my head came out of the water, the child could no longer be seen, and half of all the houses that had been floating were gone.

We decided to climb up to the roof. I had my wife and everyone else stand on my shoulders, and then my sons pulled them up. Luckily we found six or seven blankets and two futon mattresses sealed in plastic bags—they were floating in the room—so we took them up to the roof. The roof was of copper and we moved along by placing our feet against the snow stops. Our clothes had absorbed water and were heavy and cold. We held each other and, putting the blankets over our heads, covered ourselves up in them. The house was being swept farther and farther offshore. And then it started to snow. As I could see the Shiroganezaki lighthouse at the tip of Ogatsu Peninsula, we must have been carried about four kilometers out to sea.

WHEN IT WAS STARTING to get dark, an unattended 3 to 4-ton boat came drifting our way and it lined up right alongside of the roof we were on. There was an engine room the size of a tatami mat (90 by 180 centimeters) on the boat. Although the engine didn't work, we judged that we could spend the night there. We laid down the futon mats and eight of us squeezed in there and sat down like packed sardines.

"Is anyone in there?"—around 5:30 p.m., we heard a man calling. It was Masaharu Yamashita, 51, the owner of the neighborhood fish shop. He was drifting on the roof of his own house. The house was then carried farther away from us, but an hour later we were near each other again, and he jumped onto the boat and joined us. We were so glad and we hugged each other.

THE TSUNAMI CONTINUED throughout the night, and the boat drifted along with it, surging and receding, about 15 minutes each way. It bumped into the wharf many times and ran aground as well. Since I was shivering too much from the cold and couldn't go outside, Yamashita maneuvered the boat for us all night using a bamboo pole.

In the morning, the ship was drifting near the damaged wharf in the Ojima district. We managed to get closer to the wharf by rowing with bamboo poles. Around 20 people gathered to cheer us on, and they tied a rope to a fishing rod and threw it to us. The rope was tied to the boat and they pulled it until we finally made it to land. We were able to warm ourselves in the house where the Ojima residents had taken shelter.

Kyuetsu Abe and his family drifted on this fishing boat the night of March 11. They landed at this wharf in Ogatsu-cho Ojima.

Over a third of Shin-Kitakami-ohashi Bridge collapsed, cutting off the shortest route connecting Ogatsu and Kitakami. The bridge appears in stories that start on pages 175, 178, and 184. Photo taken at Kitakamicho Hashiura, Ishinomaki City, around 2:40 p.m., March 18, 2011

Motorcoach washed up on top of Ogatsu Community Center. Tsunami increased in height as it surged onshore through Ogatsu Bay. Photo taken at Ogatsucho Ogatsu around 10:50 a.m., April 6, 2011

Mother disappears in whirlpool
Water roars as it recedes

Kiyonori Naganuma
male, 51, aquaculture industry

It was the peak of the season for harvesting wakame seaweed. In the morning we had gathered in seaweed in the fishing grounds near the Shiroganezaki lighthouse. In the afternoon, we were at the fishing port ready to start loading the seaweed onto pickup trucks with a forklift when we were struck by the extraordinarily huge earthquake.

THE FORKLIFT STARTED BOUNCING AROUND like a basketball. *I can't afford to get injured*—I ran away from the spot. After a while, the quaking stopped, and I looked over at the breakwater in the bay. I could see a current like a whirlpool forming near the far end of it. *This earthquake is different from all the other ones before. A big tsunami may be on its way.* I had a gut feeling that something terrible was in store.

I saw a man working on a fishing boat far out in the bay, 200 meters away from the shore. I shouted at him, "Get out of there! A tsunami is coming!" I wanted to warn him and everyone else in my community. So, to call out to the whole district, I rushed to the fisheries treatment plant where there was equipment for community broadcasting.

Soon a major tsunami warning was announced on the local disaster radio system. I quickly drove my car to Tachihama where my fishing boat was, and secured the boat tightly with rope so that it wouldn't be swept away.

WHEN THE EARTHQUAKE OCCURRED, my father, 77, mother, 75, and wife, 51, had been working hard at removing the stems of *wakame* seaweed in the shed next to our house, which was located on high ground approximately 30 meters above sea level. During the earthquake, many things had fallen down in the shed so they decided to go outside since it was dangerous, and then headed to the fishing port.

My parents then pulled their boat (0.7 ton), which had been taken onto land, upwards to an even higher spot and secured it with rope. Meanwhile, my wife carried the containers that were outside into the fisheries treatment plant. When I came back from the Tachihama area to the fishing port, around 20 people were watching the sea with uneasy looks on their faces.

As the minutes passed, the water level gradually rose. People started to run toward an incline about two meters wide in the middle of the district that led to higher ground. Someone—I don't know who—shouted, "Get out now!" "Run, run!" When we reached a point 20 to 30 meters from the sea, my father said, "I left something in my boat," and he ran

Kiyonori Naganuma points to the spot where his parents were swept away by the tsunami. Kuwanohama district, Ogatsu-cho

back toward the boat alone.

I guess my mother was concerned about my father so she split from the people heading toward higher ground and waited in the garden of a house. Then, with a roaring sound of the sea and bizarre sounds of splitting and breaking, a tsunami rushed in toward us carrying houses and other objects on its way. My father, who had gone back to his boat, was engulfed briefly by a big wave but he managed to hold on to a nearby electricity pole. Then, by chance, his own boat floated by so he grabbed its side for dear life and was swept away.

The tsunami sweeping into our village made a roaring sound as it began to recede. It was an almost unearthly sound. The quick currents carried a lot of debris away to the sea in an instant. Fortunately, the boat that my father had clung on to was lodged on top of a house. I could see my father and prayed—*Please let him be alive!* Before I called out to him, several people who had been around and had seen the whole situation developing rescued him by spreading a ladder from a nearby parking lot to make a bridge. My father was dazed and shivering from being submerged in the sea water for quite some time.

I, TOO, COULD NOT STOP shivering and trembling—I was witnessing for the first time the sight of a massive tsunami and its horror. As the tsunami retreated, my mother, who had been clinging to a piece of debris, was washed away by a muddy current. She was unable to swim. "Hold on!" "Hang in there!"—Several dozens of people at the parking lot, including those who had saved my father, all raised their voices to encourage her. But we could not even hear her screaming, "Help!"

What is happening now? Is this a dream or is this really happening?—I wondered to myself. *I'll jump into the water and save her. I have to do something*—but my body froze. I couldn't do anything. I just stood there dumbfounded.

I don't know how many minutes passed. I could see the water swirling before my eyes and then, sucked into the whirlpool, my mother vanished. *What a failure I am as a son!* I felt guilty for not being able to save my precious mother. *That despicable tsunami!* My kindhearted mother, who raised me with loving care, is unaccounted for even now.

Hamlet becomes remote island
Five who won't be returning home

Senichiro Suenaga
male, 62, fisherman

It had been very windy from the morning that day so I quit harvesting wakame *seaweed, the task that I had started from the day before. Our house was 15 meters above sea level and located near the very back of the Tachihama hamlet, which consisted of 47 households. The earthquake happened after I had finished washing my car in the yard.*

SINCE I WAS the deputy head of the Ogatsu-cho volunteer fire company, I put on my uniform and helmet immediately and went down to the beach. There were 11 or 12 members gathered from the Tachihama fire brigade there. Based on my intuition as a fisherman, I knew without a doubt that a tsunami would come.

Our fire company had a manual detailing how to respond to giant earthquakes and the residents of our area had had routine drills to evacuate to higher ground. After telling the residents to evacuate, we firefighters broke up into small groups and went around closing the tide gates of the seawall and the gate doors of the entry to our fishing port. Even though the beach was small, there were 11 gates. At the time, we thought that all of the 110 or so residents had managed to evacuate.

We stood near the seawall as long as we could, looking out at the ocean. I think it was around 3:25 p.m. that the sea surface came rushing up with irregular movements. The wave swelled and swallowed the offshore breakwater, and then came over our fishing port.

"RUN AWAY!" We also ran from the road alongside the beach up to the nearest high ground. The wave cleared the seawall behind us, and was falling down to the road. After we had reached higher ground, all I could do was watch what was happening. Even before the first wave had subsided, the second wave arrived. *Oh, please stop coming. Let this be all the damage there is*—we could do nothing other than pray. But, our hopes were dashed when the third and fourth waves followed. It wasn't the crest of the waves that attacked us, but the relentlessly rising water level. It made such an incredible noise as it swallowed houses and turned them into nothing but debris before our eyes.

After it became dark, we went over the mountain ridge and headed toward the evacuation shelter. We all evacuated to a Shinto shrine first, but since we felt it was dangerous to be there, we ran up to the house standing at the very back of the hamlet. Actually, the only places in the whole area that had not been touched by the tsunami were that particular house and another one that was vacant at the time. Practically the entire first floor of my house was also flooded. The car I had just bought and my pickup truck were also damaged beyond repair.

About 50 people evacuated to the shrine at the other end of the beach. It was only after the next day or so that we realized some people were unaccounted for. Eight residents from Tachihama were either dead or missing. Three of them fell victim to the tsunami outside of our hamlet and the other five within our community. One of the five victims had evacuated once but returned home for reasons we do not know, and went missing. The owners of the sole shop in the hamlet, a parent and child duo, stayed on the second floor of their shop-cum-home, thinking it would be safe, but the whole building was swept away with them in it. In the house just below ours, a woman and her 95-year-old grandmother, who had trouble with her legs, could not evacuate in time. The woman's husband was swept away in front of the entrance door, but he managed to cling to a tree in my garden. My wife, 55, says that she saved him by throwing him a rope used for oyster farming and towing him in. In the end, it was the weak and the ones who didn't take the tsunami seriously enough that lost their lives.

THE FAMILY whose house was at the very back of the hamlet took in 50 evacuees and shared everything they had. But soon their provisions ran out. And the rooms in their house were packed with people. So on the second night after the earthquake, we split up, with some people staying in the vacant house that had not been ruined by the tsunami and others on the second floor of my house. We didn't have enough blankets for everyone so we spread the styrofoam debris that had washed up across the floor to survive in the cold.

The hamlet of Tachihama was surrounded by water and became a remote island—a solitary island on land. The rescue services were not able to

Senichiro Suenaga's house, center of photo, had the entire first floor flooded. On the left is the next-door neighbor's house where the residents evacuated to. Tachihama, Ogatsu-cho

reach us. We heard that relief supplies had somehow reached the city's sports and event arena, known as Big Bang. On the 13th we discussed procuring supplies via the river, using some of the boats that we had collected from the debris that still seemed usable. We thought we might be able to go to Iinogawa by entering the Kitakami-gawa River from Oppa-wan Bay after going around Ogatsu Peninsula. Later we heard that the conditions of Oppa-wan Bay and Kitakami-gawa River were not safe enough for boats to sail through. However, without any material support, even the people who had survived the earthquake and tsunami could not live much longer. So three people got on a boat and set off into the sea of debris.

But from what I heard, the boat engine broke down in the sea off Osu and they were not able to travel any further. There were many things floating in the sea, so we had been worried about the boat getting tangled in the debris and that fear came true. But a Maritime Self-Defense Force vessel found our boat and our members told them about the dire situation in Ogatsu. They promised to give support to both Minamisanriku Town and Ogatsu.

Three days after the tsunami, I was able to go to the Ogatsu Disaster Response Headquarters at long last. From that moment on, I ran around helping wherever I could and rarely returned home for two months straight.

Muddy waters reach high ground
Men rescue elderly woman

Shoji Sanouchi
male, 66, civil engineer

On that particular morning, I went to the ophthalmologist and returned home around noon. An incredibly strong quake struck when I was relaxing at home with my sister Kikuko, 84. I shivered with fear; it was a kind of shaking of the earth that I had never experienced before.

I STOOD near the entrance of our house. It was swaying a lot so I thought that it was too dangerous to stay inside the house. I shouted to my sister, "Run quickly! You need to get out of the house!" My sister who had been cooking stew at the time immediately turned off the gas and was clinging to the sink. She came crawling out of the house after she heard me call out. Inside the house, things on the wall and shelves such as the clock, pictures, and mounted turtle had fallen down. But thankfully, we were not injured.

After the shaking had stopped, I took my sister out to my vegetable field on higher ground, which was about five to six meters away from our house. Major tsunami warnings were being announced on the disaster emergency wireless system. I ran around to other houses where our relatives and neighbors lived. "Are you there? Granny?" "A tsunami is coming! Evacuate to the field right now!" I called out in a loud voice, checking to see if they were okay or not.

I don't recall how much time had passed. High waves started coming across the Ogatsu Bay. An unbelievable, unprecedented spectacle was unfolding before our very eyes. *This can't be true*—at the sight of the violence, I shuddered with fear once again. We witnessed the tsunami engulf the houses in the areas directly opposite from where we were—from the Isehata district to the Shimo-ogatsu and Kami-ogatsu districts. Ships and cars were also swallowed by the wave. I don't know how to express the sounds of crashing, splitting, and the roaring that I had never heard before. The tsunami rotated everything that should have been in the central part of Ogatsu and pushed them toward Misosaku, the interior of the bay.

THE FIELD that we had evacuated to was about ten meters up on higher ground, but muddy waters reached us. It was sleeting. There was an elderly couple in their 80s who were trying to climb, hand in hand, up the slope behind their house. They looked

Shoji Sanouchi points to the spot in a green field where the woman in the story was rescued. Funato, Ogatsu-cho

as if they had come to the end of their physical strength. The man yelled, "Give us a hand!" About ten residents had evacuated to that field. Four men grabbed the woman's head and arms, trunk, and legs and heaved her up to the field. She was completely soaked and was shivering with cold, but an expression of relief came to her face now that she was safe. Her husband managed to climb up by himself and was also safe. If the men's rescue attempt had been a few seconds later, she would have been swallowed up by the tsunami. *I'm so glad*—momentarily, everyone's expression softened.

I was so focused on the rescue, that I did not have a moment to take any notice of my house. By the time the woman was brought up to safety thanks to the cooperative effort by the locals, my house, which was nearby, had been completely swept away and had vanished. There was no anger, regret, or sadness. I was just dumbfounded. An overwhelming feeling of frustration hit me.

We decided to spend that night in the only remaining vacant house located in the highest area of the district. There was no food and nothing to drink. But luckily we had futon and blankets, and although they were worn out, we shared them among us. In spite of this, we still felt the cold so in order to warm ourselves, we went into the woods to collect firewood. We made a fire with a cigarette lighter we happened to find. However, we just couldn't fall asleep because of the fear of tsunami attacks and the hunger in our bellies. The men took turns to keep the fire going throughout the night.

We residents who had gathered together were worried about the safety of a man in his 80s and a woman in her 50s who had not been seen around since the tsunami engulfed our town. The woman's body was found later but the man is still missing.

WHEN THE LONG NIGHT finally ended, I was flabbergasted by the scene of our hometown which had totally changed. In the middle of the town there were only the reinforced concrete buildings left standing—structures like the elementary school, the junior high school, the community center, the hospital. The rest was all gone, swept away by the tsunami backwash.

My older brother's house was nearby, and his house just managed to remain standing. He shared with us a big pot full of uncooked rice, which had been soaked by the salt water. We found a pot among the debris and drew water from the mountain runoff to cook the rice. The rice balls we made were exceptionally delicious. That evening rice balls and other provisions reached us at last. From the fourth day after the earthquake, we spent one week in a shelter, the waiting room in a nearby crematorium. Then we moved to the Iinogawa First Elementary School gymnasium. At the moment we live in a temporary housing unit built in the Ishinomaki city's sports park along the Oppa-gawa River.

Man swims across waters with floating log
The tsunami was like Niagara Falls

Michio Komatsu
male, 72, former chief of volunteer fire company

The big quake started with a fearful rumbling of the earth. I was doing some paperwork at the funeral home which I managed in Ogatsu-cho Isehata. Holding the computer and the bookshelf with my hands, I was hoping earnestly that it would stop soon.

ALTHOUGH THE ACTUAL DURATION of the shaking was a few minutes, I felt that it had continued for about ten minutes. At the same time, my intuition told me, *A big tsunami is coming.* Then I received a phone call from my second daughter, 44, who lives in Tokyo. "Dad, are you OK?" The moment I responded, the line was cut off. I was glad that we could exchange words albeit only for a moment.

Around that time, a 6-meter major tsunami warning was being announced over the local emergency wireless system. What crossed my mind then were the members of the volunteer fire company, closing of the water gates and guiding the locals to evacuate to safety—it was a sense of mission in me. Every year we had conducted drills to prepare for a possible major earthquake off the coast of Miyagi, but I was disoriented for a while because of the overwhelming massiveness of this earthquake.

But I composed myself and put on my uniform and helmet. I drove to the municipal branch office, a few minutes away by car. The electricity and telephone line were both out at the office. Volunteer firefighters gathered in front of the garage-warehouse building next to the office. We could hear a fire department member announcing, "The tsunami is expected to be ten meters." Sensing danger, we went up to the open-air space on the second floor of the garage-warehouse and braced ourselves against the tsunami.

LOOKING TOWARD THE BEACH, I could see an ebb tide of about two meters. Taking this as a sign that a big tsunami was coming, I made an all-out effort urging the residents to run to higher ground.

I think it was just before 3:30 p.m. The water came over the seawall and rushed in. Trees and cars could be seen getting closer and they collided with each other, making huge sounds from the impact. Looking at houses starting to be washed away, I wished again and again that it was a dream.

The open-air space on the second floor where we were standing was 3.6 meters from the ground. The water level rose in a flash, coming to only 30 centimeters below where we were. The floor material there was tin and it had bulged up stiff from the pressure of the tsunami. We had no time left.

Of the six people that were together with me, three escaped to the storage room on the second floor, while the rest of us decided to climb onto the rooftop of the two-story structure. The roof was about 3.6 meters from where we were. I was the third one to go. I put my foot on the storage room door knob, and the last member pushed me up.

The force of the tsunami became increasingly strong, and the last member got his right foot caught in the storage room door. We grabbed his arms and clothes, making a desperate effort to pull him up. Water started to enter into his mouth, and we were about to give up hope, thinking *It's over*, when at that very moment, his foot came out and we were able to save him. This must be what is meant by the expression, "a narrow escape from death." The three who had gone in the storage room moved up to the rooftop, climbing up from a window.

THE ROOFTOP was no longer safe, now that the water had come up to our waist level. If a violent drawback came, the seven of us would be sucked right into the bay, and that would be the end. I made up my mind to swim over to the mountain in the back which was ten meters away, and waited for the best timing when a wave rolled in. At that moment, a log about one meter long came floating

Central area of Ogatsu was submerged. Photo was taken in the late afternoon of March 11 from the high ground near the foot of the mountain where Michio Komatsu evacuated to.

right in front of me. As I look back now—it may be strange to think such thoughts—I think that somebody must have thrust it over to me.

I made my dive into the sea. Perhaps because of the air that was inside of my long rubber boots, my body overturned in the water. While I didn't have to struggle for air, I felt my life was in danger. I quickly held on to the log and got my body set right. I had a strange feeling that maybe the log was there because of a favor of some god or the spirit of my ancestors. I kept my hold on the log and made it to the mountain in the back. The rest of the group had also swum to safety, and I was the last one. I was so relieved.

Making our way through vines in the bush, we climbed up to high ground at the foot of the mountain. Looking toward the municipal branch office, the surging wave had the force to nearly reach the roof of the office, but in the next moment, the drawback replaced it. The water was very violent; it was like Niagara Falls.

Around 4:30 p.m., four other people—elderly and children—joined us. The snow was falling and it was getting increasingly cold. All there was to put in our mouths was mineral water. In order to survive the night in the mountain, we gathered a lot of wood to make a fire. When that was used up around midnight, we went to gather more. Sounds of debris creaking in the darkness echoed from the sea. "Help me, please!"—cries for help reached us any number of times. There was nothing I could do and only time passed ruthlessly.

ABOUT FIVE O'CLOCK the following morning, some of us went down to the branch office by using a ladder. After a meeting among the fire company members held in front of the branch office, we started our actions, keeping top priority on saving people's lives. Because of the shortage of food and fuels, all of us fire company members were hungry and exhausted, but we were able to find 78 bodies.

It is regrettable that four of the firefighters lost their lives while being engaged in emergency actions immediately following the earthquake. I retired as chief of the volunteer fire company in June, but I remain grateful to the members for their strenuous efforts when they themselves were disaster victims.

Tsunami attacks school from two sides
Teachers save stranded woman with rope

Shigeru Tamura
male, 59, Okawa Junior High School principal

It was the day of our graduation ceremony. We finished the ceremony smoothly in the morning and after seeing the graduating students off with the school staff, 7th and 8th graders had left school as well. Teachers and other staff members who remained at school were busy with their own work, paperwork and other matters.

I WAS HAVING a little break in the principal's office when that singularly extraordinary quake struck. It was the strongest and the longest that I had ever experienced and made me think *This is no ordinary event.* Five of the framed portraits of the past Parent Teacher Association presidents fell off the wall, and the covering of the fluorescent lighting on the ceiling almost came off.

The entire school building rocked fiercely. I heard voices calling out, "Got to run!" and "Let's get out." We ran outside to the school yard for safety. Cracks ran in certain parts of the yard and a big gap appeared between the yard and the steps leading up to the front of the school building.

Although the shaking had subsided, we stayed in the yard for a while to see how things would go, afraid that aftershocks might follow. Then in order to get information about the earthquake, I went over to the parking lot to turn on the radio in my car, but I couldn't get any details.

Soon after, I instructed the teachers to check for damage to the school buildings. They found that a big drop had appeared in the second-floor corridor connecting the main building and the gym. Then four of us—assistant principal, a teacher, an administration office staff member and I—went to the gym in an effort to contact the city's board of education using the emergency hotline, but only a recorded message came on. The line was probably congested.

WE GAVE UP trying to reach the board of education and were about to go outside the gym, when a terrible roaring sound of the earth arose. The assistant principal opened the gym door, and there a tsunami was surging toward us over the embankment by the school that was as much as four or five meters high. "Water!" screamed the assistant principal, and shouted at us to run away. We ran up the stairs, went through the connecting corridor and headed for the second floor of the main building.

The rest of the teaching staff had already evacuated to the second floor. When I looked outside from the second floor, an unbelievable sight jumped into view. Rice fields stretched out beyond the school yard, but on the east side, the embankment that was behind a small hill by the school had been breached by the tsunami and a pitch-black wave was making its way toward us, pushing houses in its path, looking like it could engulf that small hill.

The school yard had turned into a river, and the teachers' cars floated up ever so easily and were carried away in the blink of an eye. The school building was being pinned by the tsunami from both sides now. The fierceness of the tsunami was such that it appeared that the whole school building could be carried away. *Is all this for real?* I could do nothing but stand there dumbfounded.

Then I found a woman who appeared to be in her 40s or 50s, calling out for help. She was clinging to a street light that was by somebody's yard, located between the school and the embankment. The force of the tsunami was increasing and she was in a dangerous situation. "Hold on!" "Hang in there!" The teachers continued to call out encouragements from the second floor of the school.

WE WANTED to go and help her, but couldn't because the water level continued to rise. She was about 30 meters away from us. Then it started to sleet. The woman lost her strength and let go of her hold of the street light. However, after being carried away, fortunately she got a hold on a tank that was in front of the school and clung to it. We could almost reach her now. The teachers thought hard to find a way to rescue her, and they found a rope that was over ten meters long, threw it toward her from the home economics room on the second floor, telling her to tie it around her body. After making sure that she had wound the rope around her several times over her soaking wet clothes, the teachers yanked at the rope with "Here we go!"

Since the woman had been in the water for some time, she looked extremely emaciated and was uttering repeatedly, "It hurts!" The teachers made an all-out effort to rescue her, bearing the pain in their hands that came from pulling on the rope.

The rescue process probably took 15 or 20 minutes. The teachers worked all together and saved a person's life. "I'm so glad you're safe now!" "Are you all right?"—they were saying to her. The woman said in her faint voice, "Thank you so much."

After rescuing her, we took down the door to the home economics room, used it as a stretcher to carry her, and took her to the martial arts gym where there was a tatami* floor and she changed into a judo uniform there.

We lit candles we found in the science room and spent the night there. The female staff members rubbed the woman's body—she was shaking from the cold—and kept encouraging her. There were some seasonings in the home economics room but no food, and we had to make do with what little snack food there was.

Morning came. The water had started to recede, but the water level in the school building was still over 1.5 meters. Since a helicopter could not be utilized, city firefighters brought over two pairs of rubber boots instead. Starting with female staff members, all the school staff evacuated to the embankment in twos with the firefighters guiding us. At last, expressions of relief came to our faces as we realized that we had survived.

*tatami: See note on p. 078

Saving two girls stranded in school
Making path with boards for barefoot girls

Hiroshi Sasaki
male, 63, fisherman

I fish freshwater clams in the Kitakami-gawa River for a living. On that day, I was at my fisherman friend's place in Ogatsu-cho Ogatsu, helping him make new rafts since some he used for cultivation had been destroyed by the tsunami triggered by the earthquake two days earlier on March 9. We were on land preparing ropes when the shaking struck. Cracks ran along the concrete seawall right in front of us.

WE STOPPED our work and were wrapping up when we heard the local emergency wireless announcing a major tsunami warning. I helped my friend and his wife, both in their late 60s, run up to the nearest hill. A while later, a big wave of over 20 meters came barreling in. I thought *How can a tsunami be so huge?* The ocean had swelled up and came surging in, reducing everything in the town of Ogatsu to rubble.

Around 5 p.m., we walked for about ten minutes over hills and moved to the Ogatsu Funeral Hall, a municipal government facility. It was crowded with 100 or so evacuees. A man who had his car parked outside let me spend the night in it.

The next morning I headed by foot for the Ogatsu-toge hill pass on National Route 398 aiming to get home in the Harioka district. After walking through the rubble that had once been a town, I reached the fork where the hill pass diverged from Route 398, and there I saw people who had evacuated from the town at a loss as to what to do. While there, I found a man in a small truck who was going over the hills to the Kamaya district and I got a ride with him. When we came out of the tunnel, the plain that we looked down on was like a sea.

When we reached a spot the locals call "*sankaku-chitai*" (triangle area) by the Shin-Kitakami-ohashi Bridge, we found, to our distress, two bodies, presumably the bodies of kids who went to Okawa Elementary School. In a small truck that was there, we saw corpses of two men. The Magaki hamlet embankment had disappeared, and I could see some people who were taking cover on the second floors in a few houses that had survived. In the far distance I could see my own house standing next to Okawa Junior High School. I was worried about my family.

THE TOWN OF KAMAYA was gone. The only buildings left were those of Okawa Elementary School and Kamaya Clinic. There an old classmate who was also a resident of Kamaya ran up to me and said that he had heard some voices when he called

Okawa Elementary School—one week after the tsunami struck

out toward the elementary school. The two of us and another person who happened to be there headed for the school. After pushing our way through debris and deep sludge, we reached the school and went up to the second floor. And there, in a severely damaged classroom were two girls, huddled together, shoulder to shoulder. They were shivering with one towel that they had found somewhere, which they shared by covering themselves. While they looked relieved when we talked to them, it seemed that they could hardly talk even if they wanted to. The stranger and I took off our jackets and helped the girls put them on.

We took them outside, but the girls couldn't go further with their bare feet, which must have been numb because of the cold. "We're nearly there, so keep up your spirits," we encouraged the girls to keep on going. We found some boards that the girls could step on and laid them in their path so they could walk, and this enabled us to barely get to the triangle area.

From what they told us, the girls were students from Okawa Junior High School, and they were at home in Kamaya after the graduation ceremony in the morning of the 11th. They were carried away by the tsunami toward Okawa Elementary School, but fortunately they were able to grab on to something like a rope or wire, which enabled them to stay inside the school building.

Later on, four or five nurses and a patient from Kamaya Clinic walked by themselves to the triangle area.

I LEFT THE TWO GIRLS at a nearby auto repair shop that had escaped damage, and then headed for my own home. Around noon, what remained of the embankment in Magaki was starting to emerge above the surface of the water which had covered the area, and I was able to walk on the embankment and finally made it to my home.

The tsunami had gone over the embankment in front of Okawa Junior High School as well, but the embankment itself was not breached. My wife, 59, had taken shelter on the second floor where she was safe. From what she told me, she first heard a strange sound of some movements—a sound she had never heard before—so she went outside in the yard, and then saw a pitch-black crest of a wave shoot upstream over beyond the river bank. At first she thought it was a black cloud that was traveling in the sky. It wasn't until after the very tip of the wave had come over the river bank in front of the junior high school and surged up to her feet that she realized that it was actually a tsunami. She then ran to the second floor of the workshop.

My oldest son, 38, had witnessed the massive tsunami running upstream in the river from the top of the river bank at a place called Yachi. After encountering the earthquake in the Watanoha district, he headed back home and was almost home when he saw the tsunami. "The wave came advancing like it was a wall on the river," he said. He also said that he could see the water that came out from the breached embankment in Magaki flow into the rice paddies around Fujinuma Pond. He immediately drove his car up a forest road and escaped the danger.

While many lives were lost in the Okawa district, it was fortunate that I was able to help save some people, if only two, at the elementary school.

Tsunami attacks from two different directions
Stranded residents rescued by fishing boat

Shigeo Ogawa
male, 62, fisherman

My house is located near the waterway that connects Nagatsura-ura Bay and Oppa-wan Bay. March 11 was the last day of shipping cultured oysters from Nagatsura-ura. I had finished work for the day and had just returned to the dock in front of my house, when I felt this shock—a sudden and powerful uplift from the bottom of the boat.

THE BOAT WAS IN FACT TOSSED UP about 30 centimeters. The extremely strong and long shake had made people come out of their homes and onto the streets. My mother, 82, and daughter, 34, were among them. I was sure that a tsunami would follow.

I had another boat, which was anchored in the fishing harbor, and, because of my nature as a fisherman, I was worried about that one as well and ran toward the harbor in the Oppa-wan, two kilometers from my house. I didn't even get halfway there because of fallen rocks that were blocking the street. I went back home once, and then headed out to the harbor again with two fellow fishermen.

There were two anglers on their way home from the harbor who were also stuck on the street. We joined up and the five of us pushed aside a huge rock and finally made our way through. I got to the harbor, and after anchoring my boat 20 meters away from the wharf, I returned home.

The radio was warning of a 6-meter tsunami. I assumed it would actually be about four meters, taking into account the level of the spring tide at its lowest, which made the sea level two meters lower. I thought my house was high enough to be all right though its foundation might get flooded. Although I had just anchored my boat at my home dock, I decided to move it to the innermost area of Nagatsura-ura Bay just in case. Then I walked home.

JUST AS I REACHED HOME, the first wave of the tsunami came flowing through the pine woods on the other side of the waterway. It didn't seem so high, but the second wave was high enough to engulf the pine trees that were at least ten meters tall. But then there was this other wave, black and muddy, that came from a different direction—over the seawall from the direction of the Nagatsura district. No sooner did the water reach my feet than it began to rise higher and higher. Just as I decided to run up to the second floor of my house, a woman from my neighborhood drove off toward the Onosaki-bashi Bridge. But the water pushed her car back, and it ended up getting stuck on a power pole in front of my house.

Despite the water being up to my neck, I managed to grab hold of the car and pull her out. Together we held on to a palm tree in my yard, waiting for the water to subside. Looking back now, I suspect that before the tsunami reached the Onosaki area, it had gone up the Kitakami-gawa River first, hit the mountainside (on the northern shore of the river) beyond the Nagatsura district, and came flooding in our direction.

I'm not sure how many minutes we were holding on to the palm tree. Once the water stopped flowing, we waded across the water and got into my house. My next-door neighbors had fled to their second floor, and they offered to have the woman who was with me stay there. I went up to the second floor of my house and changed to dry clothes. I kept myself warm with a kerosene heater which my daughter had prepared for an emergency. I had bottled water and enough emergency food supplies for one day.

I was worried about my wife, 59, who was visiting a sick relative in Higashi-Matsushima City, and my son, 30, who had gone to central Ishinomaki. It wasn't till much later that I found out that they were safe and then I was relieved.

THE NEXT DAY, I went to check my outboard which I had anchored in the innermost part of Nagatsura-ura Bay—I found it had landed on top of a pile of debris. After dragging it down with the help of my friends, I set about rescuing people trapped in houses or left stranded on piles of debris. I recovered the body of a preschooler from my neighborhood. In the Onosaki district, the tsunami had killed three adults and one child. The number of casualties was relatively small considering the magnitude of the tsunami, but it is nonetheless painful to think about each person.

I think there were around 60 to 80 people at Kaizoan, a Buddhist temple designated as an evacuation shelter in the Onosaki district—there were more evacuees there than at other places. I talked with some of the leaders of the district, and we decided that five of us would take my boat and head inland to make a request for rescue for the isolated Nagatsura and Onosaki districts.

We sailed across rice paddies which had turned into a sea, and then went through a breached levee into the Kitakami-gawa River. When we sailed up the river to the Magaki district, we saw some firefighters and other rescue workers up on the levee. We made a request for kerosene for heaters, fuel for outboard motors, food and other supplies. We then started our shuttle transport from there. A full-fledged rescue attempt by three helicopters started on the fourth day after the earthquake.

If the tsunami we experienced really is a once-in-a-millennium event, it means that for many generations hereafter, people will live their lives without experiencing something like this. It is for that reason that I think it's important to pass down the story of this disaster for posterity.

Tsunami swallows homes in Nagatsura district
Collapsing in tears while holding body in arms

Hisaji Nishimura
male, 63, fisherman

I had just finished filing an income tax return on the second floor of the Kahoku branch of Ishinomaki City Hall, also known as Big Bang. The extremely powerful lateral shaking had me conclude that this one was no ordinary event, and the thought of a tsunami attack came to mind.

I RUSHED OUTSIDE and jumped into my work truck. There was a landslide by Nakano-Maginosu-mae on Prefectural Route 197 running along the left bank of the Kitakami-gawa River. I took the other street to the north that ran along the Saragai-gawa River and got to the Shin-Kitakami-ohashi Bridge. An aftershock hit while I was going over the bridge, but I managed to get across in spite of the truck being tossed about.

The streets in Kamaya weren't crowded. I stopped by my daughter's (38) house in Nagatsura but found no one there. I hurried to Onosaki, where my house was. When I looked to the left, I saw a big white wave approaching. As I was passing the Onosaki-bashi Bridge, I noticed that the bank on the other side had dropped some 40 centimeters below the bridge. "Clunk!" I ignored the big shock that the truck sustained and drove on, shouting, "A tsunami's here!"

I found my father alone in my house. We were running out of time. I shouted to him, "Go up the hill behind!" Then I saw him climbing up the emergency ladder that was fixed on the concrete wall on the hill behind. I parked my truck near Onosaki Nursing Home and took to the evacuation path which led to higher ground. There were about 60 residents of the area there watching the sea. I learned that a bedridden woman was still in her house 100 meters away. Four of us men set out to rescue her.

We rolled her up in the futon bedding she was resting in, tied a rope around it, and carried her to a Buddhist temple on higher ground called Kaizoan.

THICK BLACK WATER came across Nagatsura-ura Bay from the northeast, engulfed houses in the Nagatsura district with roaring and tearing sounds, and struck the mountain on the south, debris and all. Then it rebounded in our direction, swelling high with all the debris that it carried. At that moment, I heard knocking sounds from the parking lot just below the evacuation path. There was an elderly woman left behind in a parked car. The car was swallowed in the tsunami once, but it came floating back up in a short while. I thought we might still be able to save her, so two of her family members and I went into the water. We swam over to the car and broke a rear window with a hammer. We pulled her out, but she was already dead. We carried her to Kaizoan Temple. She was the only person who was killed in that disaster in the Onosaki district.

After sunset, everybody evacuated to the main hall of Kaizoan Temple. Two kerosene heaters were lit, and people were huddled together—covered in blankets— in groups of ten, but there was no way we could sleep with the continuing aftershocks. I made a fire by the evacuation path and watched the condition of the sea until about 10:00 p.m. I heard voices crying out in the darkness from the direction of Nagatsura-ura Bay and saw some lights that might have been flashlights.

ON THE SECOND DAY, the sea was still swirling even after it became light. The bank on the other side of the Onosaki-bashi Bridge had been gouged by the tsunami, and that area had become part of the sea. The Onosaki district was isolated now.

Choosing places where the water had subsided, we made our way through the debris looking for people needing rescue. As we went toward the back of Nagatsura-ura Bay, we found a man on the wreckage of a roof. When I called out to him, he moved his hands up and down. There were mounds of floating debris blocking access. We found a small boat with a broken engine, and the four of us, volunteer firemen and I, paddled over to him using wooden sticks and planks we found. He was a 70-year-old resident of Nagatsura. We asked him, "Are you all right?" but he was too exhausted to produce any voice. He must have been there all night long. We carried him to the bank nearby and had him sit by a campfire.

As we looked around more, we saw something moving in the distance. It was a dark human shadow on a roof with a chimney, which rested on a mound of debris. We found a boat with a working outboard engine and went in it to his rescue. Along the way we found a young child's body floating on the surface. As we picked the body up into the boat, I saw that the face looked just like my grandson's—my first daughter's 5-year-old child. It turned out to be a different boy from Nagatsura, but at that time I had taken him for my own grandchild and I collapsed in tears while holding the body in my arms.

After a while, I remembered the person on the roof, so we started the boat again. It was a woman in her 20s from the Nagatsura area. Her feet had started to get frostbitten. There was a place on the bank nearby where some volunteer firemen were on standby with a campfire. We took the woman there so she could warm herself. These rescue efforts couldn't have been made without the cooperation of the people who were there. We took the boy's body to Kaizoan. We looked after it carefully and I stayed by it during the night.

ON THE THIRD DAY, helicopters arrived in Natatsura with relief supplies, and taking people to the Iinogawa district for shelter began. It was during this time that I learned from an acquaintance that my grandchild was safe, and I finally realized that the body I had found was not my grandson. I heard later that he had fled to the mountainside in Nagatsura with his grandmother. On the fourth day, I went to my relative's home in the Magura district where I got to pick up my grandson in my arms. I was overcome with emotion, and again I couldn't help but break out in tears.

Aquaculture farmer hangs from tree branch
Too busy struggling to feel any fear

Takashi Oyama
male, 73, aquaculture farmer

I was swallowed up in the tsunami at the fishing port in Aikawa, which is located in Kitakami-cho Jusanhama in Ishinomaki City. I barely survived by swimming to the roof of a warehouse and by clinging on to tree branches. I was fortunate because one lucky condition followed another and I was able to survive without any injury. I'm living a full life now.

ON MARCH 11, my wife, 72, my daughter, 35, and I were processing harvested *wakame* seaweed in the workshop just below our home which overlooked the fishing port of Aikawa. Suddenly, we were struck by this jolt that shook us sideways. It was so long that I was repeatedly picking up things that had fallen from the shelves.

As soon as the quake subsided, I rushed out to the fishing port to move my boat away from the wharf to anchor it. I went about these steps to prepare against the tsunami according to the old adage "When an earthquake hits, be ready for a tsunami." However, I had in fact not taken it to heart, thinking *No big deal*. I didn't hear any tsunami warning, either, for that matter.

I had just taken the seaweed boiler out from the shed by the wharf and was putting it on top of the seawall just to be sure that it would be kept from getting wet. At that very moment, a tide came surging unexpectedly. I hurriedly jumped up on the seawall, thinking that perhaps it was a high tide water—it hadn't occurred to me yet that a tsunami would actually be coming. The water level, however, kept rising. Just as I got down from the seawall thinking that I had to escape, a big wave came over me and I was completely under water, head and all.

I took off my rubber boots in the water, and then popped my head out. All around me was the sea. A forklift's wooden pallet came floating my way, so I grabbed it with my left hand and paddled the water with my right hand. Black waves surged over the breakwater one after another, closing in on the inner port. I swam in the direction of the mountain to the north of the port, going with the flow of the wave.

I SAW A FAMILIAR-LOOKING HOUSE being swept away—it was my own house. It went straight through the gap between breakwaters out to the open sea. A propane gas cylinder went flowing past me making these hissing sounds—I prayed that it would not explode. The idea of death didn't come to mind then because I had safely escaped from a capsized ship before.

In front of the mountain, all I could see were two small fishing boats and the roof of a fishing co-op warehouse that was about ten meters high. As I got closer, I could see that the boats were stuck up on a power pole next to the storage room. One of them had a tangled rope on it, so I put my foot in it to climb into the boat. I was relieved thinking that I had survived. But then, with a shove from the wave, the boat's bow stabbed the warehouse roof, and I could hear these breaking noises. Now the stern was lifted up by the wave and the boat was tilting at an angle of almost 45 degrees. I sensed danger and jumped onto the roof.

"Boom!" From under the roof, I heard an explosion, and the tin roof broke apart time and again. The fishing buoys that were kept in the warehouse apparently burst through the roof since there was no way out when they were shoved by the invading wave. Later, I was terrified to imagine what would have happened had they burst directly under me, but at the time I was too busy struggling to feel any fear. I sat down on the ridge of the roof, but then the water level rose so I had to stand up right away. Eventually the water engulfed me.

I STRUGGLED TO THE SURFACE and when I managed to stick my head out, there were zelkova tree branches hanging down by me from the hill behind the warehouse. I grabbed one of these branch-

Takashi Oyama with the warehouse he swam to in the background, Aikawa Fishing Port, Kitakami-cho Jusan-hama

es in desperation. I wanted to hold on to the trunk of the tree, so I tried to pull on the branch while swimming, but then the backwash started. It went out extremely fast and there was a strong tugging at my feet. I barely managed to hold out against it, and when the water had receded, I found myself hanging from the branch. I held on with all my strength, but eventually ran out of stamina and released my grip.

As I was falling down, there happened to be a big branch that extended out horizontally in my downward path, and I grabbed it instinctively like you would the horizontal bar. My hands grew tired again, though, and I had to let go, but there was still another branch in my falling path, and I had to hang once again. I ran out of strength this time, too, and had to let go, and fell down in the bush behind the warehouse. Fortunately, there were no bamboo growths there and I sustained no injury even though I was in my stocking feet. I was truly lucky.

I climbed up the wooded mountain—almost a crawl up the steep hill. I had leaden feet from the cold and exhaustion. A man in his 80s, who was watching the condition of the sea, found me all wet. "You're going to die if you stay in that condition," he said and took me in his small truck to his house that was on high ground. I was shaking and I couldn't even answer his inquiries. He gave me a change of clothes, lit the heater and poured me a cup of coffee. I got warmed up there and finally felt I was safe. While there I was told that my wife and daughter had safely escaped, much to my relief. I really didn't realize what had happened until he told me that it was a big tsunami.

House after house swept away in whirling waters
Warning neighbors to evacuate

Kiyoshi Oyama
male, 62, fisherman

On the day of the tsunami I had loaded rice onto my pickup truck, taken it to a rice mill and had it polished. That finished, I was returning to my home in Aikawa village facing Oppa-wan Bay when all of a sudden I felt an intense earthquake. I had never felt anything like it before, and stopped my pickup. I started the truck again, and carefully drove home even though the initial earthquake tremors didn't seem to stop.

THE LAND WAS STILL SHAKING boisterously even when I reached home. *A tsunami must be coming. There is no reason for one not to come!* In front of my house, around ten people were working on a waterworks job. I told them, "You need to evacuate!" But they responded, "Okay, after we finish this job," showing that they did not recognize how dangerous it was. I firmly declared, "A tsunami will definitely come!" and urged them to evacuate.

My mother, 84, was at home by herself. I urged her to go upstairs to the second floor for the time being. I was planning for us to evacuate together to the Kumano-jinja Shrine on the hill in the back of our house afterwards.

The first thing I did was to move my truck to higher ground. Then I ran to as many houses as I could around the neighborhood, telling everyone to evacuate. I ran as it was much easier to go around from house to house that way. An elderly woman in the neighborhood was on her way back home. She said to me, "My daughter-in law and grandchild might be at home." I told her to go up to the hill, and went to check her house to see if anyone was there. No one was there. Then, there was the house where two elderly people lived, the house beyond the lot where the mother and sister of my wife, 61, lived, and other homes—in any case, I went around everywhere searching for people who had remained and called out to tell them to evacuate.

I returned home, and the next thing I had to do was to take my mother to the Kumano-jinja Shrine up the hill. With her weak legs, it was hard for her to climb up the steep zigzagging stairs of the cliff leading up to the shrine. A resident whose home was halfway up the hillside came down and helped us. I was deeply grateful for his kindness.

The disaster emergency wireless system was forecasting a tsunami of six meters in height. *If that's the case*—I appraised the situation. *My house is about five meters above sea level and the foundation is one meter high. Even if the first floor is flooded, the second floor should be okay.* I asked other evacuees to take care of my mother and went back to my home to move the valuables in our home up to the second floor. When I finished doing that, I felt relieved and returned to the hill behind the house. That's when I saw it. When I looked back to the bay I was astonished by the sight of seawater retreating back behind the breakwater.

FIFTY-ONE YEARS AGO I saw the undertow created by the Great Chilean earthquake and tsunami, but that was no comparison to what I was seeing. The amount of water receding now was probably three or four times more than what I had seen before. The reefs usually show only the top of the rocks over the horizon of the sea. This time they jutted out like mountains in the seabed, while the crest of a huge wave was approaching from a point past the cape. I could see two of my fellow fishermen at the fishing port where the ships were docked. I screamed out at the top of my voice, "Get away from there! Run!" They narrowly escaped to higher ground.

About thirty minutes after the first jolt, the humongous tsunami struck. The waves engulfed the seawall, came over to the village, and swallowed up the fisheries cooperative building and post office. The water level rose as the waves rushed in over and over again. This water must have merged with the water that flowed through the tunnel from the opposite side on National Route 398—from the hill on the left-hand side—creating swirls of seawater in which houses floated up, and they were starting to be swept away, my own house among them. . . .

My father had once told me that my home had previously been destroyed by the 1933 Showa Great Sanriku Tsunami, with only the pillars left standing. My family continued to live in the same place by constructing a high stone wall. We had a new house built in 1996. How could the house be washed away so easily? I was watching the situation from the middle of the cliff with a dozen or so other evacuees, but the approaching water was within two or three meters from our feet. Thinking that the place wouldn't be safe for much longer, we decided to climb the stairs up to the area within the Kumano Shrine grounds. It was snowing before I knew it.

The tsunami had flooded the bay and then began to pull back out to sea. The strong undertow had washed away even the highway bridge. I heard the incredibly loud noise of objects crashing. The force of the tsunami was amazing. I still can't forget the color of the dark black waves that attacked us, scooping everything from the bottom of the sea and hurling them around.

IT WAS EXTREMELY COLD, too cold to spend the night in the shrine. Behind the shrine is a settlement of about 30 houses, built by those who relocated themselves after their community had suffered damage from the 1933 Great Sanriku Tsunami. We locals call the settlement "the Collective Area." We walked on a footpath leading from the shrine, heading for the Aikawa Childcare Support Center located in the area. The houses in the Collective Area on higher ground were unharmed, and we were warmly received and helped by the residents. I really appreciate their kindness. Each family brought us things such as heaters, blankets and futons so that we could warm ourselves.

From those families who were using the old-style wooden stoves or propane gas stoves, we could borrow some of their cooking equipment. Fortunately I was able to cook the rice that had been loaded onto my truck and distribute food to people.

Afterwards, one after another, evacuees joined us at the childcare center, including those who had taken shelter at the city's sports park on a hill. About 230 people in total gathered together. I was made Vice-Chairman of the Steering Committee in charge of the shelter, and we somehow were able to make it through our days of communal living as evacuees.

Now I am living in temporary housing, but I still want to live in Aikawa again. I hope for the development of a new residential area on high ground in the back from the beach. I'm wondering if we can have a mass relocation of our village, something like a "Heisei Era" collective relocation. Isn't it a pity to let the area go downhill by leaving it without such facilities as schools, fisheries cooperative and post office? I wish to create a new Aikawa and live there.

Screaming to pupils, "Run up the hill!"
Graduation ceremonies on the street in six different venues

Seinosuke Katakura
male, 59, Nakatsuyama-Ichi Elementary School principal

At the time of the tsunami, I was working in Aikawa Elementary School. On that day I was watching five or six children in the lower grades waiting for their parents to pick them up by the road near the sea. All of a sudden we were hit by a terrible earthquake. It was extraordinary.

STAY COOL, I told myself and rushed to the spot where the children were. Out of fear, they were crouching down on the spot and shaking. Some were crying. Hugging them, I tried to lift their spirits by saying, "It's okay. It's okay," and "Your mom's coming to pick you up." Before long, cars began to arrive one after another and the children got in the cars.

I headed to the playground and children came trotting out of the school building to evacuate. Our teachers were busy calling out names and checking the number of students. In order to receive up-to-date information, one of the teachers moved his car into the playground. On his car radio a tsunami warning was broadcasted. The school yard became tumultuous, with the matter of handing over children to the parents who had come for them. The faces of both children and teachers were white with fear.

"In any event, go to the shrine."—At Aikawa Elementary School we had a firmly established tradition for teachers and children to evacuate to the shrine on the east side of the school building in times of earthquakes and tsunamis. (The shrine was located on high ground approximately as high as the third floor of the school building.)

We had only just taken refuge in the shrine during the March 9 earthquake two days previously. Because of the high level of disaster awareness based on such experiences, we evacuated to the shrine just as the emergency procedures manual instructed. After seeing off 51 pupils whose parents had come to pick them up, all of the remaining 23 pupils and 13 teachers evacuated to the shrine approximately ten minutes after the earthquake.

LOOKING DOWN BELOW, we soon saw blackish water overflowing from the Aikawasawa-gawa River, which flows immediately in front of the school, and swelling tsunami waves advancing toward us. It was a terrifying sight. The cars in the parking lot that belonged to the teachers and the houses located between the coast and the school were swept swiftly along and the loud noise of the houses crashing into one another could be heard. Seeing the scene that defied description, I instantly thought, *It's too dangerous to stay here. We need to get out of this place.* "The hills! Climb up the hill!" I cried in a loud voice, and instructed the assistant principal, "Please take the lead and have everyone climb up the hill."

During previous evacuation drills we had gone up to the shrine, but we had never gone through the cedar forest on the steep slope. On that day, however, escape was given top priority. We crawled along the ground in the dark going along paths that were not really paths while shouting, "Turn right!" and "Go toward the right!" We were aiming for the Childcare Support Center, where Aikawa Junior High School used to be, up on the hill.

As we were going up, we came across the proprietors of the shrine, a parent and child twosome in their 80s and 60s, who had come out from their house. With a male teacher guiding them and pulling their hands, they climbed up the slope frantically. Even though the distance between the shrine and the Childcare Support Center would be about 500 meters if we measured it as a straight line, I think the distance we actually walked was about one kilometer. The whole journey took about 20 to 30 minutes but somehow, we made it to the Childcare Support Center. With no time to take a breather, I asked the assistant principal to make a roster of the children. *I wonder if the children we handed over to their parents are okay.* I was worried sick about those who were not in front of me. In the childcare center, there were blankets and provisions such as rice balls. We were lucky to be able to spend the night there.

THE NEXT MORNING, I visited our school and what appeared before my eyes was a school building that had been mercilessly transformed. I was flabbergasted by the unbelievable scene.

It was during this time that information reached us—"A first-grader boy is missing." It was a child whose grandfather had come to pick him up from school. Swept away by the tsunami, he still remains missing. This is the only thing that I bitterly regret.

On March 16, five days after the earthquake, a state of confusion still existed in the community as well as in the schools. After agonizing over what to do, I decided to hold a graduation ceremony for ten of our pupils despite all that had happened. I went around to six districts such as Kotaki and Omuro and held a graduation ceremony on the street. Although there was no diploma, I told the children, "Congratulations on your graduation." Some of the children shed tears, undoubtedly feeling joy but also dealing with mixed emotions.

The teachers sang the school song at the top of their lungs. The ceremony turned out to be one held in a drab area without the usual festive curtains or flowers, but it came to be a moving graduation ceremony of tears, tears, and more tears.

Bridge girders swept away by wave's impact
Rice paddies and villages becoming just like sea

Yasuo Sasaki
male, 53, building contractor

When I was driving along the left bank of the Kitakami-gawa River near Magura to go to my bank in Iinokawa from my house in Kitakami-cho Hashiura, I felt a tremendous convulsion.

THE ROAD HEAVED about 30 centimeters, no, it was more than that, making it impossible to drive. On top of that, the shaking continued for a long time. *With the tremors continuing for this long, I'm not too sure that my home is okay.* The embankment that I had just travelled on had huge cracks so I searched for detours along the hills and somehow made it home.

I heard the disaster emergency wireless system making announcements and when I heard the words "tsunami" and "six meters," the broadcast went dead. *Could it be that the Kitakami Municipal Branch Office might have been destroyed?* I told my parents to evacuate in their car to Nikkori Sun Park which was designated as an evacuation shelter or to go up to higher ground on the hill, and I saw them off.

My wife, 54, who worked at Ogatsu Hospital had a day off and was resting at home. "I must go to the hospital. Please take me there," she asked me. I tried to stop her, saying that a tsunami was surely on its way, but she didn't listen to me. She simply said, "I must go," so I finally decided to drive her to the hospital.

Soon after leaving the house, I ran into the son of a former classmate of mine. He was walking around aimlessly, holding his family's Buddhist spirit tablets. I stopped my car and spoke with him for a couple of minutes. "You should evacuate to Mr. K's house," I told him, "It's a sturdily built house that I made." Then I started to drive away. I thought that when the tsunami came he would be safe if he was on the second floor.

I CANNOT FORGET the scene I saw when I came up to the embankment. I saw the crest of the tsunami, in all likelihood somewhere around Tsukihama, located by the estuary four kilometers downstream from where I was. I thought, *This is getting risky.* The only place high enough to escape was the roof of the Municipal Kitakami Mizube Center near the Shin-Kitakami-ohashi Bridge. It was a facility that displayed materials concerned with the local reed fields and the natural environment of the area, and it had a rooftop observatory. I drove one kilometer at full speed on the embankment and parked the car right next to the Center, and just dashed up the stairs with my wife. Ten people had already arrived there.

As the tsunami was about to finally reach the bridge, there was a small car about to cross it. We all cried out, "Go back!" as loudly as we could. The driver eventually noticed our cries and started pulling back but when he reached the embankment, the car began to float and drift in the water. I thought he was done for, but luckily he drifted over to the Center, got out of his car, and climbed up to us.

Looking back now, I realize that our lives may have been saved because I stopped the car once and chatted to someone for a few minutes. If I hadn't stopped, we might have been in the middle of the bridge when the tsunami arrived.

REGARDLESS OF OUR ESCAPE, the largest wave to assail us came after that. I'm pretty sure that it was the third wave. I was afraid we might be swept away along with the Center. However, we all huddled together in the center of the rooftop observatory and kept our heads down while we clung to the iron railing with both hands. Crash! The horrible sounds that pierced our eardrums—However, there was no sign that the building structure under our feet would be swept away. The waves seemed to have run through under the roof by half a meter. Raising my head, I could see a part of the girder of the Shin-Kitakami-ohashi Bridge was gone. Shortly after 5:00 p.m. when it was starting to get dim, I decided that it was probably safe to get down to the ground. The rice paddies and villages that had been protected by the levee were altered completely, and now resembled the sea.

We decided to head to Nikkori Sun Park up on the hill for the time being. Along the way, I could see that the embankment road asphalt was peeling and there were a few perilous places that were difficult to pass because they had been gouged out leaving holes and gaps. Because of my job as a carpenter, I went down the embankment wherever the footing was bad and helped everyone walk down. We finally arrived in Nikkori Sun Park when it was quite dark. I looked for my parents using the light of my cell phone, but they were not there. *Where the hell are they?*—I was worried, but I had no choice but to stay put until the morning.

A few hours passed and food was distributed to us. For two people there was one rice ball and one 500-milliliter bottle of juice to share. It was not enough, but I heard that the city officials who had survived the tsunami since they had not been in City Hall's decimated Kitakami Municipal Branch Office had somehow arranged this meal. I really appreciate their efforts.

THE NEXT MORNING, we walked on the road along the hills and when we finally got close to home, we were reunited with my parents, who had come back home by car. After being sent off by me, they had set off for my uncle's house in the Saragai village. However, many neighboring residents gathered there, too, so they took off for my sister's house in the Koyo-cho district of Ishinomaki City and spent the night there.

Since then, we stayed at the shelter at Hashiura Elementary School for more than a month. Thinking about it now, it wasn't such a long time. I might have felt that the time there was short because we were all struggling hard to live. Even now, when I recall the violence of nature, I feel a chill go down my spine.

II
Onagawa Town

Damage Report of Onagawa Town (as of end of December, 2013)

Casualties	
Dead	591 (including 22 related deaths)
Missing	258 (including 255 officially declared dead)
Peak number of evacuees	5,720 (March 13, 2011)
Date all shelters closed	November 9, 2011
Extent of inundation by tsunami	
Inundated land area	3 km^2
Municipal land area	65.8 km^2
Population of inundated area	8,048
Number of damaged homes	**Number of homes**
Total collapse	2,924
Partial collapse	349
Partial damage	661
Total damaged homes	3,934
Total homes before earthquake	4,411
Temporary housing	
Number of temporary housing	1,234 (1,285) units
Occupants	2,792 (3,201)
Houses/apartments as temporary housing	409 (480) units
Occupants	1,024 (about 1,300)

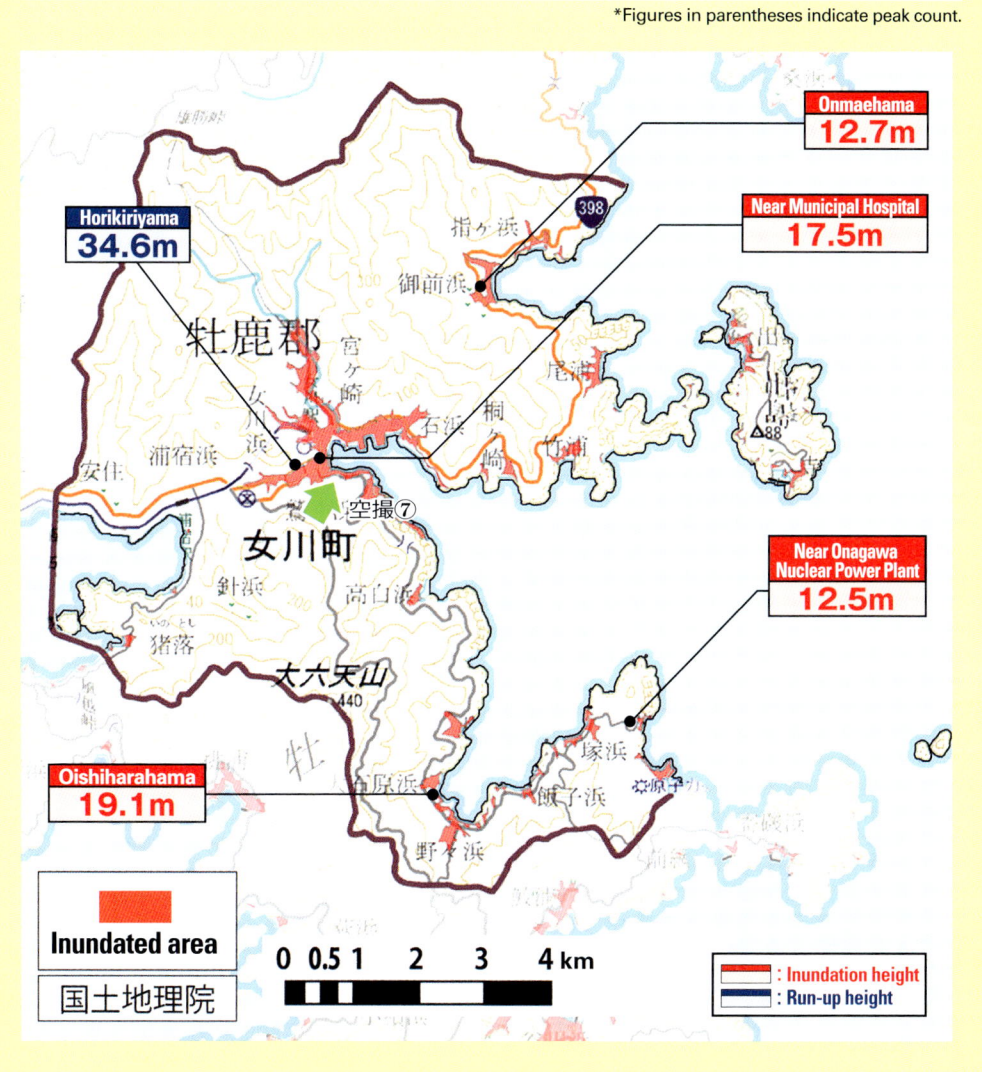

*Figures in parentheses indicate peak count.

- Onmaehama: 12.7m
- Near Municipal Hospital: 17.5m
- Horikiriyama: 34.6m
- Near Onagawa Nuclear Power Plant: 12.5m
- Oishiharahama: 19.1m

Inundated area
国土地理院

0 0.5 1 2 3 4 km

: Inundation height
: Run-up height

Aerial view ⑦
Central Onagawa

In post-disaster photo, reddish brown field at top left is athletic track field of Onagawa Town. Next to it right front is Onagawa Daini Elementary School. (Photos Top: August 2002 Bottom: April 5, 2011).

Onagawa Town

Onagawahama
- General Gymnasium
- Onagawa Second Elementary School
- Onagawa First Junior High School
- Onagawa Station
- Town Hall
- Onagawa Town Community Medical Center (Municipal Hospital)
- Kumano Shrine
- Onagawa Fire Station
- Marine-Pal Onagawa

Koganecho

Washinokamihama

Onmaehama

Oura

Izushima Island
- Onagawa Fourth Elementary School
- Onagawa Second Junior High School

Shimizucho

Onagawahama
- Onagawa Station
- Town Hall
- JR Ishinomaki Line
- Urashuku Station
- Onagawa High School

Takenoura
- Route 398

Washinokamihama

Mangokuura

Onagawa Bay

Onagawa Nuclear Power Plant

Chased up antenna tower by tsunami
Capsized fishing vessel came bearing down

Kazuyoshi Noda
male, 42, Onagawa Fire Station firefighter

A designated tsunami evacuation building, the Onagawa Town Fire Station was engulfed by the waves. One colleague was killed and two went missing. I am alive today, and the only reasons are that I was lucky and that many people helped me.

I WAS ON THE SECOND FLOOR OFFICE of the fire station which was near Onagawa Port when the earthquake occurred. It was an intense lateral shaking that lasted long. Eleven members—including the off-duty members who joined us—took on different responsibilities for the necessary contingency operations, and went about the tasks of making safety checks and moving the fire trucks up to higher ground.

While moving two of our cars—one equipped with a loud speaker and the other for emergency dispatch—to Onagawa First Junior High School which was on a hill, we called out to people to evacuate to higher ground.

Around 3:10 p.m., when we had returned to the fire station and had just confirmed that none of the locals had evacuated to the fire station building yet, we heard these dull, dragging, roaring sounds. I went up to the second floor balcony facing the harbor, and saw the water level rising as if the sea was bubbling up like a spring. The water engulfed five or six cars before it came surging into our garage on the first floor.

I called out to the three colleagues who were in the office to go up to the rooftop with me. Then I realized another staff member who should have been there on duty was missing. Although the first floor of the fire station was about the same height as the second floor of a standard home, it was already immersed in water.

The level of water was rapidly rising, forcing the four of us to climb up the ladder on the antenna tower, which stood above the staircase. A colleague and I sat astride a public-address speaker, while the other two hung on to the ladder. We were approximately 15 meters above ground. Water was rising to the waists of the two at the ladder who were below us. On the rooftop of Hotel Suzuya which was near the fire station, there were four or five people. All around us was the sea now and the only things we could see were the third story of the Onagawa Town Hall building and the fifth floor of Onagawa Town Lifelong Education Center.

In a short while, a capsized fishing vessel about ten meters long came bearing down on us, showing its blue bottom. Just when I braced myself for the collision, the tremendous impact sent us flying into the water.

IS THIS THE END? Just then, a styrofoam box used for packing fish came floating, and I clung to it desperately. When I got my head above the water, I could see one of my colleagues hanging on to a board.

I was starting to be carried away while holding on to the box. It was the speed of a bicycle ride. The surface of the water was hardly visible as it was filled with rooftops of houses, ships and pieces of wood.

I was hit by rubble again and again and nearly got squashed between two roofs. It was fortunate that I was wearing my helmet. I switched objects to cling to every time I saw something that looked stronger, such as a log or a piece of debris. I had to do this numerous times until I finally climbed onto the tin roof of a house that I collided into.

About 20 minutes had passed since I was thrown into the water, and I had been carried to the Shimizu-cho district, about 1.2 kilometers inland from the harbor to the north. Only the fourth floor of a municipal apartment building was above the water. *I can jump to that building if the course stays the same.* I was waiting on the roof for the right timing and just as I was about to jump, the backrush started, powerfully drawing me back at the speed of over 30 kilo-

Up front: remnant of antenna tower of Onagawa Fire Station that Kazuyoshi Noda climbed up
Center back and left back: Onagawa Town Lifelong Education Center and Onagawa Town Hall. Both had only top floors above water at peak of tsunami attack.

meters per hour. I couldn't keep standing.

As I looked for a place where I could jump to the hill, there was a steel beam sticking out sideways from the Miyagi Prefectural Nuclear Emergency Preparedness Center. As the roof I was on was about to pass the Center, I jumped and hung on to the beam. Luckily, a small fishing boat was stuck between the Center and the neighboring Environmental Radioactivity Research Institute of Miyagi, forming a bridge between them. I walked over the boat and reached the rooftop of the first floor of the Institute, but the water was running too fast for me to go over to the hill.

Then I heard someone calling out to me from the rooftop of the Center. I went back there and climbed a steel frame up to the rooftop. There were about 15 people including staff members of the Center and some locals. I felt relieved there but then a woman looked at me in surprise and said, "Your leg is badly hurt!" The pant leg over my right thigh was torn and the tissue of my thigh was gouged. I had been so desperate to survive I hadn't felt the pain.

We decided to call out for help to the firefighters who were at Onagawa First Junior High School that was up on the hill in front of us, so we all started to shout and blew whistles. After continuing this for over 20 minutes, somebody finally noticed us. Two of my colleagues came down with a ladder and a rope to rescue us. We waited for the water to recede and climbed up the hill.

I COLLAPSED into a car. My hands and feet were numb because of the cold. I was taken to the temporary first-aid station set up at the municipal gymnasium, where the school nurse from Onagawa Second Elementary School gave me first aid treatment. It was a serious injury that required more than 40 stitches at a later date, but the dedicated attention I received at the time put me at ease. I didn't feel any pain, but I couldn't go to sleep because of the cold. I was worried about my family.

The next morning I was carried on a stretcher to Onagawa's municipal hospital—about 20 locals offered to take turns lifting me over heaps of rubble. I was grateful that I was being helped by many people when I should have been the one to save people. My eyes overflowed with tears.

I underwent four surgeries after that. I was getting increasingly frustrated over not being able to engage in rescue operations, but finally returned to work on June 6, 2011. Since then, I have been trying to find as many missing people as possible. Thankful that my life was saved, I am determined to keep improving my skills through training in order to protect the lives of citizens.

Waiting out tsunami perched on ladder
Dozens of cars falling as if in waterfall

Kenichi Hino
male, 41, Sea Pal Onagawa administrative clerk

Anticipating a tsunami, I ran into a building facing the sea. But the water rose so quickly that I had nowhere to escape. I went up a ladder which I spotted on the rooftop of the building and waited out the tsunami. I could do nothing but pray that no more high waves would come.

WHEN THE EARTHQUAKE occurred, I was in the office of the Sea Pal Onagawa Steamships which also had a waiting room for passengers. I had just started working at the company as an administrative clerk on March 1.

The big quake hit suddenly with a powerful thrust upward. I was desperate to hold and keep documents and other things from falling from the shelves. The long-lasting shaking eventually settled down. I learned from the TV that a major tsunami warning had been issued.

I called on some ten customers who were in the waiting room to evacuate. The *Shimanagi*, a 62-ton cruiser owned by our company, headed out offshore in order to avoid the tsunami. Even though I knew a tsunami would definitely follow such a big earthquake, I still had time. I moved my car which I had parked by the pier to the parking lot of Onagawa's municipal hospital that stood on a hill, and walked back to the office. The pier had caved in and our small company car, stuck in a gap, could not be moved.

After locking up the office, I evacuated to Sea Pal One which was behind the office and was part of the tourist facility called Marine Pal Onagawa. I climbed up the outdoor stairs to the balcony on the second floor with seven colleagues.

THE SURFACE OF THE SEA had started to recede quietly, exposing the stakes which supported the pier. *A great big tsunami will come,* I thought, but no one mentioned anything about leaving the building and moving to higher ground.

Black water came flowing over the wharf. The water was rising, the windows and sign boards of the office broke and the whole building disappeared. *We may be in danger too,* I thought. We tried to escape to the rooftop of Sea Pal One, but the access door would not open.

We went through the connecting corridor to Sea Pal Two, which housed restaurants and other establishments. We ran up the stairs to try to go out to the rooftop, but the metal door was locked and we could not get out from there either. We decided to break the glass in the door with a stepladder we found in the landing and escaped to the rooftop one by one.

Kenichi Hino with Marine Pal Onagawa in the back. The tsunami nearly reached the antenna at the top of the building.

I was the second last to get out. By the time I got out, the water was up to my waist. The people who had gotten out before me had disappeared. As I looked to my side, a metal ladder came into view. Holding out against the pressure of the tsunami, I grabbed it with all my might and climbed up.

I could hear someone calling my name. It was Haruo Yoshida, 63, a senior co-worker who had come outside after me. Apparently, the metal access door was forced open by the pressure of the water rising up through the building, which allowed him to get out and go up to the rooftop. I grabbed him and pulled him up onto the ladder.

The water level was still rising. The ladder that we were on was attached to the elevator maintenance room. We climbed the ladder up to the very top. There was nowhere to go any more. *It's all over*—the phrase crossed my mind.

I looked around and saw that dozens of cars parked at the municipal hospital which stood on a high hill were falling down as if in a waterfall. The tsunami had started to draw back. We went back to the landing on the stairs. Houses that had turned to rubble were being swept away between Sea Pal One and Two, making a roaring sound. It was truly a torrent.

The surge and the backrush of the water repeated over and over, at least ten times as far as I remember. Twice we sensed imminent danger and went up the ladder. I heard fish oil tanks banging against the building, which made me really worried that the building might collapse.

It was freezing cold. As I was sitting on the landing with my body soaked, I became drowsy. "Don't fall asleep!" I woke up to Mr. Yoshida's voice. It was a moonlit night. The municipal hospital was brightly lit up by the backup electric generators.

BY AROUND 6 A.M., the water level seemed to have dropped significantly. We thought we had better escape then. We got out of the building and hurried toward the hospital, walking through the rubble.

People from the Chamber of Commerce building were also heading in the same direction for higher ground. We went beyond the hospital and climbed up the front approach to the Kumano-jinja Shrine which stood behind the hospital on a higher area, then headed for Ishinomaki City, where my home was. We hitchhiked through Onagawa Town. On the way I parted with Mr. Yoshida as he headed to his home in the Watanoha district. I think it was around 9 a.m. when I finally got home.

Regrettably, four out of the five people who had escaped to the rooftop of Sea Pal Two before us were swallowed by the tsunami and are still unaccounted for.

Massive waves go over supermarket roof
Drifting alone in sea for over 14 hours

Akihito Kimura
male, 30, supermarket employee

The earthquake happened when I was at work at Onmaeya—the name of our supermarket—in the Onagawahama district. On the first floor, merchandise was scattered all over the floor, and many glass bottles of sake and liquor were broken. It was so dark inside because of a blackout that it was dangerous to walk.

TSUNAMI WILL FOLLOW a big earthquake, I thought. I guided customers out of the shop first, and then told the 15 or so part-time workers to evacuate either to the Onagawa Municipal Hospital or the high ground of Onagawa High School.

There were seven people who remained at the supermarket—five full-time male employees including myself, the president of Onmaeya and his eldest daughter who was the managing director. The men piled up sandbags in front of the entrance since it was the area which had been flooded by the tsunami following the Chilean earthquake in 2010. Then, we set about moving the cash registers to the second floor—they were quite expensive— so that they would not get damaged. Just then, the president shouted, "Tsunami is here!"

The tsunami came over the sandbags and into the store. I heard the sound of glass breaking, the water was flowing in through the windows, its level was rising gradually, and there was no sign of it stopping.

When I looked outside from the second floor, cars were being carried away in a muddy stream. Our building started to make nasty groaning sounds. *Something extraordinary is happening,* I realized. Seven of us crawled up to the roof of the building, but soon, the tsunami came higher than the roof. I tried to keep my head above water and swim to some taller building nearby, but couldn't.

FOUR OF MY COLLEAGUES were holding on to a floating board and two of us, an employee in his 20s and myself, climbed onto some debris. Black water was all around us and the municipal hospital was the only building I could see. The town had been submerged completely.

A backwash started and everything was being swept out to the sea. This backwash and the second incoming tsunami clashed against each other, creating a tall wall of water. *We can't make it through this*—I had resigned myself to death, but in the next instant, I had gotten through that wall. But the five people who had been with me had disappeared, leaving me alone.

Because of the irregular movements of tsunami, I was tossed again and again off of the masses of debris that I had mounted on with much effort, but then again, I moved onto another mass. Eventually, I got up on a whole clay-tile roof of a house. In the meantime, snow started to fall. I was soaking wet. An intense cold overtook my body. Feeling dizzy, I collapsed right then and there. *This is it. I am going to die,* I thought.

That moment, some light hit my face. I opened my eyes and saw patches of clear sky. That one ray of sunshine felt very warm and it brought me back to my senses. I could see a fishing boat offshore. *There is still a chance to survive,* I told myself.

THE WIND WAS GETTING STRONGER as night fell. A broken half of a concrete panel was drifting on the surface of the sea. It was big enough to contain my whole body if I crouched down, so I used it to protect myself from the wind. I picked up some pieces of styrofoam and stuffed them between my body and the concrete. I put a big styrofoam over my head. I was very thirsty, so I quenched my thirst with the snow which had piled up on the roof.

When the roof I was on came within a few meters of the shore, I tried to swim over to it. But the moment I was about to jump, a landslide occurred. Apparently, big aftershocks had been hitting over and over. I had not felt them because I had been drifting in the sea. I gave up my attempt to reach the shore.

THE LONELY COLD NIGHT seemed endless. I

The supermarket, up front, where Akihito Kimura was enulfed by the tsunami. Photo taken at Onagawahama, March 21, 2011

was anxious, thinking, *Will I survive? How far am I going to drift?* When I was close to losing all hope again, a searchlight from a fishing boat shone around where I was. *I am not alone.* I felt encouraged.

As the sky started to brighten a little, the roof came to a sudden stop with a great wham. I was at the breakwater off Tsukahama in Oshika Peninsula, approximately six kilometers southeast. At least 14 hours had passed since I started drifting. I crawled up on the breakwater. Feeling relieved that I had survived, I was starting to drowse when I heard a man's voice. "Are you alive?" I answered "yes," and he said, "Wait there." Soon after, a boat came to me.

I got on the boat, and it took me to the beach. I changed clothes at a community center where the locals had evacuated to. Then I was handed a bottle of sports drink in front of a heater. I felt, *I am alive.* Drowsiness hit me and I fell asleep.

MY FAMILY was safe. However, the lives of six people—my colleagues and my boss—had been lost. *Only I survived.* The thought hit me time and time again. I could not feel truly thankful when people told me it was "good" that I had survived. Now, I am busy working to reopen the supermarket. I believe that is something I can do as a survivor.

Escaping to maintenance tower
20-ton ship closing in on Town Hall

Koya Kimura
male, 51, Onagawa Town Tax Department manager

It was the last day of the regular meeting of the Onagawa Town Assembly in March. Suddenly we were struck by a strong and long-lasting quake—the kind that I'd never experienced before, and the sturdy 4-story reinforced concrete building of Onagawa Town Hall shook and groaned. I thought intuitively, Tsunami is on the way.

WHAT CAME TO MIND when I heard the tsunami warning for waves higher than six meters was the tsunami attack that was triggered by the Chilean earthquake of May 24, 1960—four days before I was born. The tsunami surged up to just below the community center which was located in front of the town hall then—I had heard that story over and over. That was six meters high. *This town might be extensively submerged in water,* I thought. My father, 79, and mother, 76, were at home at the time, just two minutes away by foot, and they came over to Town Hall to evacuate.

A little over ten minutes afterwards, just after 3:30 p.m., the first wave of tsunami came. I was on the first floor of Town Hall and could see the car that had been parked right outside of the front entrance float up and move about. *What's coming will be beyond our imagination.* When I went upstairs to the third floor, I could see the second wave was just going over the two lighthouses, one white and the other red, in Onagawa Port. I went up to the balcony on the 4th floor with the locals who had evacuated to Town Hall.

What I saw from there was our town being destroyed. Houses were being swept away. A house next door to Town Hall came slamming into it and roof tiles of the house got scattered on the balcony we were on. A 20-ton ship came closing in on us as well. I noticed that the water was only a few centimeters below the balcony now. We came to the conclusion that if a bigger wave came, it could cause casualties. Town Hall staff led everybody up to the top of the maintenance tower. The metal ladder was the only means of access. Some of us pushed the frail elderly people up the ladder to be pulled up from those already up on the top. A woman in a wheelchair was lifted up by using a fire hose.

Waves had overfilled the residential areas of the town. A muddy brown torrent was streaming past between Town Hall and the higher ground as if it were a mighty river. A while later, the backrush began. It was extremely fast. The houses that had been uprooted by the incoming wave were now being torn to pieces. Some people, left stranded on the roofs of houses, could be seen being carried away.

AFTER WE HAD ESCAPED to the top of the tower, wet snow started falling. Many of the evacuees were elderly people. Emergency plastic rain coats that were stocked at Town Hall were passed out, but the snow relentlessly made its way through small openings in the coats and penetrated our clothes. The elderly people were shivering from the cold. The Town Hall staff, after talking among ourselves, decided to look for an escape route once the water receded. Flashlight in hand, we cleared rubble and made an escape route to the first floor.

Sometime after 6 p.m., the staff workers led all the 70 or so evacuees outside, and we all evacuated to a house on higher ground that was in the back of Town Hall. While looking for that evacuation route, I had gotten trapped in an open manhole. After confirming that everybody except for the staff workers had been led to safety, I poured out the water in my boots; it was red. I looked at my right leg and saw that there was quite a large wound on the shin and the sock had turned all red. I didn't feel any pain at all until that moment.

Throughout the night, ominous sounds could be heard from the aftershocks and the surging tsunami waves. But I had this strong determination—I'm going to survive this, and didn't feel frightened. I kept thinking, *I won't give up.*

The next morning, what I saw of central Onagawa in the morning sun was that nothing was left—even the reinforced concrete buildings had been overturned. I walked over to the municipal hospital to receive treatment for my wound, and I was astounded to hear that this hospital, located on a hill which is 16 meters above sea level, had been flooded up to nearly the ceiling of the first floor.

ON MARCH 14—three days after the tsunami—I went inside Town Hall to investigate. On the balcony where we had taken refuge from the tsunami, I found a familiar-looking wooden post. I could tell from its grain pattern that it had belonged to our house. As for our house, only the foundation remained—nothing else. My mother had taken out our family's Buddhist spirit tablets and they were safe, but we lost everything else. It was fortunate that on the day after the tsunami hit, I could confirm that my sister, 43, was also safe. At my former work area at the office, I saw a warped desk. The paraphernalia around it enabled me to tell that it was what I had been using before the disaster, but the drawers were all empty.

Town Hall had lost practically all of its function with all of its essential utilities cut off. With the telephone dead and the emergency wireless broadcast system submerged in water, there was no way to obtain or send out any information.

Life in the temporary housing units still continues. Everybody in the town is prepared to reconstruct a better Onagawa. I believe that as long as there are people here, Onagawa will come back to life.

Tsunami reaches hospital on hill 16 meters above sea
Hospital staff respond to patients and evacuees

Kaoru Cho
female, 49, director of nursing and care
Onagawa Town Community Medical Center (formerly Onagawa Municipal Hospital)

I was at work at Onagawa Municipal Hospital when the earthquake struck. We guided about ten outpatients who were there to a safe place where there was no danger from anything like glass breaking. The thirty inpatients on the third floor were also safe.

THE HOSPITAL STANDS ON A HILL which is 16 meters above sea level. The major tsunami warning was issued. One car after another came up the two access roads to the hospital to evacuate, and the parking lot was filled up. There were still more cars lined up, trying to

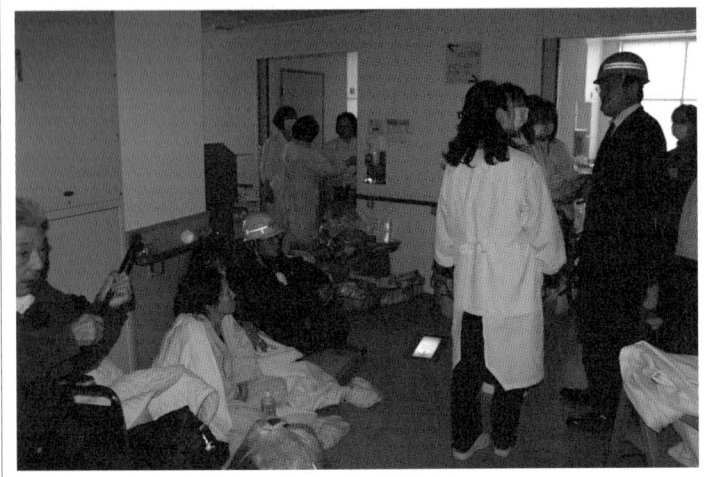

Second floor of Onagawa Municipal Hospital was filled with tsunami evacuees. Photo taken on March 12, 2011

make it up the hills. It was just after 3 p.m.

Our medical staff immediately started to prepare for triage. Triage is about deciding the priority of treatments in a disaster setting with the aim of achieving the highest life-saving result. There were about 70 staff members in total including doctors, nurses and dieticians. We all rushed to prepare for our tasks.

People who had come to evacuate were hanging around by the parking lot fence, where they could watch the sea, or trying to get information from the radio in their cars. Some people left their cars on the access roads where they were stuck in the jam and walked up the hill to evacuate.

The tsunami finally came. It approached rather gently but it was increasing its height. And then we watched in disbelief—it came closing in on the hospital building after engulfing the land in front of it which is 16 meters above sea level. *How much higher is it going to rise?*—there was no end to the increasing height or the force of the tsunami.

THE HOSPITAL STAFF directed the patients and evacuees to the second floor, and then on to the floor above for safety. There were only two sets of stairs, and people rushed there. The water was getting closer and closer, and the number of people whose whole bodies were getting drenched was increasing greatly. Some of the patients nearly drowned. Fighting against the fear of people drowning and of a possible stampede breaking out, we eventually managed to evacuate everybody without anyone incurring a major injury.

The total number of people who sought shelter at the hospital reached over 400. We had many of them change out of their wet clothes into our staff's clothes. The electricity stopped with the arrival of the tsunami, and the emergency power system was activated. For those people who were complaining of the cold, we offered bed sheets and curtains removed from windows so they could keep warm.

It was fortunate that drinking water was stored in the rooftop tank where it was safe. However, emergency food supply that we had left in stock was enough only for our inpatients. In a disaster, we were allowed to use anything at the kiosk without permission. Food items such as snacks in plastic packages as well as soft drinks in cans and bottles from the vending machines—the machines had to be broken to get them—were distributed among the evacuees. We were expecting to see many injured people, but only a few came on that day. Nearly everybody was suffering from hypothermia.

THE NEXT DAY, on March 12, we were speechless as we looked down at our town from the hill. It had been totally destroyed except for some large buildings. We had a large influx of people with injuries and those who were about to develop pneumonia after having swallowed sea water. Some people came to get medicine for their chronic illnesses—they didn't have enough time to pack their medication when they evacuated. Some of our staff went down to the pharmacy on the first floor, digging out medications buried in sludge and collecting anything usable.

But there were still problems. One was that there simply was not enough medicine. Another was that most of the patients who needed medicine didn't know what kinds of medication they were on. With medical records in paper swept away and the electronic medical record system broken down with the flooding, the patients' own stories were our only source of information.

On the second day after the tsunami, we could no longer obtain drinking water due to a pump failure. Those who could walk were asked to move to the municipal gymnasium where emergency meals were stored, and about 300 people did so. The remaining 100 people and the medical staff tried to stave off hunger with one 500-milliliter PET bottle of a soft drink, a limited amount of snacks, and rice porridge in a paper cup that was only one third full. In hopes of being rescued, we made an SOS sign on the rooftop with whatever we could find such as bed sheets.

On the third day after the tsunami, some people made an effort to report our situation to an affiliated hospital in Sendai City. But before the arrival of any support, we ran out of oil and the emergency power generator stopped.

The majority of our staff members had been working without being able to confirm the safety of their family members. And starting the next day, we took turns going out and confirming the safety of our families, giving priority to those who had young children. I managed to get a short visit home one week after the disaster. The first floor of my house had been flooded up to 40 centimeters, but all my family members were safe.

On the fifth day, we turned the hospital parking lot into a heliport, which allowed us to transfer patients in serious conditions to other hospitals. Medicine, water and food were delivered on this day.

ON ONE OF THE COLUMNS by the front entrance to the hospital is a sign that says "1.95 meters," indicating the height that the tsunami reached. Every time I see it, I remember those harsh days we went through.

Husband and wife carried away into bay
Her last words: "I want to see my grandkids"

Hayato Aso
male, 72, real estate business owner

On seeing a tsunami, we ran into our house but were washed away to Onagawa Bay, house and all. Fortunately, our house drifted to a building that stood on the wharf. However, another big wave closed in, dumping muddy water over us. No rescue came and my wife was starting to gradually lose her consciousness.

AT THE TIME THE EARTHQUAKE STRUCK, I was in my office which was next to our house. Computers and other things in the office fell down and the top half of our family's Buddhist altar inside our house was bent over. I decided to wait for my wife Sachiko, 66, to come home from the Ishinomaki Red Cross Hospital and then to evacuate to the municipal gymnasium together with my mother Kimiyo, 97.

We were about to set off after helping my mother into the car, but my wife said that she needed to get some blankets. I went in the house with her and we tried to go into my mother's room which was in the very back of the first floor, but the sliding door to her room would not budge. We went in the next room and got some blankets, but just as we were going out the front door, I saw black water surging onto the street.

My wife and I ran upstairs and fled to the very back room on the second floor. From the hallway, I could see my car being swept away with my mother in it. The water level rapidly rose, going up to our necks. We climbed up on the middle shelf of the closet and held fast to the beam above.

Our house was being shaken up and down and from side to side. We watched as neighboring houses got easily knocked over by the tsunami. A house, uprooted from its foundation and having escaped getting torn down, could be seen rotating and coming toward ours. With the big impact from this crash, our house started to drift now. It seemed like the backwash was taking us toward Onagawa Bay.

Then all of a sudden, the roof of our house split apart and our field of vision opened up all at once. I imagine that the posts and the walls of the house were gradually torn apart while being carried away. From the contours of the mountains, it seemed that we were drifting somewhere in the middle between Ishihama and Konorihama. I could see the first-floor hallway roof, and I decided that we should swim and get over there. My wife got her foot caught in the rubble halfway through, so I had to pull her out.

The slow flow of the water sped up again the moment we got onto the rooftop. Cars and rubble were rapidly being swept away. *Just how far are we going to be carried away?* Then suddenly something bumped into the rooftop we were on, changing the course of our drift.

WHERE WE EVENTUALLY DRIFTED TO was the office of Onagawa Fish Market Vendors' Union on the southern side of the port in the Washino-kami-hama district. The water was just about the height of the second-story floor. I first jumped onto the office building, removed the broken glass pieces from one of the windows, and helped my wife to get in. Just as we began to feel relieved, a tsunami came flowing into the office. We ran into the men's room behind the office. We struggled to avoid the waves by climbing onto the urinals, but after a few attacks, one wave went over our heads, dumping dark black water over us.

"Charlie got carried away!" my wife said. She had brought along our pet Maltese, carrying him in her arms. "Forget him"—that was all I could say then.

Just as I was thinking it might be over for us as well, the tsunami started to gradually weaken. We moved into the kitchenette next to the bathroom. We moved a long table from a meeting room into the kitchenette and sat on it. We were in our stocking feet. No matter how many times we wrung out the sleeves of our jackets, water came flowing out. We could hear the water approach with skittering sounds in the pitch-black darkness. I opened an overturned refrigerator, but it was empty.

AFTER DAYBREAK, around 9:00 a.m., we went around to the back of the building and climbed up the emergency ladder to the rooftop. We waved to a helicopter, but there was no response. We could see a lot of people in the parking lot of the municipal hospital. We called out to them at the top of our voice, but nobody noticed us.

It was cold. Mountains of rubble covered the roads to the hospital. The wharf had caved in. I thought of swimming toward the hospital for a second, but realized it would be impossible.

Around 2:30 p.m., my wife's consciousness started to wane, and she began to talk in her delirium. I gave her a heart massage, encouraging her by saying, "Hold on now." But her body started to struggle uncontrollably and fell from the table down to the floor. Then she started to utter the names of her five siblings, one by one, followed by the names of her nephews at the home of her birth, our three sons, our four grandchildren. . . . She drew her last breath, after twice murmuring, "I want to see my grandkids." It was 2:58 p.m.

A little after half past four, I heard the sound of a fishing boat's engine approaching. As I moved toward the sound, it was a fisherman from Kirigasaki named Suzuki. I asked him to drop me off at the wharf in front of a place called Marine Pal so that I could walk to the town center, even though he told me it would be impossible.

I kept thinking that I had to go to my parents-in-law's house in Nobiru in Higashi-Matsushima City and let them know that my wife had died. In a state of shock, I had lost my ability to make sensible judgments. I thought to go over the mountains of debris and began to walk sluggishly.

Floating away in my attic refuge
Running to shrine when waters recede

Tadashi Yamada
male, 81, former member of Onagawa Town Assembly

I ran up into the attic of our house with my family, escaping from the tsunami flowing into the house from the garden. Our house was easily dragged away by the tsunami and drifted among rubble even though we had learned to have the foundations of the house raised after The Great Chilean Earthquake in 1960.

THE 11TH OF MARCH was the last day of a regular session of the Onagawa Town Assembly. Massive shakes hit us about ten minutes before we were about to finish the meeting. The chairperson of the assembly called for an adjournment. All the assembly members went separate ways to head to their homes, and I too drove to my home in Washinokami-hama.

My wife, 80, and my granddaughter, 26, who had come back from work, were home when I arrived. Roof tiles from our house had dropped down. Things like stained glass handicrafts that my wife had created had fallen down and there was no place in the house to stand. I changed into work clothes to begin the chore of tidying up the house.

My granddaughter cried out, "A tsunami warning is being broadcasted! We'd better get out of here." I knew that a tsunami would come, but didn't try to escape. The foundations of our house had been raised about two meters when our new house was built after the old one was flooded by the tsunami following the Chilean earthquake. *Our house should be reasonably okay with a tsunami*—I wasn't being careful enough.

I saw tiny waves flowing into our garden through the entrance gate when I went outside. The same moment my granddaughter shouted, "The tsunami has come!" The three of us quickly rushed into the house. My wife tried to close the front door, but the water continued to pour in before she could shut it. We hurriedly went upstairs. Crunch! Crash!—the sounds of rubble crashing into our house. Before we reached the top of the stairs, our neighbor's house crashed into our home. Frantically, we ran up to the attic.

THE ATTIC WAS AS BIG as ten tatami* mats. We had had the room renovated for our grandchildren. There was a small window in the room from which we checked on the situation outside. Our house was tightly enclosed by a lot of debris. A gas cylinder was bouncing around, releasing gas here and there through its hose. We saw several houses on fire being carried away by the tsunami.

I saw the company housing for Tohoku Electric Power Company. It rocked from side to side as it was washed away more than a hundred meters. The wa-

The site where Tadashi Yamada with his family were washed up while in their house. The triangular roof in the left of the photo is what remained of Yamada's home. Photo taken on March 20, 2011. Courtesy of Yamada's relative Toshimi Amakura

ter in the attic rose as our house gradually sank. It reached our navels. We kept it at bay by getting on top of a bed and onto the upper section of the closet. "We won't die here like this, will we?" my wife asked. "There is no way that could happen," both my granddaughter and I said, as if we were really trying to convince ourselves. It felt like our house continued to be carried back and forth by the backwash and incoming waves. Waving a white flag made of a stick and some cloth from the window, my wife shouted, "Somebody, help us!" But there was no response.

As our house kept drifting and revolving, the amount of debris around us decreased, the water receded, and we could see some ground. We "landed" inland less than fifty meters from where our house originally stood.

We were able to see the steps leading to Kumano-jinja Shrine. The three of us crawled out of the small window and ran through the debris toward the steps. We could hear the roaring of the waves, but did not look back. While panting for breath, we ran up the steep slope without stopping until we reached the shrine.

A number of people had already evacuated to the shrine. We were able to go into the shrine office to warm ourselves. There was a heater there, and it was truly warm. This was not the only time we received support from people. During our time as evacuees, we were able to survive because we had so much support from both locals and out-of-towners. I'm extremely grateful for this.

A FEW DAYS LATER, my wife and I went to the place where our house finally ended up after being swept away. To our surprise, the direction of the house had changed. After we escaped from the house, it had been pushed around by the tsunami. If we hadn't left the house at the time we did, we might have died. Because we used the attic as a bedroom, we had had it reinforced with steel frames. Probably because of the frames, the house did not smash into pieces even though it was swept away. I have come to realize that we had survived because of the series of fortuitous circumstances.

In the town of Onagawa, nearly one in ten people died. Some of our neighbors who had gathered at the designated evacuation sites such as a park or the community center were swallowed up by the tsunami. Four of the sixteen assembly members were also victims. Were we fully prepared for an earthquake and tsunami? With the loss of so many lives, we must do some soul-searching.

After the earthquake, I was indisposed, and that was one factor in my decision to decline to stand as a candidate in the election in November and retire as an assembly member. In Onagawa, seventy percent of the buildings were either completely destroyed or washed away, and the functions that a town must carry out were nearly all defunct. I guess that a lot of difficulties are in store for us as we work toward the recovery of our town. I sincerely hope that the townspeople, the town assembly members, and the civil servants in the town hall all work with the young new mayor to create a new hometown for everyone.

*tatami: See note on p. 078

Astonished to be swept away in my home
Waiting on roof to be rescued

Miki Mochida
female, 35, homemaker

It happened just as I was thinking of doing the washing after returning from my part-time job at a convenience store. There was a first shock as if the earth were heaving upward. Then the tremors became increasingly stronger.

I HAD NEVER EXPERIENCED big earthquakes before as I was born and brought up in Sapporo in the northernmost island of Hokkaido. I heard the tableware fall down and break in the kitchen. My mind went completely blank. I had no idea what to do even though a siren was wailing and a major tsunami warning had been issued. Our two cats were so frightened that they ran into a closet. I wanted to put them into a cage and evacuate with them, but they didn't show any signs of coming out of the closet.

My husband, 40, came back home. He was a little surprised that I had not escaped yet. "Our home is on the second floor, so maybe it's okay to stay here." That is how our discussion ended so I decided to stay at home.

My husband worked for a ferry company that operated the route to Kinkasan Island. After watching the company's two ships go out to sea, he returned to the harbor to move his precious yacht to a safer place. Since he told me to make sure that I keep warm, I put on a coat and a pair of rubber boots.

Suddenly the siren and the tsunami warning announcement stopped. In its place, I heard a noise that sounded like metal bars rolling over some asphalt roads. *What are they doing at a time like this? Who is it?* Just when I said that to myself, I heard some banging noise from underneath the floor. Then, part of the floor swelled up and water burst out from there. *What on earth is that?* I opened a window to check on what was happening outside. Numerous pieces of rubble were floating by. We had a canoe that we kept beside the window. The next thing I knew, my feet stumbled and I was in the canoe. Our room was now flooded with water that came up to more than one meter.

THE VIEW I SAW from the window was different from what I usually saw. That was because the building I was in was being swept away. I saw a man, the owner of a tea shop in my neighborhood, being carried away by the waves while sitting astride the top of a roof. There was a woman waving a towel, pleading for help from her balcony. Her house continued to sink and I could no longer see her. After a while, the direction of the flow changed. The tsunami began to ebb.

My building was rapidly moving toward the pachinko hall building. *The edge of the building will stab me. I'll be squashed!* Just when my building ran into the pachinko hall building, I moved from the canoe to the balcony and jumped onto the roof. I can't remember exactly how I did it.

I heard a voice from the neighboring Chamber of Commerce building. It was the voice of a man that I knew. Before I knew it, it started to snow. The man threw three life jackets out from the building for me. I went down on the slippery tin roof to get the life jackets. I used one of them as a cushion and put the other two on over my coat.

The wind blew strongly as it became dark. I sat down as if hiding behind the roof to keep out from the wind. I could hear the voices of people who had escaped to or had been left behind at Onagawa Municipal Hospital and the Marine Pal Onagawa building. Their conversations calmed me a bit as I realized I was not the only person waiting to be rescued.

THE STARS IN THE SKY were beautiful that night. I had never seen as many shooting stars as I saw that night. Now and then, something hit the building of Marine Pal, making an eerie sound. It got colder as it got closer to dawn. After daybreak, I heard someone talking on the road and looked to see two men walking there. I blew the whistle that came with the life jacket to call for help.

There seemed to be no access to the rooftop of the pachinko building from the street. The men went into the Chamber of Commerce building and went to a lavatory that was as high as the rooftop of the pachinko building. They then leaned out through the window there and pulled me in to where they were.

Ah—I can actually survive—That's how I felt as I was being pulled about the one meter between the two buildings by the men. I went to the municipal hospital and a home-help careworker that I knew gave me something to drink and a rice ball the size of a golf ball. I happened to run into a neighbor and evacuated to the town's general athletic gymnasium with her.

On the morning of March 13, some people that I came across told me, "Your husband had come to the gym." When I checked the list of survivors that was put up, I found the name of my husband, written in his distinctive handwriting. He had come to the gym to search for me on the night of March 12, but we couldn't be reunited at that time.

My husband had abandoned his plan to move his yacht out to sea, and instead escaped far out at sea by getting on a stationary net fishing boat. It was midday of March 13 that we were able to see each other. With tears streaming down our faces, we held each other, overjoyed at the fact we were safe.

Tossed around in my ship out at sea
Saving life by jumping onto rocky tract

Hideki Ueki
male, 58, fisherman

I was overtaken by the big tsunami just as I was about to move my fishing boat moored at Onagawa Port out to sea after the earthquake. My 15-ton fishing boat did not capsize even though it had drifted while being hit by waves from various directions. I was later told that some fellow fishermen had died taking the same course of action that I did. I think it is a miracle that I am still alive.

AT THE TIME THE EARTHQUAKE STRUCK, I was on the third floor of Saito Hospital in Ishinomaki City with my younger sister, 53, to see my father, 84, who had been undergoing rehabilitation. Although I was shocked by the magnitude of the big shakes, my first thought was about the safety of my family and my fishing boat moored at Onagawa Port.

Take the boat out to sea—That was the first thing I needed to do. And that's what I decided to do. Fishermen had protected their fishing boats for generations by moving them offshore, as the deep waters lessened the impact of the tsunami. I had done this many times before whenever an earthquake struck. *My boat and I will be okay this time, too*—so I thought.

The shaking still continued as I went down the stairs to go out of the hospital. Without any hesitation, I started to drive my car. *The main roads will be jam-packed*—I chose the less crowded alternative routes. I arrived at my house along National Route 398 in twenty minutes' time. I assumed my family had already evacuated as nobody was home. I moved my car to the parking lot of Onagawa Municipal Hospital which was on high ground. I rushed down the stairs that led to the sea. I kept running the few hundred meters to the quay where I had moored my fishing boat.

I saw a 20-ton-fishing vessel close to me preparing to go offshore as I was releasing the mooring rope. Two of the seven to eight-ton class boats were also preparing to leave the port. This encouraged me a little, knowing that other people had made the same decision as me.

ABOUT THREE MINUTES after I had started to steer the fishing boat, I saw a tall white wall over on the other side of the breakwater. I didn't make it in time—I held my breath. Within a couple of seconds, the wave cleared the breakwater. I kept saying to myself—*I won't die. I can't die. I'll be all right*. The waves made movements like scooping up the bottom of my fishing boat and pushing it upwards, and then shook it violently up and down three times. I still tried to control my boat so that I wouldn't be pushed back toward the land, but my efforts were in vain.

As I looked at my surroundings, I saw that the town was completely flooded. I shuddered at the magnitude of the tsunami when I realized that the triangular rooftop and a pole that I could barely make out were a part of the five-storied Onagawa Town Lifelong Education Center. When I looked toward the direction my fishing boat was flowing, I saw the broken rooftop of the Onagawa Fish Market drifting and approaching my boat. *It's more than ten meters wide! There is no doubt that I'll sink if we crash!*—Praying fervently for the best, I prepared for the worst. The rooftop sank into the water, as if sliding toward the bottom of my boat.

While being tossed about on the waves without even a break to heave a sigh of relief, my boat got out of the Onagawa Port. It was at this time that the second tsunami wave reached me. After facing two billowing waves head-on, a wave unexpectedly hit my boat from the right. The boxes containing silver salmon fishing bait collapsed, and the massive contents were dumped out on the portside. *I can't have the boat lose its equilibrium!*—I scooped up the bait in my hands and desperately threw it all into the sea.

After a short while, the engine of my fishing boat stopped. It looked like a rope for aquaculture use that was among the debris had coiled around the screw. All I could do was just drift with the currents.

A THIRD TSUNAMI then hit my boat. This time there were three strong shakes coming from the direction of the stern. Shouting with all my might, I tried to fire up my courage and take my mind off my fear.

I realized that my boat was gradually starting to approach land. *This might be the chance I was waiting for. If worse comes to worst, I can swim ashore*—I made up my mind to do that and put on two life jackets that were inside my boat.

Under the bottom of the boat, something crashed. I could feel it. *The boat might run aground as the tide is on the ebb.* I threw a ten-meter fishing hook over a pine tree on land and then hauled the boat toward it. From a distance less than five meters away from the land, I took the plunge and jumped onto the rocky tract. I ran up a slope in one breath, making sure not to look back at my fishing boat, which had been like my "mate" for over thirty years. I stayed overnight in the mountains.

The next day, I was reunited with my only son, 27, in the Onagawa High School gym. The moment we held each other, I felt the greatest joy of life in my entire lifetime.

A few days later, one of my friends told me that a man in the fishing business who went offshore around the same time as me had died. All I can say is that I was just very lucky.

Friend's ship washed away
Salmon farming facilities destroyed completely

Yoshiaki Kimura
male, 55, fisherman

I was with my wife, 52, out at sea when the earthquake happened. We had been to Ishinomaki for shopping and were on our way home to Izushima Island from Oura Fishing Port, travelling by motor boat. We were to arrive at the island in five minutes when I noticed the surface of the sea rippling in a strange way.

THE SCREW SEEMED TO BE RUNNING idle at times, and I didn't like it. I also heard tremendous roaring noises from all directions and saw landslides happening at several locations on the mountains of both the mainland and Izushima Island.

The quay of Izushima Port was damaged here and there. We hurried to our home by the sea. My mother, 76, was at home and luckily, she was safe. Some tiles had dropped from the roof and were broken. The window sashes had come off and the shoe locker had fallen over. "A tsunami is coming. Let's move!" I urged my mother. I decided to have my wife and mother evacuate to Eisei-ji Temple up on the hill. The place was about 20 meters above sea level so I judged that they should be all right there.

After seeing them off, I got on my biggest 6.1-ton boat named *No. 38 Kompira-maru* and made my way to the floating pier which was at the entrance of Izushima Port. The pier, as its name shows, is floating in the sea. I thought it should endure the tsunami.

I met some fifteen fisherman friends on their own boats there. They were tying their boats to the pier with a number of painters, ropes used for mooring boats. I also tied ten of my painters. I hoped that way the boat would not be swept away by a tsunami even if some of them were severed.

THE TSUNAMI CAME a little after 3:30 p.m. Izushima Island is located off a peninsula in the northern part of Onagawa Town. First, the tsunami pushed its way from the north of Izushima Island. Soon, another tsunami came from the south. Then the waters started to recede, sweeping debris of houses and fish farming rafts.

The movement of the tsunami was complex and our boats and the floating pier swayed in different directions. Every time they swayed, the painters groaned. Eventually, the boat of one of my friends got washed away. I was just stunned by the massive power of the tsunami.

After the arrival of the tsunami, the roof of my house, which had been visible from the boat earlier, was not there anymore. *My house must have gone too.* I prepared myself to hear this bad news later. Surrounding houses had also disappeared. The only consolation was that I could see the temple at which my family had taken shelter remained intact so that meant they were safe there.

Just after 8 p.m., I came back to Izushima Port with my friends by sharing two boats among us. We only had dim rays of flashlights to rely on but managed to land as we knew all the geographical features around the area.

We first climbed up a nearby hill. Then we decided to move to Onagawa Second Junior High School and Fourth Elementary School. There were many construction workers who had come to the island to work on that day and they had a power generator, so the schools were lit up. There were many people who took shelter at the gym. Heaters were on, and in what seemed to be a lucky coincidence, emergency food had been supplied to the island only that morning and had been stored in the schools, so we could have a hot meal.

My cell phone had no reception, of course. I couldn't confirm the safety of my third daughter who was a student at a high school in Ishinomaki City, as well as my first and second daughters who were working in Sendai. I was worried about them but could do nothing. I decided to spend the night in the gymnasium.

THE NEXT MORNING, I found only the roof of our house on the ground. I guess we were still lucky though, because not everything had been swept away. Some memorabilia, such as our photo albums, were left on the site. Three of my four boats remained, but all of them had been damaged by the tsunami. All three of my salmon farming facilities had been washed away.

There were about 200 locals in the school gymnasium. We looked for kerosene all over the island. Meanwhile, I heard that the neighborhood leaders of the island including the head of the district were trying to find means to contact people off the island. Mr. Terama, the head of the district, apparently had a satellite phone in his house up on the hill. They used it to call "118," the emergency number to Japan Coast Guard, and got through.

Around 3 p.m., we heard a loud sound approaching from the sky. It was large helicopters of the Self-Defense Forces. Thirty of us got on a helicopter at a time. From the sky I could see that everything was gone. The fish farm facilities, which should have been there, were all gone. No houses were left around Oura Port.

The center of Onagawa Town was also devastated. Nothing was left except for tall buildings. "What is this? What happened?" Everyone was mumbling the same words.

Later, I was able to confirm that my three daughters were safe. These days I go over to the island almost every day. I am sweating and slaving away with my fisherman friends to restore the fish farm facilities.

III
Higashi-Matsushima City

Damage Report of Higashi-Matsushima City (as of end of December, 2013)

Casualties	
Dead	1,043 (including 66 related deaths)
Missing	91 (including 66 officially declared dead)
Peak number of evacuees	15,185 (March 18, 2011)
Date all shelters closed	August 31, 2011
Extent of inundation by tsunami	
Inundated land area	37 km^2
Municipal land area	102 km^2
Population of inundated area	34,014
Number of damaged homes	**Number of homes**
Total collapse	5,513
Partial collapse	5,560
Partial damage	3,506
Total damaged homes	14,579
Total homes before earthquake	15,080
Temporary housing	
Number of temporary housing	1,789 units
Occupants	4,654
Houses/apartments as temporary housing	950 units (peak count unknown)
Occupants	2,634 (peak count unknown)

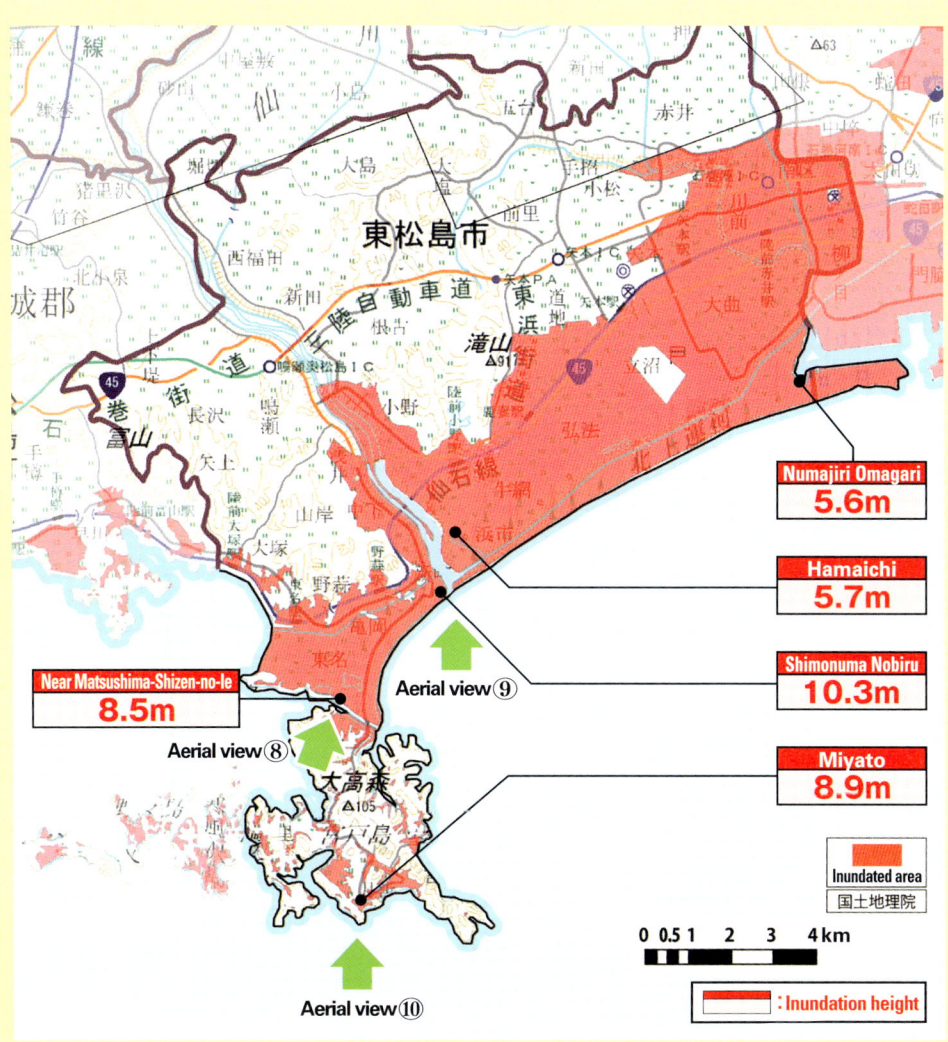

Numajiri Omagari **5.6m**
Hamaichi **5.7m**
Shimonuma Nobiru **10.3m**
Near Matsushima-Shizen-no-Ie **8.5m**
Miyato **8.9m**

Aerial view ⑧
Aerial view ⑨
Aerial view ⑩

Inundated area
国土地理院

0 0.5 1 2 3 4 km

: Inundation height

Aerial view ⑧ Nobiru District

Nobiru Beach extends from bottom right as far as Naruse-gawa River near top left. Pre-disaster photo shows marshland with Oku-Matsushima's athletic field in center, landscape rich with green. Beyond river in back is Japan Air Self-Defense Force Matsushima Base. (Photos Top: August 2002 Bottom: April 5, 2011)

Aerial view ⑨
Area around estuary of Naruse-gawa River

Right of river is Hamaichi district. Kitakami Canal runs along beach. Left is Nobiru district. (Photo Top: May 2003 Bottom: April 17, 2011)

Aerial view ⑩ Miyato District

Pre-disaster photo shows Tsukihama village in center. Post-disaster photo shows Tsukihama at bottom left, Ohama village at bottom right, and Murohama village near top right. (Photo Top: August 2002 Bottom: April 17, 2011)

Higashi-Matsushima City

Tumbling into water as house collapses
Unable to move in muddy torrent

Atsuko Ogata
female, 34, comany employee

The massive tsunami mercilessly surged onto hills which were supposed to be a safe haven. Cars were rolling, and there were shrieking screams. My father was swallowed up by a muddy torrent in front of my eyes. He clung to a house, trying not to be carried off. But the foundations of the house collapsed and he was pulled into the water.

WHEN THE EARTHQUAKE occurred, I was at my house near the mouth of the Naruse-gawa River. The quake was so strong that I couldn't remain standing unless I clung to something stable. From my experience of previous big earthquakes that happened successively in Miyagi Prefecture in 2003, I opened the entrance door so that everyone in the house could run away at any moment. My mother, 66, was holding the TV set with all her might so that it wouldn't fall down.

As soon as the quake stopped, my mother left by car to fetch my grandmother, then 85, whose house was near Nobiru Station on Japan Railways' Senseki Line. *A tsunami will surely come.* I began to prepare for it, gathering valuables and the ledger for our family business of newspaper delivery so that I could carry them with me.

After a short while my mother came back home with my grandmother, and then the three of us moved to the hill behind Cho-on-ji Temple, a few hundred meters away from our house. The hill was six or seven meters above sea level and was usually used for the residents of the community to gather during evacuation drills. It was the place where a Tohoku University professor, who had come to investigate the area after the successive earthquakes, had declared to be safe.

My father, 64, who had gone to the Yamoto district earlier in the day, came to the hill in his car after he had dropped in at the community center and our house. I seem to remember that there were 15 or 16 cars parked by then and the number of evacuees had reached approximately 40.

Around 3:30 p.m., there were cries from the people who were on the side of the hill that had a view of the ocean. "A tsunami is coming! Get out of here!" they shouted. I heard rumbling noises from the ground as well as great crashing sounds of pine trees along the coast getting torn down. I saw people being pushed around by drifting cars and swallowed up by the water. It all happened in a moment. We started to run as fast as we could.

I SAW MY FATHER being washed away. A friend of my mother's who was running with me cried out, "Where should we go?" The back of the hill was a cliff. On the hill, there was a mound where rocks and stones for masonry had been hewed, but there was no path to go up there.

"Help me!" "Mom!"—came the cries from the people who were being engulfed by a muddy torrent together with rolling cars. There were newborn babies and children who hadn't yet reached school age gathering on the hill. These sights seemed completely surreal.

I held back a minivan which was drifting toward me while stepping back. Then I resisted the current by clinging tightly to the wall of a house standing at the edge of the hill. But water gradually rose to my neck. I saw the large roof of Cho-on-ji Temple floating away. As I was watching the scene in utter amazement, the stone steps at my feet collapsed suddenly.

I saw a light above my head. I tried to get up to the surface, but I was unable to move my body freely against the current. I gulped down some muddy water mixed with oil three times. *How sickening. Is this how people die?*—I thought hazily.

Then a pillar of a house came drifting in front of me. I caught it and held it in my arms. I came above the water. The area looked familiar to me. I was being carried away in the Tona Canal toward Matsushima Bay. Grasping a floating door, I raised the upper part of my body above the water.

It seemed hard to get through the Furo-bashi Bridge, which was blocked by piles of debris. Kicking some of the debris away, I climbed up onto the bank. "Is anybody around here?" I cried, but got no reply. I tried to stand on my feet, but there was no strength left in them.

IT WAS SNOWING, and the cold was unbearable. I found a board to use as a cane, and picked up another board nearby to use as a windshield and sat down by the root of a pine tree. *I will die if I let my internal organs get cold, or if I go to sleep*—I kept telling myself.

The wind became stronger, and it became even colder. But the moon and stars that night were beautiful. *What a merciless night. How are my family members doing?* I was thinking such things vaguely. A building destroyed by the tsunami, known as Marumitsu Hall, was slowly falling down into the canal and continued making eerie sounds.

From the direction of the Yamoto district, I heard a sound like a whistle that a baked sweet potato vendor makes. The sound was alternately loud and soft. I still wonder what that was.

As the day broke, a helicopter began to whirl around in the sky. I waved the boards but there was no response. Climbing over the debris and crossing Furo-bashi Bridge, I began to walk on the prefectural road (Prefectural Route 27). I came across a man who had taken shelter at the second floor of a bicycle shop, and together we headed for Jorin-ji Temple near Nobiru Elementary School.

On the way I met a male acquaintance who told me: "Your dad was looking for you." That was how I learned that my father was alive. My mother was also safe. But sad to say, my grandmother was found dead later on. I am wearing her watch, which served as a clue to identify her body and was handed over to me as a memento.

Whirling current like a plunge pool
Clinging to floating beam

Nobuaki Atsumi
male, 33, lumber dealer

I was on my way back from a bank in Matsushima Town. At 2:46 p.m., while I was driving my truck along the prefectural road that served as a border between Matsushima Town and Higashi-Matsushima City, I was hit by a violent jolt as if the earth were heaving upward. I stopped quickly as the car before me did. I looked around to see the cars in the opposite lane did the same thing.

IS THIS A SO-CALLED MEGAQUAKE? Getting anxious about my house and office, I started my car right away. Rocks of about 50 centimeters, having apparently fallen from the roadside slopes, were in my way. Some parts of the asphalt road had been ripped up, creating bumps. I had to get out of the car numerous times and remove by hand all obstacles so I could make my way.

The news about the earthquake and a tsunami warning were continuously aired on the radio. Getting through heavy traffic jams, I came close to my house in the Otsuka district of Higashi-Matsushima City, and saw some houses were tilted. I finally got to my house and confirmed that all my family was safe there. Then, after the brief stop at home, I left again to take up my duties with a volunteer fire company, which I had joined in July of the previous year.

I was in charge of closing a water gate in Tona Canal. I got there in a hurry, but the gate would not close because of the blackout. So I switched to the emergency diesel engine and shut the gate.

I thought I would have to be on the alert at the gate for an extended period of time, and decided to get myself prepared for the long watch. I headed for Tona district's fire brigade post to fetch stocked food and heaters. On the way I felt anxious about my relatives living near the fishing port in the area. Switching to my father's car, I picked up two relatives and then stopped by the fire brigade post.

Within a minute after I went into the post, as I was checking heaters, I heard a strange noise from outside. Not knowing what was happening, I looked outside. It was hard to believe, but the car I had been driving was being carried away by water. *It's a tsunami!*

THE DEPTH OF THE WATER was still shallow. I jumped into the water to try to reach the car, but the current was terribly strong. I managed to cling to the body of the car.

Just then, the water level suddenly shot up. The current, which had turned black and looked like a thick wall, was rushing in. Looking around, I saw even houses were lifted ever so easily and getting carried away one after another.

Holding tightly on to the car, I looked inside it and saw my relatives. They looked frightened and their faces were ashen. I encouraged them by saying, "It's all right. It's all right." In spite of the violent current, the car was holding its position and floating. *The car might make it to land somewhere.* I was surprised at myself for being able to think so calmly in that situation.

But it was only until then that I was able to stay composed. The car smashed against a house, bouncing me off so that my body was sandwiched between the car and the house. I was unable to move. *It's all over.* Just when I thought so, I was drawn into the house. I was probably taken to the second floor. When I stretched my legs, they hit a floor. There was a small space between the surface of the water and the ceiling. I managed to float above the water and breathe.

Getting out of the sinking house, I again clung to the car. Although its windshield was broken, the car was barely floating in the water. I looked into the car to find no one there. I cried out in all directions, "Hey, are you there?" I heard "Help me!" followed by a long scream. Then came a strong backwash and I felt my body plunging in a rapid stream. As if caught in a plunge pool of a waterfall, my body was spinning.

It's all over this time, I thought. Then something hit my whirling body. It turned out to be a beam of a wrecked house which had flown out. I floated up to the surface of the water with the beam I was clinging to. The surface of the water was almost all covered by drifting debris. I pushed it all away with my hands so that I wouldn't get crushed. I was covered with cuts and gashes all over my body.

I heard the noisy alarms of the major tsunami warning sirens intermittently. It was getting dark, but I could still see my surroundings vaguely. Sitting astride the floating beam, I continued calling the names of my relatives. No matter how many times I called their names, there was no answer. Heavy snow began to fall. I felt cold for the first time.

A small boat without anyone on it was drifting about. I tried to get on it, but I had no strength left to lift myself up. My grip was weak too. After poking myself by mistake over and over, I was finally able to connect the protruding wires of the boat with the metal strap of my watch. Thus I established a lifeline with my body tied to the boat, and continued to drift side by side with it.

I HAD NO IDEA how much time had passed, but I must have drifted for more than an hour. I heard the slight sounds of clang-clang from a distance. I thought they could be from the crossing near Otsuka Station on Japan Railway's Senseki Line. If I was right, I had been carried away at least two kilometers from the fire brigade post. I vacantly thought this while I was losing consciousness.

When I was about to give up hope, a boat with a man on it approached me, and I was hauled up onto the boat. I was frozen, and I couldn't do anything but cling to the owner of the boat.

Thus I was saved, but felt no joy. The two relatives I had picked up are still missing. In my mind, I can still hear their cries for help.

Tsunami sweeps man into river
Hanging on to floating object for three kilometers upstream

Masaru Ogata
male, 69, self-employed

On that day my wife and I both underwent a thorough medical examination at a hospital in Matsushima Town. After coming home, as it began to snow, I set out to cover the household equipment supplies on the truck parked in the yard. Just then, a strong jolt struck—a fierce shaking, both vertical and lateral. I clung tightly to the back of the truck so as not to be shaken off the bouncing vehicle.

THE QUAKE WAS LONG and out of the ordinary. What came to mind at that time was a tsunami. First and foremost was to run. The front entrance of our house had become warped, but I managed to go inside. The cupboard had toppled down with its contents scattered all over. There literally was no room to step in the house. I shouted to my wife, "We have to run!" and we got out of the house together.

Across the street from us was an elderly man who lived alone and had difficulty walking. We went inside his house to check on him and found him pinned under the front door. My wife and I helped him get out from under it and left his care to his relatives who rushed to the place a little later. Because of this, it took us 15 minutes before we got to the designated emergency evacuation site, Shinmachi Community Center, which was located near the bank of the mouth of the Naruse-gawa River. About 20 people were already there including the locals and volunteer firefighters on watch. The atmosphere was filled with tension and anxiety.

We went outside to watch the river and the sea. Suddenly the surface of the river began to stir, and shortly the river bed became exposed at different spots. It was the first time for me to see such a sight. Because of the snow, visibility was poor. I could just barely make out a rock called Myojin-sama, a local legendary deity, which was located by the mouth of the river, some 800 meters away from the Center. But in the next instant, it vanished. It was a tsunami.

The pitch-black mass was now coming toward us with this humongous roar combined with the rumbling of the earth, the likes of which I had never heard before. After it entered into the river, the tsunami appeared rather thick with one crest overlapping another. It wasn't so high along either of the banks, but the middle part had swollen up like a mountain—it was an extraordinary spectacle.

THE CENTER, standing on the bank of the Naruse-gawa River, was about eight meters above the surface of the river water. *The tsunami would definitely reach that level.* Just as we were about to go inside for safety, the tsunami came closing in on us from behind the Center—it had gone over the coastal embankment, a structure that was expected to protect the local communities. There were about 70 houses in our community. It was a matter of a few seconds that the tsunami knocked down a house or tore one off of its foundation. The torrent came attacking the village, loaded with great amounts of rubble.

My wife was trying very hard to cling to the fence of the community center. Even though I wanted to do anything I could do to help her, the torrent kept me from moving at all. All I could do was to call out her name "Miki! . . . Miki!" The curbstone in the parking lot was just barely keeping the fire engine from being carried away. I was just putting my hand on it, when a white car that was being washed away by the tsunami hit me right on my foot, forcing me to let go of my hold. After what seemed like a slide down into the Naruse-gawa River, my body travelled upstream along with the tsunami.

The current was so fierce that swimming in it was just impossible. My body sank in the water. I couldn't breathe, and I wondered, *Am I going to die?* Then I thought, *If that's the case, I might as well try and swallow this water.* The moment I did that, my body somehow floated up. And now I was overtaken by this sheer desire to survive. A strong determination to survive came springing up from deep down in my heart. *A drowning man will clutch at a straw.* I grabbed anything that came drifting, no matter how slender it might be, one after another.

TSUNAMIS ARE FORMIDABLE. They not only flow, but form whirlpools as well. I was sucked into the water together with a wooden board I was clinging to. *If I could touch the river bottom and set my feet firmly, then I could try to bounce up.* The water, however, was rather deep. It was fortunate that I ended up floating up without touching the bottom.

And now I found a thick piece of square timber to hang on to so I wouldn't be drawn into another swirl. Up over my head, the Naruse-ohashi Bridge on National Route 45 appeared. I called out for help to the people who were looking down from it. "We're contacting the police right now!" came the reply. The current, however, would not wait.

I found a sturdy piece of some outer wall floating by. I tried to get on top of it, but couldn't because my winter jacket got caught on some nails. I was dreadfully cold. I then found a plastic container, held on to it and went on drifting.

I was about three kilometers upstream from the Center now. There were some people in camouflage uniforms along the bank in the Ono district. They threw a piece of clothing toward me to use as a rope, which I tried desperately to catch, and I did—and I survived. It was still not too late in the afternoon so I was able to see the surrounding area.

As for my wife, she had held out to the end against the torrent of the tsunami at the Center and had survived it. We were both fortunate—I can't find any other words. I will very likely remember this for the rest of my life.

When I look back now, a strange thing had happened. Our two cats were sticking close to us during the two days before the disaster struck. They are still missing.

Tree stops car from being swept into bay
Evacuating into canal's control center

Harue Kanno
female, 64, former horse club owner

Near the water gate connecting the Tona Canal and Matsushima Bay, there stands a now-withered acacia tree. That tree saved our lives.

MY SON, 38, and I were at the horse-riding club which I owned in the Nobiru district in Higashi-Matsushima City. In addition to us, a girl from the horse-riding club of Miyagi Agricultural High School and a visitor were there. Both of them were taking care of their horses after riding.

The jolt was of a kind that I had never experienced. The inside of the club house was turned into a mess, and we decided to evacuate. I didn't even get around to turning on the radio, and moved all of the ten horses into the stable. The visitor said that he would go home by train, and he walked toward Janan Railway's Nobiru Station of the Senseki Line, while the three of us headed for my home in Otsuka-Tona in my son's car. My husband, 65, was supposed to be there.

We crossed the canal in front of Tona Station and had gone some 200 meters toward the beach when muddy water came flowing out from a yard on the left side. *It must be overflowing from some broken water pipe*—I thought then, and the idea of a tsunami had not occurred to me yet. We decided to back up, but we were surprised when we looked back. Massive volumes of water and rubble were coming our way from the direction of Nobiru, accompanied with these destructive sounds, and our car began to be swept away.

THE WATER was going in a whirlpool, and our car revolved in it with rubble crashing into it. My son

Harue Kanno stands by the acacia tree which saved the people who were with her in her son's car. In the back right is Tona Canal water gate.

kept his cool, and though the engine had stopped, he held on to the steering wheel, and if the car started to lean one way or the other, he directed us to move over this way or that way many times to try to keep the car from overturning. He was extremely intent at it, probably thinking in the back of his mind *I can't have this high school kid die here.*

The car was washed away through the rice paddies by the canal, and now Matsushima Bay was only a few meters ahead of us. Just when I thought we would surely die if we got washed into the bay, the car bumped into a tree and stopped there, right behind the seawall. The tree, the rubble, and the car got all tangled up, and our car was saved from being washed farther away.

The water in the car was ankle-deep. As I was thinking about what we could do, I noticed a volunteer firefighter in the control room above the nearby Tona Canal water gate. I stood up out of the sunroof and called out in a loud voice, "We need help!" My son had probably opened up the sunroof while we were being carried away. The firefighter turned out to be an acquaintance, and he was shouting back, "You're going to be all right, so don't you get into a panic now!" I was really relieved to hear his voice.

It was only 30 to 40 meters to the water gate. Since the car doors would not open, we climbed out through the sunroof and headed for the water gate. We were surrounded by mounds of debris. Worse still, it was getting quite dark. What lay beyond the debris was the sea. I walked barefoot, carefully picking my way through the rubble. I think it took us almost one hour to get to the water gate. We walked up the stairs to the control room, where they probably had a generator since the lights were on, and they also had a kerosene heater. Besides the firefighter, there was another person who said that he was saved by clinging to a tree.

In a little while, we heard this cry "Please help!" from outside. We looked outside with a flashlight and found a woman clinging to a tree. The firefighter went out to rescue her. Her body temperature had dropped and, thinking it could be fatal if she fell asleep, I tried to keep her awake by talking to her and giving a massage to keep her warm.

Beside the water gate, there was a house, and from there, an old couple evacuated to where we were. The second floor of their house was intact, and the couple said, "You're welcome to use whatever there is up there." We took them up on the offer, and the firefighter went out to get such things as blankets and clothes. Up in the control room, we were fortunate to have a hot water pot as well, and we could drink warm water. Thanks to these lucky factors, the woman who was suffering from a low body temperature survived.

THE NEXT MORNING, we all walked to the overpass of the JR Senseki Line which was around 500 meters from the water gate. Due to the mud and wreckage, it took us two hours to get there. From the overpass, we were taken to an evacuation center by car.

I found out that my husband was all right since

he was at a hospital in Akai. My daughter, 40, had run to the hotel "Kanpo-no-Yado" in Nobiru where my grandchild had been, and survived—by the breadth of a hair.

Unfortunately, none of our horses survived. I was informed that their dead bodies had been found but I could not bear to go and see them. We had some fond memories of each horse and I could not muster enough courage to see them in their horrible conditions.

We closed down our horse riding club at the end of May. However, my son's wife had given birth to a baby girl in April. And this is our saving grace.

Narrow escape: train stopped on high ground
Caring gestures keep hearts warm overnight

Yasuko Konno
female, 74, homemaker

I was on a Japan Railway's Senseki Line train bound for Ishinomaki when I encountered the earthquake, and spent one night on the train. I had a narrow escape from the tsunami because the train was stopped on high ground and as a result it was not swallowed by the water. The anxiety, the hunger and the cold which we experienced in the dark train were considerable, but in light of the damage caused by this earthquake, I think it's a miracle that I am alive today.

WHEN THE EARTHQUAKE occurred, I was on my way home from the Tohoku University Hospital in Sendai City where I regularly go. It was a while after the train had left Nobiru Station that the passengers' cell phones started buzzing the earthquake alert* all at once. Immediately after that, we were jolted up and down, and left and right with an extremely powerful force. The train came to a stop right away, but the intensity of the quake increased, making me feel as if my body were being lifted up by somebody. I was prepared for death even.

Immediately after the shaking settled down, text messages to confirm my safety reached my cell phone from my son, 47, and daughter, 43, both living in Tokyo. I replied to them, "I'm all right. Contact Father." Since our house was rather old, I was worried that certain parts of the house might have collapsed. I remember being overwhelmed with the anxiety for the safety of my husband, 80.

Meanwhile, the train conductor went around to each car, instructing all the passengers to get off the train and directing us to an evacuation center nearby. Following the instructions, we got off the train, the older people first, and had walked about ten meters along the tracks when a man's voice could be heard from behind, "Don't go in that direction! Tsunami will surely come!" In the end, it was decided that it would be safer to remain where we were and we returned to the train. If we had continued walking, we might have been killed.

THE TRAIN had four cars with the third car being at the highest spot, and that was where all the passengers gathered together. I think there were about 70 to 80 people. Among us was one boy, third or fourth grade in elementary school, who was by himself and seemed lonely, and everybody had it in their mind to look after him.

In a little while, we saw through the windows of the last car the tsunami wave coming our way. Houses, cars and rubble were all being swept up our way in a continuous flow. It was so terrifying and all I could do was just watch it, dumbfounded. On one of the houses was a man who seemed to be in his 70s, stranded on top of the roof and calling out for help. Several of the male passengers plowed through the water to rescue him. They laid him down on the passenger seat and gave his shivering body a good rubbing to warm him up.

Since the heater was out, the cold intensified increasingly toward the evening. It was snowing now. We covered ourselves with thin plastic sheets the conductor gave us and gathered up close together to try to keep out the cold as much as possible. As darkness approached, I was overcome with a feeling of loneliness and hunger at the same time. I was planning to have lunch when I got home, and so all I had had that day was breakfast.

THERE WAS A FAMILY who said they were on their way home from Tokyo, and they passed around boxed lunch sets and other foodstuffs they had bought for souvenirs. "Please take a bite"—I was very grateful for their caring gesture. Then other people followed suit by sharing whatever food they happened to have with them.

The passengers' support of one another was not limited to food. A young man encouraged everybody by passing on the information he obtained from the intermittent Internet connection on his cell phone, saying, "We're going to be all right." A granny sitting nearby told us funny stories to warm our hearts. I felt really encouraged.

Even after it had turned completely dark, many of the people were engaged in conversations without going to sleep—talking about their families, homes, or how it was that they happened to be on that particular train. . . . If I had not been able to engage in conversations with those people, I might well have become depressed.

In the middle of the night, there was a woman who came plowing through the water toward our train. It was the mother of the boy who was on the train alone. I was deeply moved as I watched the mother crying while embracing her son. That night, the mother and son cuddled up together and went to sleep.

I BECAME AWARE that the sky was growing gradually lighter. I had never longed for morning to come so badly. After confirming that the water had receded, we got down out of the train car, the young and the elderly supporting one another, one by one. Although there was still anxiety, the sense of relief that came with being able to go outside was extremely great.

I then spent one night in an evacuation center before I got to meet my husband at home in Ishi-nomaki on March 13. The moment I saw my husband's face—he said he had been looking for me everywhere—tears started overflowing from my eyes, and I kept saying "I'm sorry, I'm sorry" as we held each other.

*earthquake alert: See note on p. 125

Swallowed by tsunami, prepared to die
Mom was saved because of a cranny

Kenichi Saito
male, 53, volunteer firefighter

I work for Hashimoto Roadwork, a construction company in Higashi-Matsushima City. I was at a meeting at our client's house in Shin-Tona 4-chome when the earthquake struck. It was a huge tremor and the concrete block wall surrounding the house fell over.

I THOUGHT I MUST go about the tasks of the Kameoka Branch of the Higashi-Matsushima City Volunteer Fire Company that I belonged to, so I drove to our post near Nobiru Elementary School. There was no one there, so I walked home. I told my mother, 80, "Be sure to go to the elementary school." I changed into my firefighter uniform and went back to our post. There were some residents gathered at the parking area of the Kameoka District Community Center which was next to the fire company post. They were saying things like, "Well, we have to make provisions of rice balls for people." No one seemed to be worrying about a tsunami.

One hour after the earthquake, I was standing in front of the entrance to the gymnasium of Nobiru Elementary School. I heard someone calling out, "A tsunami!" I perked up my ears. I felt a faint tremor. *Is this a rumbling of the ground?*

A few cars broke into the school yard smashing right through the stoppers at the front entrance to the yard. I wondered what was happening. When I looked down, I saw that the tsunami had arrived. I shouted, "A tsunami! Run!" and called out to people to escape, guide light in hand.

The tsunami became powerful and started to swirl in the yard. About a hundred cars were floating and slowly swirling counterclockwise and the movement was becoming stronger and stronger. It was like a scene from a movie. A blue car faced me and started drifting toward me. *I'm going to be crushed!*—Sensing danger, I ran into the right side of the gymnasium.

There were four or five people huddled together on the basketball goal post. My mother was among them. As soon as I stretched out my hand to her, the water level rose to my chest and went up above my head at once. My body was rotating as I floundered in the water. *I was born in Kameoka, and I will die in Kameoka*—I remembered that I had said that to my friend at a pub. *So, is this where I am going to die?* I was prepared for death.

Is there something I can grab on to? I moved both of my arms frantically. My left hand hit an iron bar of the second floor balcony. I grabbed it desperately. I came up to the surface and spit out the water. Someone was holding my right hand in the water. *It's my mom!* I moved my hand. *No, the size of the hand is different.* I decisively pulled the hand up to find a man come up to the surface. I pulled him up out of the water.

I somehow managed to climb onto the balcony. My lips were shivering due to the cold, and I couldn't say a word. I resigned myself to the fact that my mother had been swept away.

Thirty to forty minutes passed. I heard a woman's voice crying out, "Help!" It was our neighbor who had been with my mother just before the tsunami came. She said, "Your mother is also here." Their heads were in the sole space of 50 or so centimeters that was between the surface of the water and the underside of the balcony. With the lower half of my body submerged in the water, I rescued them.

There were close to two hundred people on the balcony. Because the water started to recede in the gymnasium, we took the stairs to go down to the first floor. "Help me!" There was a woman on top of the heap of cars in the yard. She was one of our neighbors. "I want to look for my child!" But the water was still as high as my chest. I carried her over my shoulders and headed toward the gymnasium. When she called her child's name, there was a response, "Mom!"

THERE IS ONE SCENE that I cannot forget. Some men came into the gymnasium and called out the names of their children repeatedly. Only one name got no response. The father of the child continued to shout out the name. Ten times. Twenty times. That child is still unaccounted for.

"Nobiru Elementary School! Don't give up! " "Let's hang in there!" The voices of children echoed throughout the gymnasium. I believe this encouraged many people.

At around 9 p.m., we started moving to the school building. There were seven or eight dead bodies on the balcony. They had been all right just a while ago, but I suppose they died from hypothermia. I felt as if I was in another world.

I started to guide people in the passage connecting the gymnasium and the school building. The water was still waist high. I carried children over my shoulders. I led some people by the hand. I was numb from the cold. I got to the point where I was even thinking, *I could have escaped to the hills if I hadn't been part of the volunteer fire company post.* Ultimately, it was five hours later when we completed the task of evacuating everyone.

A friend asked, "Are you okay?" to which I answered, without thinking, "A cigarette." I didn't think the cigarette tasted good, but maybe the reason is partly because it was a brand that I don't usually smoke.

I LOOKED OVER the Kameoka district from the rooftop of the school building next morning. Houses were gone and the land was full of rubble. The scenery of my hometown had changed, and for the first time since the earthquake, tears flowed from my eyes.

Since then, I have continued working hard, rescuing people and searching for dead bodies. The Kameoka Branch of the Volunteer Fire Company lost three of its twenty members. They lost their lives while they were guiding or helping people. That is such a great shame. I appreciate my employer for understanding my activities as a volunteer firefighter. Right now I still cannot believe that I am alive. I'm living every day with the awareness that I was allowed to live.

Losing elderly residents in tsunami
Engulfed during transport to evacuation center

Teruo Oizumi
male, 62, Higashi-Matsushima City temporary social services worker

I was at work as a part-time staff member at a nursing home for the elderly called "Furoen" in Otsuka, Higashi-Matsushima City, when the earthquake happened. I was engulfed by the tsunami on the way to the evacuation center while driving residents of the facility there. Due to a series of coincidences, I managed to get out of the car, but they sank in the water with the car and I could not save them. I was overtaken by a sense of powerlessness and of remorse.

WHEN THE EARTHQUAKE HAPPENED, I was about to help a bedridden female resident take a bath. It was such an intense quake that I was barely able to keep standing. "Staff members, protect the residents!"—an announcement was aired over the speakers. I threw my body over the female resident to protect her so that she would be safe even if items from the ceiling and wall fell down, and waited for the shaking to stop.

Soon we received information that a tsunami had reached the city of Kamaishi in Iwate Prefecture. We started to prepare for evacuation. We decided to move some 50 residents sequentially to Nobiru Elementary School, the designated evacuation center, by vans. It was decided that I would take the role as a driver. Two female staff members and I put three bedridden residents—two females and one male—and one female resident who could walk, but with slow steps, into the back of the van. We were caught in a massive traffic jam but managed to get within 200 meters of the evacuation center.

SUDDENLY THE SURROUNDING CARS started to change directions to the left, to the right. *How strange. . . .* Then I realized that the volume of water had increased to the point where the tires were submerged a bit. *If the size of the wave is like this, it won't be such a big problem*—the moment that thought crossed my mind, the front windshield suddenly turned pitch black.

It then registered that the sludge-filled tsunami had overtaken our vehicle. I was prepared to die. Our van was swept up by a muddy torrent and carried along, crashing into debris and other cars over and over. Then it crashed into a railroad crossing gate and stopped. But it was tossed about once again by the receding wave. Shortly after, I heard a big noise. The right backseat window had been smashed, apparently by a falling power pole. The black water came bursting inside the van. Through the rear-view mirror, I saw the water cover the four residents.

In no time the water came up to my chest. I knew that the glass could not be smashed, but I pounded the front windshield and the window on the driver's side with all my might. I think I was panicking.

The van was tilting backwards from the weight of the water and the passenger door opened about 20 to 30 centimeters. Frantically, using both of my hands I pushed the door open. More water rushed in and I swallowed it many times. I had the two female staff members get out of the van first and then followed them.

A big tiled roof floated over in front of my eyes. When I tried to grab on to it, I saw the van right behind me, carrying the four elderly residents, sink with a bubbling sound. *I'm so sorry! I'm sorry*—I repeated again and again in my heart.

The female staff members and I climbed onto the roof. They were exhausted. I thought that if I, the oldest among us, were to whine about our situation, they would break down. I was filled with anxiety, but I said undauntedly, "Don't worry! Someone will come to help us."

There must be people like us, who are drifting or have been trapped in houses. I heard voices from different directions asking for help. "Here I am!" "Can someone help me?" I looked around but could not see anyone. I heard the cries "Help me!" made repeatedly by a presumably elderly man, but the cries gradually became weaker until I could hear them no more. It was frustrating that I could do nothing

THE SNOWFALL became heavier and the cold became more intense. There was no rescue. It was getting dim and I started to worry about waiting for rescue on the roof. I checked the depth of the water by using a long wooden stick. *Chest level of an adult.* Making myself believe that I could walk and move around, I decided to go and ask for rescue.

I headed for Nobiru Elementary School, slipping into the deep waters several times. The water level quickly decreased. Along the way, I stopped by a house and got a dry blanket to wrap around myself. People started to gather in the garden of the house. They went with me to bring back the two female staff members, and we spent the night around a bonfire we had made.

The next day, I finally reached Nobiru Elementary School. I was too stunned to speak when I saw the horrific scene of dead bodies here and there.

A few days later, we started the task of confirming the status of our residents. We identified the bodies of more than half of the 50 some residents who had died or were missing. Each time a body was identified was a heart-wrenching ordeal. I have made a daily habit of putting my hands together toward heaven every night. I am not able to remove the complex feelings within my heart.

Tsunami goes over first floor of school
Classroom packed with 400 evacuees

Satoko Ishimori
female, 48, farmer

I am a full-time farmer. At the time the earthquake struck, I was packing vegetables with my husband to sell at the local farmers' market. We were in the wooden workshop on our property, located about one kilometer inland from the coastline.

IT WAS TRULY an intense quake. I could not keep standing. I could not do anything. I really wished that the shaking would stop. When it did stop, I checked if my mother-in-law, who had been inside the house, was okay. I was relieved to find her safe.

I also checked the inside of the house. We had firmly secured things such as the kitchen cabinets and drawers, drawing on our experience during the series of earthquakes that occurred in Miyagi Prefecture in 2003, in which Higashi-Matsushima City was heavily damaged. Our preparations had paid off; the furniture did not fall down. We did not find any damage in the house either and it seemed that the overall damage was kept to a minimum.

After a short moment of relief, we thought about how to deal with the situation next. The shaking was definitely out of the ordinary. Anticipating the arrival of a tsunami, I thought of evacuating to the high ground at Takiyama hills which was quite some distance away from our home. But at that place there was a risk of a landslide. We had had a big earthquake just two days earlier. I remembered that we had agreed what to do as a family: Evacuate to the nearby Hamaichi Elementary School.

My husband, a member of the local volunteer fire company, left to go on duty. I grabbed a bag, locked up our house, and took my mother-in-law and an elderly neighbor in my car, and then headed off to Hamaichi Elementary School which was 500 meters away. I think I was able to act calmly.

The community's emergency wireless system kept warning us of a major tsunami. We were some of the earliest to arrive at the school. Guided by the teachers, we went into the building with our shoes on. Residents arrived one after another. One hundred, two hundred, and eventually the number reached four hundred including the pupils. The special classroom on the third floor was packed full, leaving nowhere to sit. But even so, we did not panic.

OUTSIDE THE CLASSROOM WINDOW, snow was falling. The expected time of arrival for the tsunami came, but there was no tsunami. I could hear the voices of people chatting as usual. The atmosphere was relaxed.

Maybe this is going to be a long battle—I thought vaguely, casting a glance out the window once again. Something was hanging over the pine forest along the coast on the east side, but I couldn't quite make out what it might be. *A fog? Some kind of bubbles?* It completely covered the trees, seven to eight meters high, including the very tips. *The tsunami!*

As the tsunami got closer, I could clearly see the thick black color. The school yard was submerged instantly. The school was close to the Matsushima Base of the Japan Air Self-Defense Force, so the school building was soundproofed against the noises of flying aircraft. We could barely hear the noise that accompanied the tsunami attack.

In the schoolyard, the muddy torrent was swirling and blustering. Houses and cars that had turned into debris were pushed by the wave and were turning around. We couldn't hear that either. The cruel scene in front of us was like an illusion—*all this is of a world in another realm.*

The water went over the first floor and nearly reached the second floor of the building. The imminent dread. . . . Shrieks arose from the evacuees all over, regardless of age. "We'll be okay," I said to the people around me, trying to convince myself. "This building had seismic reinforcement work completed. It did not collapse from the big earthquake. It won't collapse from the tsunami either."

While the tense situation continued, the water level started to settle. It was completely dark in the building because of the power outage. The special classroom we were in was packed with people and it was stifling. So the men moved down to the second floor after checking for safety. There was no heating. We were assailed by an intense cold, even though it was March. We took down the curtains from each classroom and used them as blankets to keep us warm.

TEACHERS AND STAFF MEMBERS of the school brought miniature light bulbs from the science room and used them as flashlights. They set up temporary toilets for both sexes on the rooftop by using materials like tin roofs that had been washed up. The response measures the school took were appropriate in that emergency. It was fortunate that there was an ambulance attendant of the city's Fire Department among the evacuees. We felt reassured that the person would respond appropriately should there be a need.

We shared the snacks that we had brought along. We also shared the water that was brought to the shelter by drawing a line on cups and limiting the amount that one person could drink. What really came home to me was the strong bond of the people of the community, caring for and cooperating with one another even in a major disaster.

Yes, we can hold on. I found some peace of mind. The night sky that I looked up at from the rooftop was full of stars.

Plowing through water to nursery school
Late night rescue of sleeping children

Akihiro Onodera
male, 30, civil servant—Higashi-Matsushima City Hall

March 11, 2011—it was almost one year since I was transferred to the Welfare Department of Higashi-Matsushima City Hall. I was working at my desk in the City Hall building when the fierce earthquake struck at 2:46 p.m. Computers and papers were scattered everywhere on the floor, leaving no space to step in.

I BELONGED to the Child Care Support Team of the department and was in charge of 21 institutions—ten nursery schools, nine after-school care centers and two child care support centers. When the major tsunami warning was issued, we focused on tsunami response measures. We divided into two groups in order to check the conditions at the facilities located near the coast and to ensure that the staff at those institutions were aware of the warning. A colleague and I got in a car and headed for the Nobiru district.

Although we knew that a tsunami was coming, we drove down from higher ground to the street by Nobiru Elementary School, then went along the canal toward the Naruse-gawa River. There were no traffic jams on our way, which was lucky.

Everybody was safe with no injuries at the nursery schools or after-school care centers in the Nobiru district, although some children were crying from the shock of the gigantic earthquake. Then we went on to the facilities in the districts of Ono, Ushiami and Yamoto-Nishi and went about checking on the situation at each facility.

When we returned to City Hall, the place was abuzz with evacuating citizens. In a state of general panic, I was in a rush to carry out the tasks of guiding the evacuees and setting up tents in the parking lot. When I started to make a roster of the evacuees, I noticed there were parents who were intently trying to find out about the whereabouts of their children.

AT 5:30 P.M., while the radio was continuously reporting on the major tsunami attacks with the announcer at a loss for words now and then, I got a text message on my cell phone. It was from a staff member of Omagari Nursery School. "We have taken shelter in the hall of our nursery." Then at 6 p.m., I received another message which reported the number of people evacuating at the nursery: "Eleven children, seven local residents and twelve staff members." Phone calls via land lines and cell phones were out, but the mobile text network was working. I received another message at 7 p.m. and saw an unbelievable passage. "Water level is waist-deep outside. We are using buckets to remove water from hall. We can only use stage. There are children with fever."

That's impossible! The nursery school was as much as 2.7 kilometers from the coast in a straight line. On top of that, the place was on the inland side of National Route 45 that goes through the city center. *The big tsunami had surged that far inland!*

The place was isolated now. *We need to do something.* A sense of urgency and pressure was mounting within me, but I got caught up with such tasks as looking after the evacuees—they kept arriving at City Hall in a stream—and taking out emergency supplies. I kept in contact with the nursery via text messaging. Text messaging function was truly a lifeline.

The messages that arrived had no punctuation. "we placed children on desks lined up on stage to keep them from getting wet" The tense situation continued. I replied, "We will find a way to come over. Keep your spirits up and hold on until we get there."

The last message I received had a list of the names of all the children there. That was at 7:51 p.m., and the connection went out.

WE WILL GO as far as we can by car. I gathered information about road conditions using the City Hall's wireless network. Then I got approval from my supervisor, and departed on a four-wheel drive vehicle with a colleague. It was 8 p.m.

Main roads were blocked with wrecked cars and logs among other things. We looked for a detour, but could not find one. So we went back to City Hall and organized a rescue team of ten staff members, mostly young ones. We took a van and headed off to the facility again at 10 p.m.

Our advance was blocked near the residential area of Gomikura, one kilometer away from the nursery school. So we left the vehicle there and started walking. The water was chest deep at some points. With a few flashlights guiding our path, we plowed through the water in a line. At the bottom of the water were cables which I suspected to be electric wire cables.

Around 11:30 p.m., after walking for about 30 minutes, I called out loudly toward the nursery school which loomed vaguely in the darkness, "We are here to rescue you!" We pried open the hall window and went inside one after another. The water inside was knee deep. The flashlight showed the stage that was like a floating island, with the evacuees huddled together in one lump. The children were kept from getting wet, and were fast asleep on top of the desks lined up on the stage. "Thank you for coming under these conditions. Thank you." Some people, probably relieved, were moved to tears.

Prompt decisions had to be made. Because of the fear of intermittent aftershocks and tsunami, we decided to have everybody evacuate from the nursery school. Using the curtains as straps, City Hall members carried children on their backs. Those evacuees who still had the energy to walk were asked to do so.

A little after midnight, all the people had made it to the minivan that had been left on the road. The children and the evacuees were then shuttled to City Hall. It was while waiting for the next shuttle that I felt the cold for the first time.

When we got back to City Hall, a call to rescue some people left stranded on a rooftop in the Nobiru district was waiting. Without any time for rest, we hurried to the site.

Evacuation with elderly on back
Muddy dental records used to identify tsunami victims

Hiroshi Kawashima
male, 41, dentist

On that afternoon, I was treating a patient. Sensing that it was going to be a big earthquake, I raised the reclining backrest of the dental chair that the patient was sitting on. Shortly after, the electricity went out.

THE THERAPEUTIC APPARATUS was firmly fixed to the floor with bolts and I was sure that it wouldn't fall down. I sat down on the floor with my two assistants and waited for the shakes to stop. I had experienced the two previous big earthquakes in Miyagi Prefecture in 1978 and 2003, but there was no comparison between those and this one in terms of intensity and duration of the earthquake.

Once the tremors settled, I went outside. It was a little chaotic with people coming out of their homes too. A woman I knew was walking toward Omagari-hama with her two children. "Take care," I said to her. I had no idea then that the tsunami would come. Later I heard that the woman and her two children died in the tsunami. I regret that I could not stop them at that time.

Of the three patients who were at my dental clinic then, two men returned home immediately while an elderly woman who lived on her own opted to wait with us until the situation settled.

I turned on the radio inside the clinic, but strangely I don't remember hearing any information about the tsunami. I could not hear the local disaster warning radio either. The road in front of my clinic was getting jammed in both directions—the one leading to National Route 45 and the other heading for Omagari-hama. I saw quite a few cars driven by parents who came to pick up their children from Omagari Elementary school just north of my clinic.

A WHILE LATER, there was further commotion outside. I saw someone running away, shouting, "The tsunami is coming!" I looked in the direction of the coast and saw the sky misted with what looked like a cloud of dust. *How could it get here?* I rushed into my clinic and told my assistants to move quickly to Omagari Elementary School. When I came out of the clinic carrying the elderly female client on my back, I saw a spray of water. The roads were still congested. "The tsunami is nearly here. Get out of your car and run!" I told the drivers stuck in traffic as I ran. Some drivers, who understood what I said, abandoned their cars but others remained in their cars.

We entered the school and went up to the third floor. Looking out from the window there, I saw the tsunami had already flooded the schoolyard. Cars of the parents who came to pick up their children floated and were washed up against the school building.

In the building, there were 40 to 50 evacuees in each classroom. Other evacuees overflowed into the corridors. I think there were at least 300 people altogether. Meanwhile, teachers were carrying out head counts of their students. Each classroom was allocated one radio, which was carefully listened to. It was very cold. We took the curtains from the windows and gave all of them to the elderly and children to cover themselves up. Being unable to sleep, I was leaning against the window and looking outside all through the night.

I heard the sounds of helicopters flying above us a number of times. I also saw a fire in the direction of Ishinomaki City. I learned later that the fire had broken out in the Kadonowaki-cho district. But at that time, I worried if the fire would spread to the area where we were, as I couldn't figure out how far it was in the dark. Each time I checked my watch during the night, just five to ten minutes had passed.

The sight I saw when the sun finally began to rise was horrifying. The tsunami had wreaked havoc on cars, ships, warehouses and just about everything.

At six o'clock in the morning, I left Omagari Elementary School with my two assistants. They headed home and I went to search for my wife and son, who were supposed to have been out shopping in the center of Ishinomaki City the day before. I got a text message on my cell phone from my wife just after the earthquake, saying, "We'll evacuate to Yamashita Elementary School." But I couldn't stop worrying about them until I could see them.

However, I couldn't go any further than Ishinomaki Technical High School as the area had been flooded. I searched for an alternative route to walk toward Ishinomaki Kobunkan High School, but had to retreat on the road I had walked on earlier that day because it was getting dark. I stayed the night at Aoba Junior High School.

On the third day from the disaster, I walked along the railway tracks of the JR Senseki Line and the freight line of Nippon Paper Industries, as many other people were also doing. I saw an elderly man and woman walk hand in hand. A male stranger said to me, "I'm going in the same direction as you. Let's walk together." I was impressed how people were reaching out to each other.

I finally arrived at Yamashita Elementary School and found my wife and son there. We stayed at the school for a week.

I STARTED TIDYING UP my dental clinic by the end of March. The walls and framework of the building remained, but the medical instruments were completely damaged by the tsunami. The shelves on which I had kept patient records had been toppled down by the quake and many of the records had gotten covered with mud. *I am sure the dental records would be needed to identify some of the victims later.* I dried out the ones that were just wet and tried to preserve as many of them as possible.

As it happened, some families who thought they had found deceased family members contacted me after I put my home number and other details on the front door of my clinic. There would be up to two or three families a day asking for dental records. I gave them the requested records whenever I could. I also went to a temporary morgue several times and examined the teeth of the deceased when they did not quite match with the records I had given to the family members. I feel these actions were the least I could do as a dentist.

Big wave hits car in traffic jam

Washed away in car, prepared to face death

Keiko Sato
female, 54, homemaker

I experienced the earthquake while I was driving to Sendai on the Sanriku Expressway. I got off at the Matsushima Beach Interchange and drove back toward Ishinomaki City. In Higashi-Matsushima City, I headed for the coast from Route 45 because the prefectural road by the sea along Kitakami Canal was a shortcut to my house.

A REPORT CAME through the car radio that a ten-meter tsunami had reached Ofunato in Iwate Prefecture. But I thought it would take a while for it to reach Ishinomaki. I could not really imagine a ten-meter tsunami either. I just wanted to go home as fast as possible, I guess. I got caught in a traffic jam around the intersection near Jogawa-bashi Bridge. Then I saw a large number of people running from the coast. *Why are they running?* I looked to my side and immediately knew why. A wall of massive mud-colored wave was closing in on us.

There was no way I could escape. *Am I going to die?* I asked myself. The next moment, my car began floating and was washed over to the rice fields, which had turned into a sea. People, timber from destroyed houses and cars were also carried away by the tsunami. Propane gas cylinders made noises as the gas leaked out. I prepared for death. I took out a diary from my bag and wrote a note to my family.

WHEN I LOOKED OUTSIDE from my car, I saw that a boat with some people on it was coming toward me. I was able to open my car window because both the car's engine and electrical system were still working. I asked them for help from the open window. However, the boat couldn't control its direction as it didn't have a working motor. While seeking help, I was at the same time trying to help some people who were drifting away near me. I threw my muffler toward them to use as a rope, but it didn't reach them.

Luckily, just then the boat came close to the hood of my car, so holding my coat, I jumped onto the boat. There was a family of four on the boat. Later, three men and a three-year-old girl, named Karin Ando, were also rescued into the boat.

Our boat twirled around the rice fields, and was taken toward Jogawa-bashi Bridge by the backwash. We saw a truck and some people on higher ground at the foot of the bridge. We tried to maneuver the boat toward them by grabbing some pieces of timber that were floating on the surface of the water. When we reached the bridge, some people up on the bridge lowered a rope toward us and pulled us up. They let seven of us, mainly women and children, get into the

Kitakami Canal in Omagari, Higashi-Matsushima City. Keiko Sato was hit by the tsunami while driving her car on the road to the right. March 19, 2011

driver's side of a truck. There was no driver there, but we found a blanket, futon and some curtains behind the driver's seat and used them to keep us warm.

There in the truck I introduced myself to the rest of the people. As I had been doing volunteer work around group activities (facilitation activities), I thought this was an opportunity to use that skill. I asked others what their names were. This is how we started communicating among ourselves.

Two large ships—under construction at the time of the tsunami—were washed up parallel to the bridge girder. A man who was staying outside found a room with walls and a ceiling in one of the ships. We all moved in there. There was a radiator there and it worked when turned on, so we were able to keep warm. However, the space was too small so I ended up spending the whole night standing.

THE NEXT MORNING, the owner of the truck returned. Of the people who were there with me, six decided to evacuate with him. We made clothes and a baby holder out of curtains and rope for little Karin to wear and the driver carried her on his back. We walked over debris toward the Self-Defense Forces Matsushima Base. As I was barefoot, some people took turns lending me their shoes.

It was extremely hard to walk over the piles of debris. Even for the adult man it was a real struggle to walk there with the three-year-old child on his back. Along the way, we saw a truck with a woman inside it. We left little Karin with her, promising we would request rescuers to come and pick them up without fail.

Around the gates of the Self-Defense Forces base, we met a friend of a man in the group. The friend drove us to the Higashi-Matsushima Community Center, which had been designated as a shelter. When we got there, the driver requested the rescue of Karin and the woman in the truck. They couldn't do it that day but I heard that the two were finally rescued the following day, on the 13th.

I remember that first night when little Karin was about to burst into tears. As I encouraged her saying, "Let's hang in there," she tried hard to hold back her tears. If I could see her again, I'd like to say to her, "You did so well." I too had so much support from so many people. I want to tell them once more how much I appreciate their help.

Family rushes to truck to avoid tsunami

Huddling together in attic to survive cold night

Kana Takeda
female, 36, homemaker

Swarms of birds were crying incessantly around my house. I had never seen such an unusual sight, and it was bothering me. That was the day before the outbreak of the Great East Japan Earthquake and Tsunami disaster.

MARCH 11—After my appointment at the beauty salon in Ishinomaki, I went to pick up my oldest son at Yamoto-Nishi Elementary School and was waiting for him in the school parking lot. The earthquake started out with a fierce lateral shake, and was followed by a vertical quake with a strong uplift. My car had a high roof. It started to bounce a lot and it felt like it could tip over at any moment. I was determined to keep my hold on the assist grip in my car.

When the long quake settled down and I got out of the car, I saw that the mother in the car next to mine was all pale. "That was big, wasn't it?" Her voice was shaking. As I looked toward the school building, children came dashing out one after another crying. I found my son and we both jumped into the car to rush home.

When we got home, the inside of the house was scattered with dishes and other things. There was no room to step inside, so we couldn't go in. Because of aftershocks, I decided to leave the cleaning till later, and we evacuated to the greenhouse on our property. Except for my second son who was at the kindergarten and my father-in-law who went to pick him up, there were five of us there at the time.

My husband is a member of the volunteer fire company, and he headed for the nearby post to keep watch. After confirming the safety of the local residents, he came running back home yelling at the top of his voice, "The tsunami is already there! Grab winter jackets in the house and evacuate!" I found some jackets for the kids, and moved the farm truck we used for carrying harvested vegetables alongside the house. I did that so we could climb up to the roof of our one-story house.

AT THAT POINT, the tsunami came surging into our land, even though we are two kilometers away from the coast. All our family members got out of the greenhouse to dash to the truck that was some 20 meters away. The water was at first about 30 centimeters high, but it rose to 1.5 meters in the blink of an eye. We climbed up on the truck bed one after another, but my husband's grandfather got directly hit in the leg by some driftwood that was in the tsunami before he got to the truck and was being washed away. My husband went to his rescue, but his grandfather's leg was pinned tightly with more and more rubble piling up around it, which made the rescue extremely hard.

The water level continued to rise and it easily went above the truck bed. My son and daughter nearly got carried away so I clasped them tightly. *I am their mother.* I pulled them toward me desperately. Rubble came surging our way relentlessly. A large shelf came bumping on me, nearly crushing me. The water continued to rise, but the force of the muddy torrent was subsiding now. This was fortunate for me—the force of the shelf pushing against me stopped as well. I could now use this shelf as a foothold for me and the children, and we climbed up to the roof of the house.

My husband, in the meantime, was still continuing his desperate effort to rescue his grandfather, but with the freezing water, the falling snow and the wind whipping on them—it was impossible. *If we continue this way, we'll all freeze to death.*

In order to protect the family, my husband pounded on the clay wall that was underneath the roof with his bare hands, over and over. He then kicked it with his foot and broke through the wall. Through this opening, we went inside the space that was the attic. Surprisingly it wasn't as dark inside as I had thought it would be. Still as we went deeper inside, we had to use the faint light of the cell phone to guide us. We climbed down into the futon mattress closet and looked for cushions and futons that had escaped the flooding and took them up into the attic.

The attic was filled with the freezing cold air. We tore out what little segments of the cotton in the cushions and futons that were still dry, wrapped them around our bodies and huddled together. As time passed, the battery in the cell phone that was the source of the faint light died, and now it was a world of total darkness. From outside, these strange, glugging sounds could be heard incessantly. Another tsunami might attack us—that fear kept me from getting any sleep at all.

THE AREA AROUND OUR HOUSE was submerged in water. My husband would call out in a loud voice to the people in our neighborhood who were also left stranded. He did his best to encourage us saying, "Rescue is sure to come." I voiced my concern about my second son and my father-in-law, "Are they safe now?" My husband replied firmly, "My father is tough and he's a dependable person. He's definitely protecting our boy." I trusted what he said.

At five o'clock the next morning, a dim light of dawn found its way into the attic. My husband, who had gone outside, shouted—"There's the Self-Defense Forces!" We were finally rescued and taken on their truck to Yamoto First Junior High School. However, I was at a loss for words—our grandfather was gone, and all the surrounding areas were left in this unbelievable devastation.

Two days after the disaster, I met my second son, still in his kindergarten clothes, and my father-in-law who was holding his hand. Their figures blurred as my eyes filled with tears.

Tsunami smashes through walls and windows
Withstanding onslaught by holding on to staircase handrail

Masayuki Okuda
male, 68, seaweed farmer

I was at my friend's office in Yamoto in Higashi-Matsushima City to discuss the funeral arrangements for one of our softball teammates who had died in February. All of a sudden we were hit by an intense jolt which was nothing like we had ever experienced before.

I SPREAD MY LEGS wide apart and put my hands on the table, but even then it was hard to keep standing. So in the end we went under the table and waited there until the shaking subsided. When the long-lasting quake stopped, I knew right away that a big tsunami would follow. There were several people in the office, and after confirming that every was all right, I hurried back home to Minami-Akasaki in the Nobiru district in my car as I was worried about my wife, 67. I got home in about half an hour. I could see my wife by the front entrance, and was opening the car door when I heard over the community wireless system "major tsunami of 6 meters" being announced. I felt certain that this would turn into a major disaster.

"Put on your rubber boots, get work gloves, a hat, valuables, leave the car here, and run to Nobiru Elementary School—on foot!" I said to my wife. On my way home, I had seen the traffic from Tona in the opposite lane was already heavily congested. I, too, switched to rubber boots, got my valuables including my registered seal and left home with my wife.

There were many elderly people living in our neighborhood. So I parted from my wife, and ran around the neighborhood calling out to people in a loud voice, "A big tsunami's coming! Don't use the car! Evacuate by foot!" Later a neighborhood family I met at the evacuation center told me that they were preparing to evacuate by car, but they heard my voice and decided to evacuate by foot instead. They thanked me saying, "We were able to survive thanks to you." I will always remember that.

NOW I WAS HEADING toward Nobiru Elementary School via Kameoka-bashi Bridge and the First Kita-Akasaki Railroad Crossing. The street was heavily congested as expected. I was running while I helped to direct the traffic to the school yard. Then I returned to the railroad crossing, and found the crossing bar was down. About ten local residents were stranded there, so I lifted up the bar to let them pass through. As the last one to go through, I turned around and pulled the bar back down—and there an incredible sight caught my eye.

About 100 meters ahead along Tona-unga Canal, two white boats were being carried away on a black tsunami from the direction of Naruse-gawa River. The wave must have been at least ten meters high. It

Masayuki Okuda stands in front of the former site of the osteopathy clinic which he had run into for shelter. To the left in the back is Nobiru Elementary School.

was approaching at a breakneck speed. It was too late to escape to Nobiru Elementary School even if I ran. There happened to be a two-story house which was also an osteopathy clinic less than a hundred meters before the school. The owner of the house was by the front door, and I said to him at the top of my voice, "Please let me in!" and we rushed inside.

No sooner had we shut the door than the tsunami came attacking. The dreadfully destructive force smashed through the walls and the windows, flooding the first floor up to nearly two meters. I somehow managed to grab the staircase handrail, floated on my side and withstood the attack for about 30 seconds, but unfortunately I couldn't see the owner of the house any more.

I went upstairs soaking wet, and found the wife of the house owner, the son who ran an osteopathy clinic there, and one of my softball team friends who happened to be evacuating there. The wife offered her husband's clothes for me to change into. I was really grateful for that.

The four of us were managing to fight the cold into the night, but around midnight, we heard cries for help from two women—one who sounded like a mother in her 50s or 60s and her daughter in her 30s. Although it was completely dark outside with the blackout, my softball friend and I went out and rescued them.

I COULDN'T STOP WORRYING about my wife all night, so I decided to walk to Nobiru Elementary School before dawn, the shining stars in the snowy sky as my guide. The school was only half a hundred meters away, but it was so hard to get there—the wreckage of houses and cars was scattered all about.

When I got to the school, I found that my wife wasn't there. While I searched around the neighborhood, I heard from a person I knew that she was at a friend's house. I finally got to meet her in the afternoon, and we found ourselves just hugging each other.

I learned many things from this past disaster, including the importance of the bond among local residents. I'm very sorry that quite a few residents were killed by the tsunami while evacuating in their cars. I think that many of them would have survived if they had evacuated by foot.

In hindsight, I can't help but wonder if enough disaster prevention measures had been taken. As one who had narrowly survived, I feel that a thorough review of the event is necessary.

Jet black wave assaults car
Car eventually lands on slope of mountain

Koki Yamauchi
male, 62, retired

One of my favorite activities is to drive around in my car and enjoy the scenery of my home town. I was out on one of these scenic drives by an estuary near Nobiru Beach, and was looking out the car window at what the fishermen were doing when I encountered that sudden and fierce shaking.

THE IMPACT WAS like nothing I had ever experienced before. My car shook from left to right, and it seemed that it would turn over any minute. I couldn't even open the driver's side door. I clasped the steering wheel tightly and waited for the shaking to settle down. I'm not sure if the quake lasted for a minute or two, but it felt really long.

A police car came around shortly after this and the officers gave me this instruction: "A big tsunami is coming, so you have to evacuate from here." I myself thought that this was going to be a major disaster, and rushed back home. I checked for damage to my house without getting out of my car, and since there wasn't any obvious damage on the outside, without going inside the house, I went straight to the home of an elderly neighbor couple who are my good friends—Tetsuya Ono, 75, and Yasuko, 73—to pick them up and evacuate together.

We drove to Nobiru Elementary School, the area's designated evacuation center. There was no traffic jam on Prefectural Route 27 running along Tona-unga Canal at that stage. We passed through Daiichi-Kita-Akasaki Railway Crossing with no problem. Although we were caught in heavy traffic for ten minutes as we neared the elementary school, I felt greatly relieved when I could finally park my car in front of the school's swimming pool. My friends wanted to use the toilet by the swimming pool so I waited for them in my car. I think it was about 3:10 p.m. When the two of them were coming out of the lavatory, I was looking out the front windshield at nothing in particular when this unbelievable scene caught my eye.

A JET BLACK WAVE several meters high was closing in from behind the swimming pool at a fierce speed. Yasuko had just barely sat down in the back seat, when my car floated up in no time with a tremendous force of the water—it was just like a water fountain. The destructive power of the tsunami was truly frightening.

As I looked around, great amounts of rubble along with five or six cars had also floated up and were being washed away. Looking at the people that were being swept away, I thought, *What's left for me now is to sink in water, my car and all. It's over.* I was about to give up all hope.

But then I noticed something. Even with the lapse of time, the water had not entered my car. Looking out the driver's side window, I could see that my car was mounted squarely on top of some wreckage that looked like a house. *Maybe I can still survive*—there was a gleam of hope.

My car eventually landed on the slope of a mountain several hundred meters away from the swimming pool. The area was scattered with loads of debris and so the doors could not be opened. I used a tool I had in my car to break the driver's side window and got out. Once outside, I helped Yasuko to get out, and we were both happy that we could come out of it safely.

Standing by the slope and looking down over the area where we had been swept by the tsunami, the whole surrounding was just like a sea. I thought deeply to myself—*It's astounding how we got to survive this!* Although I was thinking to stay there until the water receded, Yasuko was worried about her husband's whereabouts—he had been separated from us when he came out of the toilet. She and her husband had always been good to me, and I sincerely wanted to do whatever I could to be of help to her. I decided to walk to Nobiru Elementary School by walking along the side of the mountain.

IT WAS COMPLETELY DARK, and the weather was at its worst with snowfall. Because I had to walk along the mountainside, I slid a number of times, and it took hours just to make a few hundred meters. Even so, I was able to get to the school without incurring any major injury. I informed the volunteer firefighters about the need to rescue Yasuko who was waiting on the side of the mountain. They went out by boat early in the morning and rescued her. As for her husband, I learned that he had survived the tsunami by clinging to a tree by the lavatory. When they got to meet each other around noon on March 12, I was told later, they fell into an embrace.

As I look back now, the only words I can find are that I was truly fortunate. If I had unlocked the front door of my house and gone about getting my valuables, food, change of clothes, stuffing them in my backpack, I probably would have been stuck in a traffic jam and been carried away by the tsunami. And if the Onos had not gone to the toilet, the three of us probably would have gone inside the school gym to evacuate—and that's where many people died.

It feels like I was saved by a very minute bit of time lag. It truly was a paper-thin margin of survival. I can't help but think—*My ancestors protected my life*—even now.

Saved by running up hill
Dumbfounded at wretched sight

Keiko Kikuchi
female, 41, homemaker

I had worked in the Nobiru Community Center in the morning. I felt some kind of premonition on the way home. If I turn right after leaving the Center I go toward my house. If I turn left, I can go to the Nobiru Childcare Center where my second son Hayato, 6, is. *Although it was not time yet to pick him up, I wondered which way I should go.*

MY VAN WAS BEING REPAIRED and I had planned to pick it up past 3 p.m., after my first son Kento, 8, returned home. But for no particular reason, I called the repair shop at 1 p.m. and picked up the car. When I think about it now, it turned out to be the right decision.

When I was about to open the box of cookies that Kento, who had returned home, and I were going to snack on in the family room, the earth started to shake. It was a tremendous shake, one that I had never experienced before. I instantly took my handbag with my driver's license and other valuables inside and ran outside without even stopping to put on my shoes.

The first floor of our house consisted of a garage and the office of our gardening business. We lived on the second floor. Carrying Kento in my arms, I could only think about rushing down the stairs. The shaking didn't stop. I was afraid that the ground would crack.

How is he? He isn't injured, is he? I was sick with worry about Hayato, who was in the childcare center. I put Kento into the car and drove at breakneck speed to Nobiru Childcare Center about three kilometers away. I was so afraid and my heart was pounding. There was no traffic jam on the road, but I felt it took longer than usual to get to the center. On the way, I saw a car in the other lane, telling me that one child had already been picked up. When I got to the center, I saw two cars parked there. Teachers were doing a headcount in the yard.

I put Hayato into the car hurriedly, but strangely I didn't feel like leaving the center immediately. I watched one person, then two people walk past the gate. I was the last person to go out the gate. As we were leaving, a teacher asked me, "I wonder if you would take some children to the evacuation center." Agreeing to do that, I let child after child squeeze into my car.

It started to snow and it was getting cold. I was frantic so I don't remember how many children got into my car. On the way to the evacuation center at Nobiru Elementary School, the children were quiet, and I clearly remember some small children were trembling.

As I thought that the schoolyard would be crowded, I stopped at the site of the old childcare center that was nearby. Carrying a toddling two-year-old in my arms, I got all the children to evacuate. With my two children still in the car, I drove southwest from Nobiru Elementary School to our home.

SOON AFTER WE ARRIVED HOME, a tsunami carrying debris rushed toward our house, making a tremendous noise. It was an unbelievable sight. When my children shouted, "Dad, a tsunami!" my husband Takahiro, 48, who was in the office shouted back, "The hills! Climb up the hills behind our house!"

The four of us ran as hard as we could to the hill behind our house. The hill is about 3 meters high and a rugged cliff that was practically vertical. It was hard to climb but we used trees to push the children up and we somehow managed to get to the top. There were already more than ten of our neighbors there.

When I looked in the direction of my home, I saw it was floating, making a 90 degree spin as it swept by. Its first floor had been crushed. *The home that was full of so many fond memories of us and the children was destroyed!*—My mind went blank.

"Yaaa!" "Help me!" We heard the screams and pleas for help from all directions. *I can't believe that what is happening now is real.* I could only stand there dumbfounded.

NOTHING TO DRINK. Nothing to eat. A dark and cold night. We collected things like the styrofoam containers that had been carried by the tsunami and made a small bonfire using the lighter that my husband had. Then we warmed ourselves by it. "Let's stick it out till morning." "We should be ok." "We'll be ok." We encouraged each other throughout the night. My children didn't say anything like "I'm hungry!" or "I'm thirsty." I felt proud of them as they were holding on without making any complaints.

The beautiful scenery of Nobiru was completely changed. Boats, cars, and furniture were scattered all around. The area turned into a mountain of debris. There were also dead bodies on the roads, and we had to cover our eyes. Helicopters were flying about in the sky.

Wrapping the ropes we had brought around our waists, we used ladders to carefully descend the hill one by one. Children and the elderly were first. They seemed to be relieved that they had narrowly escaped death.

Entire car engulfed in muddy stream
Prepared to die as car started sinking

Sonosuke Endo
male, 70, restaurant owner

I was cooking in the kitchen of my restaurant when the earthquake struck. So this is what a violent tremor is like. *It felt as if I was lifted up and blown away. A freezer two meters high fell on its side. It was as if heaven and earth had turned upside down.*

I SAW CARS BOUNCING so easily like ping pong balls in the parking lot outside. There were three customers in the restaurant but they weren't injured by the tremor. I checked that everything was safe in the restaurant and then closed up the shop.

Soon after the quakes had subsided, I checked my house and the restaurant building. I didn't find any damage despite the intensity of the quake. I did find, however, water belching out at a height of 50 centimeters at four places on my property. Sand was blowing around the points. The water was clear as spring water so I thought that the water pipes had burst. But, it was ground liquefaction that was a result of the mammoth earthquake. *Water outage!*—the thought crossed my mind. That's because water is indispensable for cooking. To tell the truth, a tsunami had not entered my mind. Turning the water tap, I saw that there was still water flowing. My wife earnestly collected water in cooking pots and plastic water containers.

There were continuous announcements on the community emergency wireless system but I couldn't make out clearly what was being said. Then, when the firemen on the fire department's command vehicle came around shouting, "Evacuate now!" I realized for the first time that a major tsunami warning had been issued.

Already more than fifteen minutes had passed since the earthquake struck. I urged my wife to get in the car and we set off for the inland on the other side of the Tona canal. The Kameoka-bashi Bridge over the canal was full of cars trying to evacuate. As we were late to start evacuating, our car came in on the tail end of the traffic jam. I remember that we were in the jam for nearly twenty minutes.

Our car couldn't move at all but strangely, we did not panic, but rather felt calm. We would have been alarmed if we had seen bent electricity poles and collapsed houses as a result of the strong quake. But we were looking at a beautiful pine forest from the window. It was no different than usual. Our conversation in the car was also normal. Time passed quietly in the car. This is probably the reason I was able to calmly decide to change direction to escape the traffic jam. I steered right into a detour before coming to the bridge. The pine forest along the coast came into view.

I COULDN'T BELIEVE my eyes. I saw the crest of a wave easily crossing over the trees which were seven to eight meters high. We were lost for words as we watched the black wall of waves coming toward us. The gigantic tsunami hit the right side of the car. Surprisingly, it wasn't a big shock. The surging wave came underneath the car and lifted it up. Because the car was floating, it seems that the shock was mitigated. The windows didn't break and the water that seeped into the car stayed minimal. The tsunami filled the canal with water in no time. Our car was facing in the direction of the waves, and I think this helped us.

Huge uprooted pine trees and the debris of houses came toward our car. I held on tightly to the steering wheel of the car, which was floating in the muddy stream, and shouted, "Please, please, please! Turn!" Surprisingly, the car turned. If I turned the steering wheel to the right, the car turned right. If I turned to the left, the car moved to the left. I could avoid the obstacles, as if I was driving on the road. Although my car had been pushed continuously in the waters, the electrical system of the car was still working. And that was probably why operating the power steering was still possible.

We might have moved 250 meters in the muddy stream avoiding drifting objects. The car was taking in more and more water as it went, and the water level in the car rose close to the roof. I swallowed water many times. The car started to sink from the front. *It's all over*—we both prepared to die.

WE SAW A CAR and motorboat floating in line right in front of us. *If we can get on them, we might have a chance*—I squeezed out of the car through the broken window in the rear seat, and pulled my wife up out of the car. We moved to the car, to the motorboat, then to floating lumber, and somehow reached the second floor of a house where the first floor was completely submerged.

We had a moment of relief but it didn't last. It was so cold that we couldn't help shaking. My coughing was bad. I was almost losing consciousness and didn't even feel the pain from my broken ribs. Worrying about my condition, my wife left the house to call for help but gave up, hampered by the piles of debris. We stayed the night in the house with other survivors around us.

Our dog, a Shih Tzu who escaped from home with us, was crying like a cat but passed away that night. The next morning, we were rescued one by one by a Self-Defense Forces helicopter. We saw our neighborhood from the air. There were very few buildings to be seen. The tsunami had snatched everything away.

The appearance of silent black water
Rescuing three people from veranda

Yoshiaki Ninomiya
male, 35, fisherman

In the one hour between the first earthquake tremors and the arrival of the tsunami, I talked with my family and then went to close the floodgate, a task assigned to me as a member of the volunteer fire company. We managed to evacuate to the Naruse Branch office of the Prefectural Fisheries Cooperative just before the black, three-meter-high tsunami was about to attack us. The lesson I would like to convey to the next generation from this disaster is: "If there is a huge earthquake, evacuate immediately!"

"IT WAS A HUGE EARTHQUAKE!" "Do we need to go to the evacuation center?" Just after the earthquake struck, I talked with the six members of my family at our home in Nobiru Suzaki, Higashi-Matsushima City. We checked to see if there was any damage to the house. Then we heard this information on the radio—"a three-meter-high tsunami was observed in Onagawa Town." I thought our house was okay because it was two kilometers from Nobiru Beach, and my family was not alarmed enough to think that a tsunami was coming. When I look back now, I remember there were seagulls flying round and round above us after the earthquake and calling like crows. It might have been a sign telling us, "A huge tsunami is coming! Run away!" We should have heeded nature's warning.

I drove my car to close the floodgate of the Tona canal. It was snowing and cold, so I went back home to get a jacket. I told my family to evacuate and we went on our separate ways. At the Tona post for volunteer firefighters, I changed cars to the fire pumper truck. As I was driving toward the fishing port, I heard people at the floodgate shouting, "There's the tsunami!"

I looked toward Nobiru Beach and noticed small waves in a rice field which was two kilometers from the coast. *Oh, not a big deal. The water will just cover my legs.* I didn't think it would be serious. But just to be on the safe side, I evacuated to the second floor of the Naruse Branch office of the Prefectural Fisheries Cooperative, which was about five meters high. There were around 50 people there as the building was always used as an evacuation center for our evacuation drills. A lot of the conversation among people was about the safety of family members—"Is everyone in your family OK?"

IT WAS ABOUT ONE HOUR after the earthquake struck, and a few minutes after I ran into the second floor of the branch building. As I was looking outside through the balcony which was facing the area opposite from the Nobiru beach, a low wave washed in with cars and fishing boats, and then, a black wave of more than three meters high suddenly appeared in front of me. I couldn't hear any noise but I heard people around gasping, "Oh!" I saw the fire pumper truck, the same one that I had ridden, sinking, drawn into the whirlpool. I would have been dead now if I had stayed in the truck.

From the balcony I saw an elderly man and two women floating on the road in front of the branch office. "Help us! Save us!" they called out desperately. One of them was clinging to a bag, so I called out, "Let go of the bag!" so that she could be lighter. We tried to rescue them by extending our hands out to them and by throwing them towels tied together like a rope. When we held out a 1.5-meter table from the balcony, two people could grab on to it. Some ten people including myself pulled them up. We also rescued the other person but I can't remember much about how we did it because I was so absorbed in the task.

In the confusion, I was trying so hard to save my own life, but my mind was filled with thoughts about the six members of my family. The water level kept rising. *All of my family and I might die*—I had about abandoned all hope.

"Should we climb up to the roof of the branch office?" We discussed this option among ourselves. *What about jumping to the roof of the house next door?*—I thought deep down inside. We ended up staying on the second floor of the branch office as the water started to recede in the evening. But we couldn't go out because the water level was still estimated to be around waist-deep and there was a danger of backwash.

WE SHARED the bottled water we had brought up from the first floor. There was no food. We were chilled to the bone. We spread cardboard on the floor, wrapped our legs with plastic bags, and wrapped newspaper around our bodies. We huddled together to keep warm. We heard the shorted-out horn of the submerged fire pumper truck and the community emergency wireless system of neighboring Matsushima Town alerting of tsunami attacks throughout the night. We stood ready every time we felt an aftershock.

Around 8 a.m. the next morning I left the branch office on foot, and walked to National Route 45 passing over the foundations of the houses that had been washed away by the tsunami. I met my younger brother, 31, by chance. "Oh, so you survived!" I was surprised because I had thought he had been killed. I was so relieved to hear that all my family had taken refuge in the home of an acquaintance in Shin-Tona 2-chome and were safe.

Narrow escape from tsunami
Taking 25 elderly people to shelter on bus

Kazuo Suzuki
male, 64 years old, guest house owner

Are the grandkids all right? I was in a meeting on the first floor of the Miyato West Branch Office of the Prefectural Fisheries Cooperative, discussing the seasonal spring event of clam picking when the strong lateral shaking hit us. I immediately thought about my three grandchildren who were living with me—11-year old Kaito, 10 year-old Nanami and 9 year-old Hayato. They were fifth, fourth, and third graders at Miyato Elementary School.

I JUMPED OUT of the meeting room at once. My colleagues tried to stop me, but I was very worried about my grandchildren as it was about the time that they would come home in Tsukihama from school. Holding on to the wall, I went downstairs and then headed home in my lightweight pickup truck. The ground was still shaking while I was driving. *This must be the great Miyagi earthquake that we've been waiting for,* I thought.

My wife Chieko, 63, was at home, where seven of us lived and operated a guest house business. "I think all three of them are still at Miyato Elementary School," she told me. I rushed to the school which was one kilometer away.

Children were evacuating in the schoolyard where snowflakes were falling, and my grandchildren were among them. They were frightened, crying and shivering with cold but safe. I was so relieved to see them. A teacher said to me, "We have decided to have the children remain at school because it is designated as an evacuation center." As I think of it now, it was good that the teachers did not hand the children over to their parents.

When I went back to Tsukihama, there were 50 to 60 people gathered in the parking lot on the hill, the designated evacuation spot for the community. They looked cold, so I brought my guest house minibus, which could hold up to 30 passengers, and turned the heating on. I told them, "Please get inside as it's snowing and cold." About 25 elderly people got in the bus.

Just after they got on, we heard a TV report that a six-meter tsunami had reached Onagawa. I made a snap judgment that the area where we were was not safe enough and decided to move to Miyato Elementary School. I thought the priority was to move to the highest place possible in that kind of situation.

I REMEMBER people were excitedly talking about the earthquake in the bus. At the intersection in

The devastated Tsukihama village in the Miyato district, Higashi-Matsushima City

front of the school, we passed a fire pumper truck that came from the direction of Ohama. Later I heard that they were going to the school to escape the tsunami after closing the floodgate.

Just when my bus had climbed up the hill to the entrance of the school, I saw a black muddy torrent flowing into the road where we had just been as well as into the rice fields around it. From the school yard, I saw houses and cars flow past in front of us. A power pole had fallen down.

Later I heard that the water had reached the parking lot in Tsukihama. If my decision to move from there had been made later, we may have lost our lives. We escaped the tsunami in the nick of time. I usually have trouble making the hairpin curve in front of the school but this time I managed it. Good luck followed one after another.

My son Masaru and his wife Miki, both 39 and living with us, evacuated to the school yard but then went back home to get some blankets. They got caught in the tsunami there and had to wait it out on the roof of the house. I was so worried about them, so I walked to our neighborhood after the water receded in the evening. To my relief, we could be reunited there.

When I looked around our community, houses that had been broken apart were pushed inland and houses along the coast were washed away into the ocean by the receding waves. My guest house was thoroughly destroyed and only the steel frame was left. At the time of the Great Chilean Earthquake in 1960, the tsunami didn't reach my house, which had been the farthest inland in the neighborhood. I had never imagined that a tsunami would come that far. I also lost six fishing boats that I had used for *nori* seaweed farming and some equipment including a machine for processing *nori*.

STILL IT WAS FORTUNATE that all my family members survived. If we are all well and healthy, it should be enough. I could always rebuild my home and guest house but I would never be able to recover the lives of my family once they were lost.

Although most of the houses in Tsukishima were completely destroyed by the disaster, not one of the 174 residents was killed. This must largely be due to the fact that we had been preparing for a tsunami hazard, based on the advice given by Professor Fumihiko Imamura from the Disaster Control Research Center of Tohoku University.

We had decided in advance the evacuation route and spot in preparation for the tsunami, and conducted annual evacuation drills. We had built a new road for evacuation and had set up a system to help elderly people to evacuate in accordance with the advice from Professor Imamura. Because we had heard that a big earthquake would be occurring soon in the sea off Miyagi Prefecture, all of us had been well aware of the dangers of a tsunami.

It actually worked. During the disaster, some of us assisted elderly people to walk to safety. We also checked on one another to see if there was anyone missing. We could have lost someone if the whole community of Tsukihama had not developed a high level of awareness toward the dangers of a tsunami.

Chased up the hill by tsunami
Climbing over huge rock to reach even higher ground

Kenichi Inatomi
male, 65, business owner

On March 11, 2011, I had planned to work from 3 p.m. at the Miyato West branch of the Prefectural Fisheries Cooperative located in Miyato-Satohama, sorting bamboo to make rafts for oyster farming. After taking an afternoon nap at home, I was getting into my lightweight pickup truck in the yard a little past 2:45 p.m. when the earthquake struck.

IT WAS AN INTENSE SHAKING, swaying the ground horizontally and then vertically. I was literally bounced about. There was no sign of it settling down. I was worried about my wife and

Kenichi Inatomi's house protected the family from the gigantic earthquake, but the massive tsunami uprooted it from its foundation.

grandchild who were inside the house. Our two-story house had escaped damage even in the successive earthquakes that hit Miyagi Prefecture in 2003. I didn't think it would collapse, so I barged into it in spite of potential dangers. My wife and grandchild were under the table, doing what they could to protect themselves.

Anything could happen. The three of us stumbled along the wall and managed to get out of the house. My eldest daughter also came outside. She worked in the office of the conveyor belt replacement business that I owned, which was located on the same property.

It was an incredibly long quake. It seemed like it would stop, but then got strong again. I had no words for the rumbling sounds coming from the ground and the squeaking of the house. The mountains around the house buzzed. My legs trembled from this fear that I had never experienced before.

The shaking finally stopped. The Miyato district is surrounded by the sea, so the residents had a high awareness that an earthquake meant a tsunami. My wife had already prepared a backpack full of emergency supplies as we had had a big earthquake just two days earlier which was followed by a tsunami warning.

WE TOOK THAT BACKPACK and drove in two cars to a hill about 800 meters away. We could hear the warning sirens from the community emergency wireless system. We hurried along in the snow, calling out to our neighbors to evacuate as well.

As we drove up a narrow slope leading up to the hill, we were blocked by a landslide that was caused by the big earthquake. There was a small open space nearby. Our neighbors came one after another and parked their cars in the same space, too, and waited. The place was at least seven meters above sea level. According to the community's emergency wireless broadcast immediately after the earthquake, the tsunami would be six meters high. So we all thought we would be safe even if a tsunami came. "It was a big earthquake, wasn't it?" We exchanged such smalltalk but we weren't really in a tense atmosphere.

The next moment, however, we were taken aback. Although it was hard to tell the condition offshore due to the labyrinthine coastline, one of the evacuees noticed an abnormality. Down below the hill, what should have been rice fields had turned into a wide-open sea.

Rather than pitch black, the torrent was more brown. The surface of the sea rose just like spring water would. Because of the many small coves in the sea of Miyato, the surging waves of tsunami were crashing against one another in the maze of the sea, sprays of water shooting up here and there. Some of the houses were carried away with only the roof showing above water, but most houses had turned into debris and were drifting about.

The tsunami came closing in on us at the open space in an instant. In order to get to even higher ground, we had no choice but to go over the landslide site where a rock of over three meters in height was blocking our way. I had to move with my grandchild in my arms. A young man went first and from the top of the rock he pulled people up one by one. Meanwhile, the water was surging higher and higher, engulfing the cars that we had left in the space one after another.

Eleven of us who were at the open space had successfully forced our way through the landslide site that was wet and slippery with snow, and now we were to aim in earnest to get to a spot that was higher still.

We reached the rise, some ten meters from the sea, and then the water finally stopped rising just below our feet. It was nothing short of a narrow escape.

Where I looked down, there was a hole that used to be a quarry. Cars and rubble carried by the tsunami were getting sucked into the dark mouth of that hollow. I could hardly believe that this eerie spectacle was of this world.

After we regained our composure, we took shelter in a house on the hill, which had narrowly escaped the tsunami attack. It was already completely dark all around. We could hear the blunt sound of the tsunami as it came ever so easily over the seawalls along the coast. I heard another distinctive sound of the water—I wondered if that was the backwash. Maybe because of the landform, I remember more distinctly the furiously reverberating sound of the tsunami that came around 9 p.m. rather than the first wave in the afternoon.

The owner of the house kept watch in front of the entrance door, lighting up the darkness with a flashlight. "There's a tsunami again!" Every time he alerted us, we all ran to the hill behind. Although it was March, it was a cold and frosty night as if it was in the middle of winter. Then checking to see how the situation was, we would go back to the house. We repeated this all night, and we couldn't get any sleep.

IN THE MORNING, we went back home. My house, which had saved my family from the huge earthquake, had been uprooted and washed off its foundation because of the tsunami. Our home wasn't what it used to be any more, not at all. As the memories of our daily life came back to me, my eyes overflowed with tears.

Helicopters washed away from SDF Base
Frustrated rescue staff use dinghies instead

Momoei Koseki
male, 49, member of Self-Defense Forces Air Rescue Squadron

I was in a meeting with a group of 20 people including several team leaders on the second floor of the Japan Air Self-Defense Force Matsushima Base building. At 2:46 p.m., we were hit by a violent shake. It seemed to calm down at one point, but then started again to jolt the ground strongly side to side. This sequence was repeated for nearly five minutes.

WHEN IT FINALLY STOPPED, we lined up in front of the building so that we could check the presence of all staff members. In the operation room of the head office building of Matsushima Air Rescue Squadron, which had a staff of 76, various sorts of equipment were scattered everywhere by the massive quake, leaving no space to step in.

In and outside the hangar of the rescue squadron, we had six helicopters for search and rescue, but they couldn't take off immediately. We needed to check the extent of the damage to the runway. We also had to carry out detailed checks on the helicopters themselves—examining parts such as the rotor blades, which were just two meters above the ground and could have been damaged if they had touched the ground.

We had repeatedly undergone training drills for emergency situations. However, we would need to allocate around 30 staff members including mechanics to carry out their jobs before a helicopter could be allowed to take off. In addition, we had to think about the effect of continuous aftershocks. There was an increased risk that a helicopter would overturn if it was hit by a quake just before or during take-off. These difficult conditions prevented our helicopters from departing.

As we had anticipated, a major tsunami warning was announced. The base was located close to the coast. At 2:56 p.m., we were ordered to leave the base, which was a difficult decision for the staff.

Our helicopters had high-performance equipment and sophisticated technology that helicopters owned by municipalities and used by police and firefighters did not have, and were considered as "the last resort" in rescue operations. But we were not allowed to dispatch them at this crucial moment when a major earthquake disaster hit Miyagi and Iwate Prefectures, the areas where we were supposed to be in charge.

We felt so frustrated. A heavy atmosphere filled the room. We were rescue specialists who had trained very hard. Every member of the team looked grim. No one spoke but we all shared the feeling of deep disappointment. Some members had red eyes. We couldn't find any words to express our feelings.

HOWEVER, WE HAD TO SWITCH our frame of mind to prepare ourselves for the next mission. We took out marine and mountain rescue equipment sets—each weighed more than 30 kilograms—one after another from the depot and storage room where our rescue equipment was kept. We also set up a temporary command office on the third story of our home affairs team's building, located about 300 meters away.

It was hard to see the ocean because it was snowing. At 3:54 p.m., a huge tsunami suddenly emerged from a curtain of white snow. The runway was on the coast side of the base, so there was nothing to block the tsunami. The jet black muddy stream, engulfing cars and houses, came sliding slowly into the base. Strangely, I did not hear any sound of the tsunami.

Six minutes after the tsunami came, my cell phone rang. The display showed that it was from my eldest son, who worked in a shipyard in Ishinomaki City. In a desperate tone of voice he asked, "Dad, please help." But I could not do anything but tell him, "Hold on and stay alive." Then the telephone was disconnected. *It's the power of nature. There is nothing we can do.* I prepared myself for the worst.

At the base, 10-ton F2 combat planes were getting washed away one after another. We could do nothing but watch them go. Because of the power blackout, we had no light after sunset. I knew I had to sleep to preserve my physical power but I couldn't go to sleep. In the darkness, I heard the sound of a helicopter in the distance. It made a heavy noise that was different from ordinary helicopters. *It's from our Hyakuri Base in Ibaraki Prefecture.* We contacted them using the wireless system and reported the damage. We also asked for equipment and other supplies.

I COULD BARELY SLEEP that night. The next morning, we left the building wearing dry suits designed for marine rescue. Even a night after the outbreak of the disaster, the entire area was still submerged. We hurried to the rescue squadron's operating base. The rescue helicopters that had been outside were washed 300 meters away and completely destroyed. The hangar was in a terrible condition too. Most of the eight sturdy doors to the hangar, 10-meter high and 5-meter wide each, were destroyed by the tsunami, leaving the hangar filled with debris, ships and wood that had been washed up there. Our rescue function capability had vanished.

Our helicopters—the very ones we had trained in and maintained with great care—were almost unrecognizable. *I wish I could rescue as many people as possible from the air.* Thinking about those who would be waiting for rescue after that massive earthquake and tsunami, I was overcome with sadness and tears came to my eyes.

We lost one colleague at our Matsushima base. A total of 28 machines including rescue helicopters and fighter planes became unusable.

But we needed to stay strong. We started going on missions using rubber dinghies. We checked the situation at Higashi-Matsushima City Hall, while responding to requests from survivors in Yamoto Second Junior High School where more than one thousand people had taken shelter. We transported a medical team there.

IT TOOK THE MANPOWER of some 2,000 Self-Defense Forces members including those sent from other bases to remove the piles of debris from the runway and secure enough space for air transportation. From early morning on March 16, planes could be dispatched from there.

We shifted our rescue command into full swing, using planes and helicopters from other bases. We searched for people in four areas – Ishinomaki, Kinka, Oppa and Kesennuma. Each expedition was four hours long. We flew extremely close to the ground and checked visually if there were any survivors.

I was able to reunite with my son four days after the disaster.

I still regret that we were unable to take action immediately after the disaster occurred. For this reason, I would like to dedicate the rest of my life to rescue operations in places where there is a need.

[Volunteer translators]

松尾裕美子／門田裕美子／松本和也／陳偉熙／藤井由美／大場登／栗原隆太郎／今村順一／山田英二／井上真吾／菱田暁／佐藤悠美／木村素子／金丸悠子／酢谷桂子／西坂美奈／阿部弥生／五味麻子／木村たえ子／岡田裕子／木戸斉／佐々木美緒／会田美雪／木村比呂子／トレパスキス里美／佐藤夏子／＊中西仁美／Emma Williams／Sibyl Kane／Melissa Uchiyama／Pauline Busch／Shirin Sane／Christie Harvey／Chris Raymonds／Jessica Hallams／Nadine Eram／Edie Young／Alexandra Tolmie／Evan Jones／Patricia Silvestre／Andrew Trevaskis／Fumiko Shimizu／Peter Materne

* Coordinator of volunteer translators

[Messages from volunteer translators]

Natsuko Sato

I learned about this project in the college alumni group of Facebook. Immediately, I decided to participate in it. One year after the Great Tohoku Earthquake, I went to Cairns, Australia with my students at the university where I work. We had the opportunity to sell goods from Japan at the local community market. Many people visited our booth and bought goods. Moreover, they got interested in a magazine that showed the pictures of the Great Earthquake. We were surprised that many people including those who did not buy anything were willing to donate some money to the affected areas. They were also eager to listen to what happened to people in the affected areas and what we actually felt. We talked about our experience and the stories we had heard, but I strongly felt that we need a book for such a people. For this project, I contributed only a little unfortunately. Still, even if what each one could do was only a little, collected effort will bring about something great. I am very happy I am a part of this wonderful project.

Pauline Busch

I became involved in translating the original Japanese book "Surviving Tsunami" into English as a way of helping my daughter-in-law, Hitomi, with English grammar. We met weekly for several months and worked our way through many chapters. Initially, I treated it as an academic exercise but as the weeks went by, I became much more caught up in the personal dramas being brought to life before me.

All the storytellers began from the same point. A normal day, just like every other day and then the earthquake and tsunami and the dawning realisation that, even if they were used to and prepared for such occurrences, this time it was different.

So many of the stories reflect a society which is orderly and well disciplined: the radio warnings, the sirens, everyone aware of exactly where to go in an emergency and their struggles to get there. But alongside this, I was really impressed by the immediate concern for others. Old people were collected, neighbours checked, strangers rescued, as a matter of course. Food and clothing were shared, even floorspace was allocated on a needs basis. Could there be a greater contrast to the chaos after Katrina in the US? Perhaps we in the west could learn from the altruism and stoicism of the Japanese people.

Nadine Eram

Someone must have been watching over me back in March 2011. I was travelling around Japan that month and had planned to be in Karakuwa, Miyagi on March 12th for my students' graduation ceremony. But about a week before March 11th, my plans changed and I had to fly out of Japan the day before the earthquake and tsunami hit. Around 70% of Karakuwa (my old hometown where I had worked as an ALT) was completely destroyed.

Since escaping that experience through a random twist of fate, I've tried to do as much as possible to help this country that has given me so much. I've organised fundraisers in Australia and volunteered with Peace Boat in Ishinomaki twice. Helping out with the 'Surviving Tsunami' book project has just been another way I've tried to give back to Japan.

Reading some of the moving and heartbreaking stories in this book was really upsetting, but it was also amazingly inspiring as well. I am in awe of the strength that the survivors have shown and the courage that it must have taken to write their stories down. This book is a work of art and I'm so proud to have played a small part in it.

Thank you.

Edith Young

My name is Edith Young. I work at the National Gallery of Australia, in Canberra, organising events particularly for Asian Art. I often work with the Embassy of Japan, organising Japanese cultural events at the National Gallery.

I really wanted to keep the voice of the writer in the text. It was important not to sound too matter of fact when the content was so dramatic, and the fear, worry and concern for family and others could be detected and felt in their stories. It was important to keep their voice in the writing. It was their story, in their words, so I did not want to lose that.

News reports on war and natural disasters sound bland, briefly listing the numerical statistics, and the reporters seem so distant from the human aspect of stories in their reporting. Through these tsunami accounts I had the opportunity to hear individual stories for a better understanding of what the people endured. I was often moved to tears.

I am grateful I could read their accounts and for this chance to help with this project. I commend them for their bravery and hope they are recovering well and returning to normal life again.

Satomi Trevaskis

Being from Sendai, it was an honour to be involved with this translation project. I had wanted to do something for some time to help the affected area.

To be honest, I initially thought it would be just another big earthquake when I first heard the news, as frequent earthquakes were not unusual while growing up in Sendai. However, I was devastated when I saw images of the tsunami on TV as the news was being updated.

As I read the stories of individuals while translating this book, it was excruciating to think of the frightening time locals experienced when the tsunami attacked. Publishing this book is a great opportunity for people from around the world to learn about the horrific nature of the tsunami. International media has focused on the nuclear plant and radiation leakage, rather than how the affected people survived and recovered from the tsunami. I hope this book will begin to alleviate this.

I imagine a complete recovery from the disaster may take some years. However, I hope the situation of those affected by the tsunami has improved. I hope they can start to feel safer and happier as the years pass.

Andrew Trevaskis

Individuals from abroad will be impressed with the strong will of the Japanese people. This strong will carried them to survival during the aftermath of the tsunami, and has allowed them to make some sense of what was a horrific series of events. Gaman, or to persevere, is important to people from the Tohoku region, and we can get a sense of this from this work.

Reading each of the stories, I saw how precarious life can be. Survival largely depended on being in the right place at the right time, or the availability of a generous neighbour. Survivors showed an appreciation for the importance of life, and accepted the events of the tsunami with dignity and pride.

I would like to thank everyone involved with this work for giving people from around the world the opportunity to hear the survivors' stories. I hope that through telling their stories, the survivors and indeed their families, can begin to heal from this horrific series of events. I believe this text is an important way to preserve the history of events which indelibly shaped the nature of the Tohoku region.

Melissa Uchiyama

The project immediately became a privilege and honor—to listen to those with such harrowing experiences, help them to share and loosen their fearful grip—to experience even a bit of healing. We who were fine get to come alongside and listen. Simply listen. And then be so thankful that they survived—that they are able to tell. These survivors are not alone; they have a listening audience and community.

Where normally language would separate us and I might miss out on hearing these stories, here I have a spot at the table, thanks to the work of those who have translated. What an honor to hear firsthand and be a part of this work.

Of course it is saddening and horrifying. These stories bring about emotion. There is so much more under the surface that these survivors saw and took in. Some writers describe the face of someone swept away, people on rooftops, confused and cold. They bring us where the news could not reach or bring us, like a little camera or a small, damp, peeling journal describing the moments, hours, and days following the tsunami.

Emma Williams

I wanted to understand more about how individuals were affected by the tsunami and to help share their stories so that we begin to understand the impact of decisions made today on future generations. I was devastated to read about the tragedies and hardships that these people endured.

Keiko Sudani

When the Great Earthquake on March 11, 2011 struck, I did not know the size of it or where the worst of it was until I went home and turned on the TV. Everyone in Tokyo was fortunate to have been safe from the path of the tsunami but those in the path of the water would be forever changed. As days after the tragedy passed I began to get a picture of how individuals were affected. Some people lost nearly everything but were still holding on to what they had left. Seeing them, I felt that I had to do something to help. I found that one way I could offer support was to help translate peoples' stories to help spread the news that people in Japan needed help. The stories would also show people how individuals were affected by the earthquake. Providing personal stories would help others understand the threat and would encourage people to be better prepared should another earthquake strike. The stories moved me, how heroic people were working to help so many affected by the tragedy, how people were offering support with money and food. The stories showed me that even in tragedy, what gets us through is the support we receive from those we know and even those we don't.

Sibyl Kane

I volunteered for this work because it was one small way I could contribute to helping the people affected by the tsunami. Being able to use my English-language skills to help someone tell their story and have their voice heard was so meaningful to me. I know it was such a small contribution, but I was so happy to be able to help in any way.

I was deeply moved by the stories. Reading the stories was the first time I've had a truly first-hand account of that day and the tsunami. I felt I got a glimpse not only of the individual's story, but also of some of the character of Japanese people as a whole. I was struck again and again at how thoughtful and mindful of others everyone was in the face of such an overwhelming event. These stories are such a gift. I hope they reach a wide audience.

Mina Nishisaka

I remember my legs shaking in front of the TV, watching the Tsunami take everything as I held my 11-month old son. I knew I was lucky to be alive in Tokyo, but it hurt me to think of the many, many people who lost their lives in the disaster. I wanted to do something, but I felt so helpless.

Since then, we as WaNavi Japan have been empowering international residents on disaster preparedness to prevent lives from being lost if people had the right knowledge. I believe disseminating the actual experiences of 3.11 is very important in this empowerment, and we hope to share these experiences to the world in order to save as many lives as possible.

Yuko Kanamaru

The devastating great earthquake in March 2011 was a great shock to all Japanese people and to the world. I have been seeking for a way to take part in whatever support I could as a Japanese for the situation. Participating in this project of translating the stories of the reality that the people has faced in stricken area was challenging for me but if any of my ability could support deliver their words, I thought I would happily take this opportunity. The stories are very personal that I believe were very hard to share for those who suffered. I felt strong responsibility to correctly translate the words spoken with a lot of emotions that are behind them. I hope I could help convey their live words to the readers. From then and to the future, I will be praying for and thinking of those who suffered and would like to keep on doing what I can to support them. I would like to thank those who has given me the chance to take part in this project.

Motoko Kimura

After 3.11, the articles and images of the tragedy through various media urged me to go to Tohoku right away and help in anyway possible. However, with my own nursing daughter, I felt stuck and helpless. I volunteered for this work because I thought it was one small way that I can contribute to helping the people affected by the tsunami. The story that I translated happened to be the one of a mother who experienced the tsunami during her final stages of pregnancy. I was deeply moved by her courage. She turned fear into a sense of responsibility as a mother to give birth to a new life. I was also struck how the people around her supported her so thoughtfully. I am so thankful for the people who took their courage to speak about this overwhelming event. I hope to turn this encounter into a sense of responsibility of my own, to disseminate the lessons learnt by 3.11 to the world and empower people to be prepared for disasters.

Christie Abel

I am a Japanese teacher at an Australian high school and I had been at work on the day of the Tohoku Earthquake and Tsunami. The first time I heard about it was a comment by another Japanese teacher on Facebook. I turned on the TV to see what had happened and couldn't believe my eyes. I hadn't expected anything like the magnitude of the disaster I was watching. I felt so full of sorrow that this was happening to Japan and her people, a country I love nearly as much as my own and people who had always been so kind. I offered to help with this project as I felt it was something small I could do to support the survivors willing to share their stories. The thing that struck me most in reading the stories was the strength of the human spirit demonstrated and the way in which people worked together, unselfishly and unconditionally, to help and support each other through an incredible tragedy. My heartfelt thanks goes to the survivors for sharing their stories and to the publishers for making them accessible to us.

Patricia Silvestre

Hi, my name is Patricia. Japan has been my second home ever since I stepped foot into the beautiful and amazing country for the very first time in 1999. Ever since my first visit, I felt a strong connection with Japan, its culture and the Japanese people even when I am living in Australia. I participated in the Surviving Tsunami Book Project because I felt that I could contribute a very small part to assisting the survivors of the Tsunami tell their story of what really happened. When I read the six stories that were assigned to me for proof reading, I felt incredibly emotional and was at a loss for words by the detailed encounters told by the people who actually saw the disaster. I look forward to reading the published copy of the countless stories in the book and hope that perhaps one day, I could somehow have a closer connection with the six incredible Tsunami survivors by meeting them face-to-face.

Asako Yamamoto-Gomi

Two and a half years ago, the pain and sorrow of 311 was so close to me, although I was in Tokyo and not directly attacked. I felt sympathy with people in disaster everytime I suffered daily inconveniences like power and commodity shortages and the fear of radiation contamination. Although I did not share the true loss and disaster they experienced, 311 was OUR pain, not only THEIRS, to be endured and overcome together by all Japanese. However, such a sense of sympathy was getting lost, as the daily life in Tokyo coming back to normal. It was in such days when I got this offer of translation, and I decided to take it not to forget 311.

A year after that offer, Tokyo is now in a jubilant mood of hosting the 2020 Olympic. However, people in Tohoku are still suffering and abandoned. Reconstruction and decontamination has not been carried forward. The government and media are arousing people's expectation for economic benefits as if they forced us to forget 311. It might be blessing for Japan to step forward, but it should not mean to forget the tragedy and to leave all unsettled things in Tohoku.

Yumi Fujii

I was in deep sleep in my home in New Jersey after a nice celebration of my birthday just a few hours earlier. Suddenly, I was jolted by a sudden phone call from my sister in Hawaii. She told me there had been a strong earthquake in Japan and a strong tsunami had hit. When struck by such an unimaginable image on the television, my only way to cope was to sit in front of it and fall into deep depression. Day after day, I would flip through channels that were reporting the surreal site of what was once a beautiful coastline. I also had the feeling of guilt, for not being able to do anything for the people who lost everything. Since the great earthquake, I was given the opportunity to visit the Tohoku region twice. It is very hard to explain in words, the emotion it evoked, trying to imagine what it was like before the disaster. It was through this translation, that I was able to overcome the sense of helplessness and feel like I was contributing just a little in my own way, and for that, I am very grateful.

Aida Miyuki

News on the earthquake and tsunami was aired everyday for a few weeks after March 11, 2011. I thought I knew about it but I learned a lot more through interpreting the notes by two fishermen. Not only their notes, I watched as many documentaries as possible for the interpretation. As a mother, I took it very emotional to learn about children there. I was shaking to see adults being worried about their children's survival.

The earthquake and tsunami are devastating enough, but there is Fukushima, the nuclear catastrophe. I am still wondering if the fishermen's lives have become what it used to be before the earthquake.

Evan Jones

My name is Evan Jones and I participated in editing some of the survival stories for the book. I was asked to help by the Canberra Japan Exchange Teacher (JET) alumni association. I left Japan for good after living there for 12 years and arrived back in Australia on Friday the 11th of March 2011. My family picked me up from the airport in Canberra after 10 hours of flying. The first thing I did was switch on the TV to relax after the long flight. The show immediately switched to breaking news and I saw the shocking helicopter footage of the East coast of Japan being swallowed by a swirling black monster. I sat there crying as I watched country side and whole towns I knew disappear before my eyes. I lived in Chiba, Ibaraki and Tochigi for three years so I had many friends who were directly affected. I spent the next week frantically calling and emailing my friends to see if they were safe. It took many days to hear back from all of them. All of my friends were safe but I knew some of them had lost relatives and close friends.

Shirin Sane

In 2011 at the time of the Tohoku disaster, I was working as an English teacher in Fukuoka, Japan. I remember refreshing my internet browser that day, only to be stunned by what was unfolding so near, yet so far from where I sat in my office. The next few hours were spent reassuring family and friends that I was far away and safe. Sadly for many, this was not the case. Together with the English teachers in my prefecture, we did what we could to raise money and donate food and supplies. I was back in Australia when I heard about the opportunity to assist with translating for this publication. This was my first experience translating from Japanese to English. I translated carefully, trying to do justice to the original stories. Each sentence was confronting and emotional, but it was only on completion that tears came to my eyes and I realized the full impact of the story I had just re-told. I feel lucky to have had the opportunity to re-tell these amazing stories of human strength and resilience. My thoughts are with the victims, their families, and my hopes are with the brave and resilient survivors of this tragic disaster.

Noboru Oba

A Prayer for Peace and Restoration

When the earthquake struck, I was in my office in Yamadera. After the shaking had subsided, I dashed out to look up at the Godaido observation cabin on Mt. Hoju. If it had collapsed, it would have meant that Risshakuji Temple had been ruined, and beautiful Yamadera forever changed. But Godaido was standing firmly there and looking down at the world below as tenderly as ever.

I knew that many volunteers were gathering at the disaster-stricken areas to help, and I wondered what I myself could do as a volunteer. Last December my niece told me about this "voluntary translation" program, and I decided to apply for it. I have translated five stories in all, from writers who narrowly escaped the disaster. When translating, I make it a rule to be calm and self-possessed, but this time I found that a challenge. Reading of suffering and sorrow moved me to tears, and made it difficult to continue with my translating.

I am glad to have been involved in this program. Now, I pray that the souls of the dead may rest in peace, that the damaged areas can be restored, and that peace will return to the hearts of the Japanese people at the soonest time possible.

Fumiko Shimizu

When I first read the stories that I was provided with, I couldn't stop crying. I was absolutely overwhelmed by the fact that people in my country have been experiencing such tragedy. After translating I read them with my students who are learning Japanese in Canberra, Australia. They read them all with tears. They learnt how catastrophic it was and how they have contributed to the reconstruction by supporting each other in the affected area. It is such a privilege to be involved in this project. I'm praying for them and wish them all an early recovery and reconstruction.

Hitomi Nakanishi

On 11th March 2011, at 2.46pm, the Great East Japan Earthquake and Tsunami changed the lives of many people. A significant number of people ricocheted between life and death. This book is the record of one hundred people who survived the tsunami. Japan has suffered from a number of disasters through the ages. However the survival stories haven't been disseminated widely to other countries. To my knowledge, this book is the first attempt to translate the real stories of Japanese people who survived a catastrophe. Although these stories are personal experiences, there are many implications for disaster prevention, land use, community etc. This book contains knowledge which we need to pass on to the next generation. As an expert in urban planning, transport planning and disaster management, I have gained many insights into how we could enhance the preparedness for future disasters. Catastrophes will occur. It is our mission to utilise the knowledge which the victims of past disasters passed on to us.

This book project started by accident. We say in Japan 'en', which means an invisible relationship or destiny. I feel that this was a mission given to me. I first discovered the Japanese version of this book in Ishinomaki, one of the most devastated cities, in August 2012. I was visiting Ishinomaki to conduct a survey for my research. I was so impressed that the stories of the one hundred survivors, which were originally serialised in the local newspaper, had been published as a book. This is a significant record of the disaster. When Mr Nishikawa, the president of the Sanriku Kahoku Shimpo told me that he wanted the book to be translated into English, I had no hesitation in saying, 'I would be more than happy to do this'. However, my schedule was already full for at least next six months and I was not sure if I could really manage. Thanks to the help of my long term friend and the director of an NPO that is supporting the recovery in Ishinomaki, I could find volunteers from Japan who translated the stories into English. The next thing was proofreading of the translated texts by native English speakers. I was lucky to have the help of JETTA (Japan English Teachers Alumni Association) ACT, to find volunteers. The English translation of 'surviving tsunami' could not have been produced without the help of volunteers from Japan and Australia. I sincerely appreciate their efforts.

I wish to thank Mr Yoshihisa Nishikawa, the president of Sanriku Kahoku Shimpo for giving me the opportunity to organise this book project. I thank Ms Miori Kashima and Mr Peter Materne for helping me to find volunteers from Japan and Australia. I also thank Mr Shunichiro Fujimura, Sanriku Kahoku Shimpo and Naomasa Tanabe, Junposha for their efforts with maps and edits. The support from the University of Canberra for my activities in North East Japan is acknowledged. Finally, I hope this book will be read around the world by as many people as possible. This will be a prayer for the 20,000 people who lost their lives in the disaster.

[Supervising translators]

*Koji Shidara
Brenda Hayashi
Makiko Kimura

*Coordinator of supervising translators

[Messages from supervising translators]

Makiko Kimura

I would like to thank Sanriku Kahoku Shimpo and Junposha for letting me to take part in their efforts to deliver the voices of 100 brave people to non-native speakers of Japanese.

While working on the testimonies of the tsunami survivors, I often asked myself: Would I be able to do this if I was in the same situations? -- The answer was almost always "No." So many times, I was amazed at how people can be so brave and caring when their lives were in absolute danger. The stories also taught me that in a mega disaster like we experienced on March 11, 2011, there is often a very thin line between life and death, and some people cross that line to the side of life, not only because of pure luck but also because of their strong determination to survive. I will also remember that there are so many other people who were not lucky enough to make it.

I truly hope that a peaceful daily life will return to all the people who lost it so suddenly in the tsunami disaster.

Brenda Hayashi

This book is an attempt to convey the stories of 100 survivors of the unprecedented earthquake and tsunami that occurred on March 11, 2011 to the English-reading public. The translation of the testimonies from the original Japanese to its present English form could not have been carried out without the selfless, cooperative spirit of everyone involved in the project --- from the staff of Sanriku Kahoku Shimpo and Junposha to the original volunteer translators and others who worked on the English manuscripts.

Reading the stories both in Japanese and the various pre-finalized English versions, I was struck at how hard every translated version tried to best express not only the objective facts of the storyteller's flight to safety but also the person's emotional state during the intensely stressful days.

I believe that we can learn a lot from the responses that the survivors took, and in some cases, are still engaged in. As the third anniversary of the Great East Japan Earthquake approaches, I fervently hope that people outside of the affected areas remember that Ishinomaki, Onagawa and Higashi Matsushima are still in the process of reconstruction. The road to recovery is considerably long.

Koji Shidara

As one who oversaw the last stages of the translation project of this book including the main body and all the other components, I am glad that so many people from both Japan and abroad volunteered to make it into a reality. Disasters bring various latent elements in society as well as in humans to surface, making them visible to the general public. The range of what was brought to surface during and after the 2011 disaster that befell East Japan is quite wide, but one such instance is the linguistic skill of the people who took part in this translation project.

Being faithful to the intent of the original Japanese version was the guiding principle of the final proofreading task. The testimonies being what they are, it stands to reason that the survivors had been through extremely extraordinary situations, and this gave rise to instances where specific expressions being used do not sound very natural, even in the Japanese original. Often the survivors were at a loss how to express what they had gone through, not clearly remembering how they dealt with whatever dire conditions they were in. There were passages that defied the final proofreaders in this respect, but all of us involved with the project did our best keeping the basic principle in mind.

When Mr. Yoshihisa Nishikawa of Sanriku Kahoku Shimpo first contacted me about this project, I had just finished translating into English a book describing how an emergency shelter was managed at a Buddhist temple in Ishinomaki. This temple appears in the testimony under the title "Restored 17th century sailing ship survives tsunami," where the reader can see the bonds of seaside community at work. The disaster-stricken areas have been fortunate to have received so much support from around the world. The book about the shelter life at the temple was one way I joined the victims in trying to show appreciation to the people overseas for what support they had extended. This book of testimonies is my second such attempt.

Many of the survivors still live in temporary housing units, living one day at a time with uncertainty about their future. *The Ishinomaki Kahoku*'s effort to record the survivor experience via the pens of reporters has assisted the survivors in disseminating what was most essential, which may have been lacking in other forms of media. And now the same essence—human capacities for dealing with critical situations and for caring and compassion—is available in the English language through the bold initiative on the part of the publishing house Junposha. It has been my privilege to be part of this project.

"My March 11" serial project team

The Ishinomaki Kahoku, a daily newspaper published by Sanriku Kahoku Shimpo

[Sanriku Kahoku Shimpo's editorial office staff writers]
Hiroto Asakura
Yoshifumi Hisano
Takenori Osu
Koya Suda
Sachiro Hamao
Hiroshi Ito
Norio Sato
Kazuhiro Shirahata
Izumi Sakurai
Toshiaki Kikuchi
Mikiko Aizawa

•

[Kahoku Shimpo's Ishinomaki Bureau staff writers]
Yoichi Otomo
Satoshi Tsuchiya
Keisuke Yoshie

•

[Freelance writer]
Seiji Watanabe

(Affiliations are as of the time of writing)

All aerial photos courtesy of Tohoku Chiikizukuri Kyoukai

Sanriku Kahoku Shimpo Co.
Established in January 1980 as an affiliated company of Kahoku Shimpo Publishing Co. serving the six prefectures of the Tohoku Region, Sanriku Kahoku Shimpo has been delivering the daily newspaper *The Ishinomaki Kahoku* to the Greater Ishinomaki Region including two cities and one township since April 1980. The paper had a circulation of 47,000 copies at its 30th anniversary in April 2010, but it dropped drastically following the Great East Japan Earthquake. The circulation has since been recovering, reaching 41,000 copies as of January 2014.
Corporate headquarters: Sengokucho 4-42, Ishinomaki City, Miyagi 986-0827
http://ishinomaki.kahoku.co.jp

SURVIVING THE 2011 TSUNAMI
100 Testimonies of Ishinomaki Area Survivors of the Great East Japan Earthquake

2014年3月11日　初版第1刷発行

編者	Editorial Office of The Ishinomaki Kahoku A Daily Newspaper of Sanriku Kahoku Shimpo （三陸河北新報社「石巻かほく」編集局）
ブックデザイン	宮脇宗平
発行者	木内洋育
編集担当	田辺直正
発行所	株式会社旬報社 〒112-0015　東京都文京区目白台2-14-13 電話（営業）03-3943-9911 http://www.junposha.com/
印刷・製本	中央精版印刷株式会社

© Sanriku Kahoku Shimpo Co. 2014, Printed in Japan

ISBN978-4-8451-1351-4